SUNLIGHT ON THE OCEAN
A MOTHER'S MEMOIR OF LOVE AND LOSS, HEARTBREAK AND HOPE

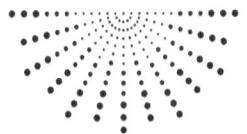

RHYL VENNING

Copyright © Rhyl Venning. The moral right of the author has been asserted. First published in Australia in 2023 by Rhyl Venning, Rosemount, Australia.

sunlightontheocean.com

ISBN Paperback 978-0-6459221-0-3

Large print 978-0-6459221-2-7

Ebook 978-0-6459221-1-0

All rights reserved. No part of this book may be reproduced or transmitted by any person or entity (including Google, Amazon or similar organisations), in any form or by any means, electronic or mechanical, including photocopying, recording, scanning or by any information storage and retrieval system, including AI training, without prior permission in writing from the publisher.

Live Forever, Words and music by Michael W. Smith & Wes King © 2004 Curb Word Music (Admin. by CopyCare Pacific Pty. Ltd.), Lotterthanme Music (Admin. by Music Services, Inc.), Smittyfly Music (Admin. by SHOUT! Music Publishing Australia)— Text of *Live Forever* by Wes King and Michael W. Smith Copyright © CopyCare Pacific Pty Ltd, PO Box 314, Ourimbah, NSW 2258 Australia and used by permission.

This Is Your Time, Words and music by Michael W. Smith & Wes King © 1999 Deer Valley Music (Admin. by Capitol CMG Publishing) (Admin. by SHOUT! Music Publishing Australia), Sparrow Song (Admin. by SHOUT! Music Publishing Australia), Uncle Ivan Music (Admin. by SHOUT! Music Publishing Australia), Sony/ATV Milene Music (Admin. by Sony/ATV Music Publishing)—"This Is Your Time" Written by Michael W. Smith and Wes King © Sony Milene Music Licensed by Sony Music Publishing (Australia) Pty Limited International copyright secured. All rights reserved. Used by permission

Scripture quotations marked (NIV) are taken from the Holy Bible, New International Version®, NIV®. Copyright © 1973, 1978, 1984, 2011 by Biblica, Inc.™ Used by permission of Zondervan. All rights reserved worldwide. www.zondervan.com The "NIV" and "New International Version" are trademarks registered in the United States Patent and Trademark Office by Biblica, Inc.™

Scripture quotations marked (ESV) are from The ESV® Bible (The Holy Bible, English Standard Version®), copyright © 2001 by Crossway, a publishing ministry of Good News Publishers. Used by permission. All rights reserved.

Publishing Consultant/Managing Editor: Belinda Pollard

Cover portraits of Kari-Lee and Rhyl Venning © Tahlea Blunt Photography

Further cover images via Bigstock copyright © Lilun (butterfly) and siriratsavett (frangipani)

RESPONSES TO SUNLIGHT ON THE OCEAN

Rhyl shares her story of loss with authenticity and vulnerability, not shying away from the parts that are painful and ugly. She honestly addresses the struggles, intense emotions, and unanswerable questions faced by parents who have experienced child loss, but then demonstrates how God can redeem these things by bringing purpose from the pain. Rhyl will be a warm and understanding companion on your own journey through suffering.

JILL SULLIVAN, Executive Director, While We're Waiting

In *Sunlight on the Ocean*, Rhyl fearlessly shares her heart-wrenching and transformative journey through the illness and ultimate loss of her beloved daughter, Kari-Lee. As a clinical psychologist well-acquainted with grief and loss, I was deeply moved by the honesty and vulnerability of Rhyl's account, and the captivating way in which she described Kari's unique and vibrant spirit and captured the profound impact our loved ones leave on our lives. Rhyl's own expertise as a health professional adds depth and wisdom to her account; one that will provide hope and guidance to those traversing the daunting terrain of love and loss.

DR GEMMA ROUX, Clinical Psychologist

∽

In *Sunlight on the Ocean*, Rhyl Venning journals a vivid account of her remarkable daughter's life with cystic fibrosis and her entrance to Heaven. Readers hold a front-row seat as Rhyl writes of the joy and adventures of Kari-Lee and family, followed by the devastating grief and deepest sorrow that any parent could ever face. With transparency and insight, Rhyl tackles many of the difficult questions that face bereaved parents, and testifies of God's faithfulness through the journey.

LAURA HOUSE, Associate Director, Our Hearts Are Home

∽

I consider Rhyl a friend even though we live more than half a world away from one another and have never met in person. We were introduced as fellow grieving mothers some years ago and immediately our hearts were knit together. We share a desire to be faithful, honest and transparent guides for anyone following behind us on this path of child loss.

Rhyl has written a beautiful and hope-filled memoir of her journey from infertility through delighted birth and on to a life of caring for a medically challenged child. I am so thankful that she chose to share with the world the ups, downs, delights and dreadful heartache of loving Kari-Lee even though she knew she'd likely get to Heaven before her. If you are looking for truth, encouragement and hope for this journey, read this book! I can't recommend it highly enough.

MELANIE DE SIMONE, Author of the blog
thelifeididntchoose.com

Sunlight on the Ocean is an eloquent yet raw account of Rhyl Venning's reflections on yearning to become a mother, many failed IVF attempts, and finally receiving the most precious gift of all, her daughter Kari-Lee. Yet this gift came with a price, as Kari-Lee was diagnosed with Cystic Fibrosis (CF), a life-limiting medical condition, when only weeks old. Rhyl shares the profound joy of watching Kari-Lee, despite CF, grow into a vivacious, curly-haired woman full of life and love and trust in Jesus; whilst balancing the grief of knowing she would one day have to give her daughter back to her God. *Sunlight on the Ocean* shares the myriad of emotions that have woven their way through Rhyl's life as a mother, before and after the death of her daughter. Rhyl describes with brutal honesty a journey through the depths of despair, jubilation, heartbreak, brilliant love, and the emergence of hope and light. This memoir will be a gift for those seeking solace in listening to, and learning from, a mother who has encountered the greatest joys, yet the unbearable pain of loving and losing their child.

LEIGH DONOVAN, PhD, BSW, Churchill Fellow, Former Bereavement Coordinator, Children's Health Queensland, Consultant in Thanatology

*This book is dedicated to my adorable granddaughter
Kari Florence:
May you always have a happy heart
just like your namesake
Auntie Kari.*

*And to her mother
my awesome daughter
Tiana
who bravely presses on
through the challenges and joys of life
without her beloved sister by her side.*

Isaiah 43:2

THANK YOU

I wrote this book because I had a burning desire to share my precious daughter Kari-Lee with the world and never let her be forgotten. I felt prompted by God to share my story in a way that might give hope to others who are thrust into the world of child loss.

Without my faithful friend Gaye, my book would have remained a great idea. Not only did she live out much of the story with me, but she read the first fledgling chapters I wrote and gave me honest feedback. I'll always be grateful for her friendship, her encouragement and her belief in me.

Her husband Bruce wrote the beautiful song that gave me a perfect title for my book. It may have taken many years, but it was worth the wait. Thank you.

My talented editor Belinda Pollard did so much more than guide and advise me. She saturated my book in prayer, something which means more to me than all the advice in the world. She made me believe in myself, in my ability to write and in the value of sharing my story. I owe her deep gratitude.

To my beta readers both here and overseas, thank you for taking the time to read my book (some of you twice!) and give helpful feedback and guidance. Melanie De Simone and Gemma Roux, you went the extra mile. Jill Sullivan, Leigh Donovan and Laura House, thanks for taking time out of your incredibly busy lives to read my book.

Proofreading is not always an exciting task, so I'm grateful to Janine Smythe and Val Donovan for the time they invested in making sure my book was as error-free as possible.

I appreciate the great start I was given as a part of Goodlife

Writers Group. I was listened to, encouraged and guided. Special thanks to Suzanne Strong.

Thank you to all my friends and family who stood by me through these challenging years, who prayed, encouraged, listened and stayed. Although you may not all be named in my book, you are all treasures to me.

Leanne and John: Peter and I deeply appreciate the love and friendship you generously give to us.

I want to publicly thank all the doctors, nurses and other staff who cared for Kari-Lee through all the ages and stages of her life. Many of you face the daunting prospect of seeing those you care for leave this earth at a young age. I admire your bravery and willingness to persevere and make a difference in the lives of these children and young adults.

I thank Peter and Tiana for allowing me the time and freedom to pursue this dream over many years. Holidays were interrupted, dishes weren't done, quiet was needed for me to concentrate. I hope you feel I've done our Kari proud.

And lastly, but by no means least, I want to say a huge thank you to Kari's multitude of friends, near and far. Please know that even though most of you aren't mentioned by name in this book, that isn't a reflection on the value you brought to Kari's life. She loved you and treasured your friendships. I could tell multitudes of stories that would fill countless books, describing the adventures and escapades you had with our unforgettable Kari. However I was constrained to writing just one book. I hope you enjoy learning about parts of her life which you may not have been aware of.

AUTHOR'S NOTE

As a mother's memoir, this book is *my* recollection of events and feelings over a period of years. Some parts of the narrative, especially those clouded in intense emotion, stand out to me in vivid detail even now. Others have been pieced together from my detailed diaries, photo albums, and the memories of family or friends combined with my own. Some of the people involved may remember the events differently.

The intention of my book is to share my unforgettable Kari-Lee with the world and keep her memory alive. My other aim is to be a voice to support those coming behind me on the traumatic and grief-filled journey following the loss of a child. I benefitted so much from others who have walked this path before me.

I've done my very best to be kind to anyone I've written about, while at the same time presenting truthful, sometimes painful aspects which are necessary if I am to be an authentic support to other bereaved parents.

I'm also aware that many friends will know a different side of Kari-Lee from what I've presented. Again, this is my story as her mother.

I have deliberately named very few people and have changed the names of some to respect their privacy. Not being named is not a reflection on the importance of many people in Kari-Lee's life, in my life and during the events described.

May my story be received in the spirit in which it is intended.

PROLOGUE

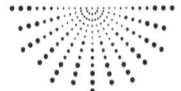

AUGUST 2014

"Woooohoooo!"

Kari-Lee's joyful cry echoed from the respiratory function lab as she skipped down the corridor towards me waving the printout high above her wild curly hair.

"Ninety-seven percent!" she boasted, her big green eyes dancing and her trademark smile wider than ever.

"That's amazing!" I exhaled a shaky breath and briefly basked in the relief washing over me. "Next time, one hundred percent."

"For sure, Mum," said Kari, her face becoming serious for a moment. "Who could believe that only a few weeks ago my breathing function was only twenty-seven percent?"

"Well, that's all behind us now." I smiled. "X-ray's done, blood tests are done, no dressings to change, no nurses to see. Hopefully the doctor doesn't take too long. Let's hurry up and get out of here and back to real life."

The sterile, sickly-yellow walls and row upon row of uncomfortable chairs in the waiting area brought back some of the heaviness of hospital. We endured yet another long wait – the hardest part of clinic days, even after doing it for all of Kari's twenty-five years. To lighten the mood, we took bets on which transplant doctor might be on duty.

Pleased to see it was Dr Hopkins who was always very positive, we took our seats in his office to find out the results of all Kari's tests. Everything was looking good. Most exciting of all was the continuing improvement in Kari's lung function.

"These results look great. With the type of bacteria that was in your old lungs, transplants can go two ways," Dr Hopkins told us. "It's usually either a complete catastrophe or a tremendous result, with not much middle ground. Everything's pointing to a great outcome for you and a wonderful life ahead."

As he turned to his computer to check the X-ray images coming through, Kari and I snuck a cheeky thumbs-up and grinned at each other.

Abruptly, our attention was gripped by a long, drawn-out "Ohhhhhh..." escaping from his mouth. I felt like I was falling through space from a great height. On that one word, the world turned more slowly and the room faded into blurry darkness.

Everything in our lives was about to change.

CHAPTER ONE

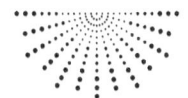

I was born to be a mother. For as long as I can remember I've adored babies and small children: their innocence, their big sparkling eyes, their sweaty little hugs. I find joy in the funny things they say and do, their innate sense of curiosity, their infectious giggles and belly laughs. It's like music to my soul.

One of my most treasured Christmas gifts was a baby doll given to me by my beloved Nana when I was four years old. I named her "Belinda" and carried her everywhere. She appears in family photos, cradled in my arms, right up until I was on the brink of teenage years. I couldn't wait to have my own baby and planned to call her "Belinda".

So, when I married Peter in 1983 after travelling the world, I was really looking forward to having babies of my own. At twenty-five I was considered old in those days, much like Toula from our family's favourite movie *My Big Fat Greek Wedding*. Her Dad was always saying, "Get married, make babies," and that was my plan.

After our first year of marriage we headed to New Zealand to live and study for a year in a Christian community called Orama, on Great Barrier Island. A wonderful but challenging year. Following that, we felt the time was right to have a baby. And right on cue, we found ourselves "expecting" in March 1986, shortly after arriving back in Australia. I immediately began planning for our future with a sweet little baby.

It felt like all my long-held dreams of being a mother were finally coming true, so our world was shattered when the pregnancy ended in early miscarriage. I deeply grieved the loss of this precious little person, but believed we'd soon be pregnant again. Isn't that how life happens?

The months rolled by and still no sign of a baby. A year passed, the longest year of my life up until then. Caring and generous family members included me in the joy of their babies, letting me wash their slippery little bodies, rock them to sleep and play lots of silly games of peek-a-boo. I didn't let them see the hot tears I cried into my pillow at night as my arms ached to hold my own cherished child.

Ladies at the nursing home where I worked offered helpful suggestions. My favourite came from a very prim and proper lady who suggested that Peter and I should "do it" with his work boots on, because that had worked for her!

After what seemed a lifetime but was in fact just over a year, it happened. I was pregnant. Hope built. Joy rose. Friends and family were ecstatic on our behalf, knowing how much this meant to us. But before I had the chance to really settle into my new role of mother-to-be, I was told that this pregnancy too had tragically ended in miscarriage. I was sent off to the hospital for another D&C – minor surgery often required after a miscarriage. I'd had some early bleeding and pain and suspected it might be an ectopic pregnancy, but when I visited a locum GP she said it was probably "wind pain".

As I groggily struggled through the fog to consciousness after the procedure, questions pounded through my brain, preventing sleep or peace. Why me? Had I done something to cause this? Was there something wrong with me? How had this happened again? When would it be our turn for a baby, something that so many others achieved so effortlessly?

This was just not fair. We'd waited and prayed for so long. It wasn't right that our baby should leave us again.

Peter decided to take me away for the weekend to give us some time to grieve. We'd planned to allow the beauty of God's creation at the beautiful Gold Coast beaches to begin to heal our souls, but even that wasn't to be. I was unexpectedly in too much pain post-surgery to travel the three hours, and reluctant to be so far away from my own doctors. Instead, we booked a cabin at a Christian camp centre in the nearby hills of the Sunshine Coast hinterland. Being out of season we knew there'd be hardly anyone there, offering me the peace and rest I needed.

That night I struggled to fall asleep, tormented by the loss, the questions, the ever-increasing pain in my belly. Finally, I drifted into a fitful, broken sleep, until, "Aaaaarrrrhhhh!" I woke in terrible pain, escalating pain, washing over me in waves as I fought to understand, not sure where I was. Excruciating pain had been building in my abdomen all night but was now unbearable.

I was reluctant to wake Peter but I had no choice. Crying in distress, I begged him to drive me to the hospital. He tried to help me out to the car but I collapsed on the grass outside, unconscious.

Who could help? Nobody was around. It was two in the morning. What could he do? Ring an ambulance. How? Mobile phones weren't invented. Find a pay phone. Where? With his contact lenses soaking in sterilising solution, he was close to blind. He groped his way along the sides of the building in the dark for a long time, round the different blocks of bunk rooms and kitchens, until finally he found a public phone and rang the ambulance.

He somehow managed to find his way back to me, still on the grass but now conscious. When he told me the ambulance was coming, I panicked. I'd worn an old tracksuit to bed so I'd be warm and comfortable, but now ridiculousness slipped into my addled brain as I thought about everyone at the hospital seeing me like that. I made Peter go and get my "decent" nightie from my bag and help me change into it right there on the grass at two-thirty in the morning, as I continued to slip in and out of consciousness. I've never really considered myself vain, but that scenario does beg the question.

The ambulance arrived and they carted me off on a stretcher. Peter had to follow in the car – still with no glasses or contacts. All he could do was follow the tail-lights of the ambulance as we made our way down the winding mountain road to the hospital. We both made it and I was rushed into emergency surgery for a ruptured ectopic (tubal) pregnancy at three in the morning. The doctors had misdiagnosed a miscarriage when in fact I'd had an ectopic pregnancy all along. Surprisingly, they hadn't picked it up even when they did the D&C.

This time I was very close to dying. I'd lost a huge amount of blood, which had pooled in my abdominal cavity causing the terrible pain. Even after several blood transfusions, my mother remembers my face the next morning being the same colour as the hospital pillowcase.

It took a long, long time to recover. I was in hospital for a week and then needed six weeks off work to recuperate physically. I eventually returned to work at the nursing home, where the residents were very concerned about me. Unfortunately, to protect my privacy, they'd been told I had a bad flu. While grief made my body ache like the worst flu imaginable, it meant I couldn't share my true feelings with them. That was when I slipped into what I now know to be depression. I struggled along for the next six months, spending my lunch hours crying in the toilet at work, counting the days until I could go back to the obstetrician and try to become pregnant again. Finally, the day came and, full of nervous anticipation, I headed off to see him.

As I sat down in front of him, he asked why I was there. Surprised, as he'd been the one to perform my emergency surgery, I reminded him that he'd instructed me to come back in six months following my ruptured ectopic pregnancy.

"You didn't have an ectopic pregnancy," he said.

I couldn't believe it. While the uppermost topic in my brain for the past six long months had been my experience and my upcoming visit to him, he'd completely forgotten it.

After checking his notes and finding I was right, he told me to come back in another six months. I left there vowing to find another doctor who'd understand that I needed to do something now, not wait another six long months.

What could I do to achieve my lifelong dream of being a mother? Who could I find to help me? Would it ever happen for me?

CHAPTER TWO

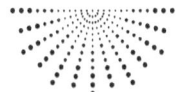

I walked unobtrusively into the church, searching surreptitiously for my friend. She made eye contact, silently indicated towards her bag, then turned to walk away down a long corridor. I followed a few feet behind, into the women's bathroom, stepped into a cubicle with her, made sure no one was watching, then shut the door.

I handed over the vial of liquid as she drew a syringe from her bag. I lowered my waistband to allow her clear access to inject into my hip muscle and pondered how this might look like a seedy drug deal.

I never thought this would be part of my life, but these were the lengths I was willing to go to in my quest to become a mother. Several months earlier, following the frustrating meeting with my former obstetrician, I'd found a new doctor who was willing to treat my infertility proactively. We started on the long and often painful road called IVF (In Vitro Fertilisation), which in 1988 was still relatively new. It's a gruelling experience – physically, emotionally and relationally – and much more complicated then than now. Back then, we had to travel two hours to Brisbane for all consultations and treatments.

The trauma and grief of early pregnancy loss in preceding years added another layer of emotion to an already bubbling cauldron. At the same time, friends around us were becoming pregnant, often without meaning to. Adorable babies appeared everywhere. The deep yearning for my own child made it incredibly difficult to be around other people's babies. I didn't want to make anyone feel guilty about enjoying their own babies or feel that they couldn't share their joy with me. It was an emotional mine field.

Initially, in hopes we could avoid the intrusion of full IVF, I was started on an oral medication called Clomid, used to stimulate the ovaries. The list of possible side effects was long and frightening. While not all of them happened to me, Peter had to deal with a nauseated, bloated, depressed, hormonal wife, on top of "performing" at prescribed times for sex. Instead of being a romantic and loving act, it became functional, dictated by the calendar, rather than by mood or desire. Not conducive to marital bliss.

It quickly became obvious that Clomid alone was not going to work, so we began down the road of full-blown IVF. Our hopes were high on that first round in early 1988. We'd proven we could become pregnant. It seemed that the problem was the destruction of one of my fallopian tubes, caused by the ruptured ectopic pregnancy.

IVF was the only way to circumvent that, but everything else was in working order. It should be simple.

We had a wonderful doctor, who was very kind and listened to our personal, moral concerns about IVF. He agreed to implant all our fertilised eggs as we didn't want any to be frozen or destroyed. On our first round of IVF, four embryos were going to be implanted.

I CLOSED MY EYES. Voices swirled around me as my IVF doctor was joined at the far end of the bed by people I'd never seen before. Scientists, medical students and nurses gathered, focused on the task at hand. I gripped the sides of the cold, narrow theatre bed, resisting the urge to run, or to at least grab my surgical gown and wrap it tightly around me.

Heart thumping and mouth dry, I obediently placed my feet in the stirrups at the end of the bed and opened my legs wide, exposing places I longed to protect. As all eyes focused on my most private parts, now illuminated by an intense beam from the overhead light, I reminded myself why I was enduring this painful, humiliating and confronting experience.

For the chance to have a baby of my own, I would willingly pay this price.

After the transfer and resting in hospital, it was time to go home and wait. I am, by nature and by training, a patient person, but there are some things that are intensely difficult to wait for, and this was one of them.

All we could do was wait and hope and pray that all the pain, trauma and expense would lead to the outcome we so desperately wanted. We fully expected that pregnancy would follow and we could get back onto the planned path for our lives. Along with many friends and family, we were praying for this precious baby, or babies, knowing it was God who gave life, while the scientists and doctors were skilled tools in His hands.

When the phone rang, I casually answered without any suspicion, "Hello?"

"Hello, this is the nurse from the fertility clinic, just ringing to let you know that your IVF round was unsuccessful. I'm sorry. We'll let you know when you can book in for another round."

The devastation was magnified by having to share it with friends and family. Many of them wept for us, knowing how much we'd longed for a baby. I've since read several books where IVF is referred to as one of the most stressful experiences that a couple can go through. They refer to a high rate of relationship breakdown – understandable, considering all that's involved. Still, we decided that we weren't ready to give up yet, but knew we had to wait a few months for my body to recover.

And so, in September 1988, now knowing what to expect, we embarked on our second round of IVF. At the time, we were both working full time as well as volunteering alternate weekends at the Pavilion of Promise, the Christian pavilion at the Expo 88 World Fair in Brisbane. Every second Friday night for six months, we'd finish work, drive two hours, catch some sleep overnight, ride public transport to South Brisbane, volunteer all day, repeat the next day, then drive back to the Sunshine Coast to prepare for the next week at work.

It was such a busy time in our lives that it probably wasn't ideal timing for the roller coaster of IVF, but we were eager to try again.

CHAPTER THREE

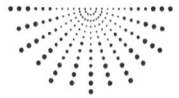

This time, the outcome was different. This time, the phone call came to tell us that we were, in fact, pregnant. This time, the scan at seven weeks showed a baby growing inside me, with a tiny, beating heart we could clearly see. Our joy was immense.

Deep inside, though, was the niggling thought that I'd been here before and it hadn't ended well. So, when the bleeding started, although I was devastated, I wasn't really surprised. That's what always happened to our babies, in one way or another. This baby, too, was probably going to leave us.

My obstetrician advised bed rest for a short time. I took it very seriously. I resigned from my job as an Occupational Therapist (OT) to give this baby every possible chance at survival. And so began my sojourn of several months in bed – because it turned out that this baby did want to stay. The bleeding calmed down and morphed into full-blown morning sickness, which I took as a great sign. I spent my time praying constantly that this little life could stay here with us, in between vomiting and feeling nauseated.

Once the magic three-month point passed, so did the bed rest and the morning sickness (apologies to all those women who suffer with it throughout the whole pregnancy). I felt great. My doctor approved me resuming normal life. In fact, the next six months of pregnancy became one of the happiest times of my life. I began to epitomise the "blooming" associated with pregnancy. I relished my expanding body, knowing that inside me a treasured life was growing. I ate healthily, swam a kilometre a day, slept and rested well. I did absolutely everything within my power to make sure that this baby had the very best start in life. I even had extra scans to check the spine of my baby, because my sister had a son born with spina bifida which gave me a higher chance of having a child with a neural tube defect. Everything looked fine. As far as anybody could tell, my baby was thriving.

One day, at a church camp during the latter part of my pregnancy, we were having a time of worship and started to sing the chorus:

> "The steadfast love of the Lord never ceases. His mercies never come to an end. They are new every morning, great is your faithfulness."
>
> — LAMENTATIONS 3:22-23 (ESV)

As we sang, I had an overwhelming sense of God's presence. He impressed a message on my mind, saying, "You need to give this baby back to Me."

This wasn't a common experience for me. There'd only been a couple of times before when I'd heard very distinct messages that I knew were God speaking directly to me. I tried to ignore the feeling. Very clearly, I heard the message repeated. This baby needed to be given back to God.

I was shocked and appalled at what I was hearing. I'd been through so much to get to this point. Surely God wouldn't ask me to give this baby back. I must be mistaken. But, no. The message was unambiguous.

I wish I could say I was a lovely submissive Christian girl – like Mary, the mother of Jesus – but that wouldn't be true. I resisted, wrestling with God throughout the song. Eventually, I did surrender. I recognised that my baby had only come through God's hand and belonged to Him. With tears streaming down my face and a heavy heart, I surrendered this miracle baby, who meant absolutely everything to me, back to God.

Things progressed well until three weeks before my due date. A visit to the obstetrician led to great excitement when he told me that our baby could be born any day. We quickly rang Peter's parents in Adelaide, who jumped in their car and drove twenty hours to be with us for the momentous event. Then we waited. And waited. And waited. Each morning, I'd walk warily into the dining room in my dressing gown, knowing the greeting that would come from Peter's Dad. "Still here, Rhyl?" After a very long three weeks of this, we reached the baby's due date.

By now, my increasing size was becoming uncomfortable and I was ready for this baby to be born. However, my baby had other ideas. The obstetrician decided that if the baby hadn't made an appearance by ten days past my due date, I'd be put into hospital and induced. I really wanted to avoid that, because I'd dreamt of and prepared for a natural birth with no medical intervention. Finally, the day before delivery day arrived. This was it. I decided to try everything I knew, including a few old wives' tales, to get this baby moving.

"Peter, I'm walking home from church."

"What? You're crazy! You're nine-and-a-half months pregnant and there are huge hills to climb."

"I need to get this baby moving. You know how much I want a natural birth."

"Okay, if you're determined. I'll follow behind you in the car to make sure you're okay."

An hour later…

"Well, that didn't work, so I need you to take me for a long drive on a bumpy road."

"Seriously? Alright, jump in the car."

Two hours later….

"Hmmm, still no action. I'm just going to go and bounce on the mini-trampoline for an hour or so."

"What?! Oh whatever. Just do whatever you think."

"And could you please cook me a really spicy curry for dinner once I finish drinking my Epsom's salts? This baby's just chilling in there and I really need them to start moving before tonight. I'm getting desperate."

But no, this baby was enjoying the current conditions and was quite content to stay there. It was the first indication I had of the laid-back nature of the child to come. That night, I spent a restless and uncomfortable night in the local hospital, before being taken to the labour ward to be induced at nine in the morning. As is often the case, once the infusion of oxytocin was started the labour was hard and fast.

At 12.06 pm on Monday 19th June 1989, the most precious and adorable little girl was placed into my arms and I knew that life would never be the same. We named her Kari-Lee.

CHAPTER FOUR

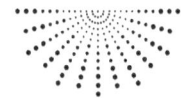

This was the happiest time of my entire life. At last, all the broken dreams and shattered hopes were behind me. I held my precious baby girl in my arms and revelled in the joy of her arrival. She was absolutely perfect, an adorable cherub with a button nose and sweet rosebud lips, tiny fingers that curled around mine and gorgeous big eyes that gazed up at me. My heart would never fully be mine again.

Life was perfect and we luxuriated in being a little family. Kari blossomed, captivating our hearts and the hearts of everyone she met. She went everywhere with us and was admired by friends and strangers alike. Everybody commented on how beautiful she was and said, "What a good baby!"

Out of the blue, into this blissful existence came a tiny rumble. Just before Kari-Lee's six-week check-up, we received a phone call from the paediatrician to say that "something" had shown up on the Guthrie heel-prick test. This blood test is done on newborn babies before they leave the hospital, to screen for certain genetic conditions. The paediatrician was quick to assure us that it was most likely a false alarm, which occurs fairly regularly. Kari was obviously healthy and flourishing, but we needed to have the test repeated, just to be sure.

I wasn't overly concerned but, being the curious OT that I am, I decided to go to the babies' ward where I'd seen some information about this test. I read about the various conditions that were tested: phenylketonuria (treatment leads to a normal life), congenital hypothyroidism (treatment leads to a normal life), galactosaemia (treatment leads to a normal life) and cystic fibrosis (no cure and a significantly shortened life).

As soon as I saw that last one, I knew.

A sick feeling clawed at my insides. Even without proof, I somehow knew that the idyllic honeymoon with our adorable newborn was about to be blown apart.

The test was repeated and we prayed it would come back clear, but deep in my heart I wasn't surprised when the result was positive for cystic fibrosis (CF). The paediatrician remained unconvinced because Kari was a picture of health. Chubby, rosy-cheeked and growing beautifully, she didn't fit the picture usually presented by babies with CF. They were often sickly, lacking energy, with breathing problems, and had difficulty putting on weight.

To confirm the diagnosis, we needed to do what's called a sweat test, because that's how diagnosis was established in 1989. Babies with CF lose much more salt through their sweat glands than others. In medieval times, it was called the kiss of death.

> "Woe is the child who tastes salty from a kiss on the brow, for he is cursed and soon must die."
>
> — EUROPEAN FOLKLORE FROM THE MIDDLE AGES

Initially, we had to do the sweat test Sunshine Coast-style, which, we soon discovered, was very primitive. On a sunny day in late July, we dressed our unsuspecting baby in as many warm layers as we could, strapped her now-bulky body into her capsule and drove around with the car heater on as high as possible, to make her sweat. Very soon, this became uncomfortable for Kari and she made her feelings known in the only way she knew. The discomfort of driving around in a superheated car for an hour was compounded by a screaming and very unimpressed baby. We then had to rush to the pathology lab where a sample of her sweat was collected for testing. Despite the reassurances of the paediatrician, the results were – as I expected, but desperately hoped against – positive for CF. We were referred to a children's hospital in Brisbane for further testing.

Through all of this, Kari continued to thrive. She was such a cheerful baby and made our lives so easy. When I'd finally become pregnant with her, one of the older ladies in our church home group told me she'd been praying for our baby to have a "happy heart". At the time I was surprised she wasn't praying for a healthy baby, like so many others. Yet from the beginning her prayers were answered. Through all that Kari had yet to endure in her life, this happy heart would become a standout feature of her nature.

The sweat test in Brisbane was much more sophisticated. Chemicals and a small electric current were applied to Kari's skin to induce sweating. Again, positive for CF. This was a definitive result. Our lives would never be the same again.

∼

HOW HAD THIS HAPPENED? I'd been so careful before and during my pregnancy. I'd done all the right things: eaten healthily, exercised right up until the birth, prayed for my baby. What had gone wrong? We soon learned all about how a baby can end up with CF.

Cystic fibrosis is a genetic condition and one in twenty-five people in Australia is a carrier. There's no indication you're a carrier and it doesn't usually have any implications for your own health. If both parents are carriers, there's a one-in-four chance that each child born will have CF. Of course, I'd been blissfully unaware of this as I basked in the warm glow of long-awaited motherhood. Peter had a nephew with CF, whom I'd met just once, but I'd never considered his condition could have any implications for our own child.

We found ourselves swept along on a tidal wave of medical intervention. Kari-Lee was admitted to the babies' ward for a week of testing and parental training. She endured so many blood tests and other procedures that would have upset any adult who had to suffer through them. As usual for Kari, she continued to smile and thrive.

Peter and I were trained in CF dietary needs and the various medications Kari would require all her life.

Most dramatically, we learned airway clearance techniques, specifically percussion, sometimes known as chest physiotherapy. This involved tipping Kari into twelve different positions, most with her head down a 45-degree slope and clapping a cupped hand very firmly on her back or front repeatedly, for an hour or more each day. She sometimes objected loudly to this, mostly because of being kept still for so long when there were better things to do. Yet Kari-Lee handled it more easily than either Peter or I did. It felt instinctively wrong to be "hitting" our tiny six-week-old baby, although we were assured it wasn't painful if we used the correct technique. In fact, after only a few days of this, Kari obviously found it soothing enough to fall asleep and this became a pattern throughout her baby years.

Understanding why airway clearance was so important helped us to persevere daily. The genetic abnormality in CF means that salt and water can't move through the cell walls as they should. This leads to thickened mucous which builds up in various organs of the body, particularly the lungs and digestive system. It becomes a breeding ground for bacteria, causing repeated lung infections. Eventually, most people with CF will die of lung disease caused by these repeated infections.

We were told that even with the best care, Kari's life expectancy was only thirty years. We took our responsibility to do daily chest physio very seriously, as we planned to beat those statistics.

Physically, it was challenging for Peter and me to continue chest percussion at the speed and force required for a full hour. I soon developed great biceps and never had to worry about developing "tuckshop-lady arms". It was also a huge time commitment, but one which we never shirked even when we were travelling or on holidays. Sometimes Peter would watch the footy or cricket to help pass the time while doing physio. This often led to arguments as I'd be able to hear the regular "patting" from whichever room I was in (good) and then I'd hear it stop (bad). Sometimes the pause only lasted a short time (maybe a cricketer hit a four), but other times it became extended (maybe an AFL mark which led to someone kicking for goal) and I'd have to step in and remind him that he was actually doing chest physio, not just watching sport.

Eating went from being a simple, enjoyable activity to one fraught with hazards. Children with CF require up to twice the recommended calories for children their age. There's an increased calorie requirement associated with lung disease and more energy is needed to fight infections. Thick, sticky mucous blocks ducts from the pancreas which supply enzymes to the digestive system to break down the food, especially fat. Because of this, people with CF don't digest fat. It ends up in the toilet, resulting in frequent smelly, fatty stools – another unpleasant side effect of CF. The main problem, though, is not the smell (although it's a challenge), but all the nutrients and calories that are lost.

To counteract that, Kari-Lee had to swallow digestive enzymes every time she ate or drank anything other than water. These came in capsule form, yet Kari had to have them even as a baby when all she was consuming was breast milk. We did this by opening the capsule and pouring the "beads" inside into an acidic medium, usually fruit gel, which would then be spooned into her mouth. Every time Kari-Lee had a breast feed, even in the middle of the night, we needed to have on hand some fruit gel and digestive enzymes. This need for digestive enzymes would continue for her entire life, with the number of capsules increasing as she grew.

In days gone by, children with CF were fed a low-fat diet to prevent these issues, but it was found that a high-fat diet is better for providing the large amounts of calories needed. This is one of the very few bonuses of CF. Right from a young age, Kari-Lee was encouraged by the hospital dietitian to eat a very high-calorie, high-fat diet, including lots of butter, oil, cream, cheese and even chocolate.

This went against all the general health advice at that time. In the 1980s a low-fat diet was considered best for health. Since our wedding, I'd been gradually educating Peter about the dangers of a high-fat diet in relation to heart disease. After six years he was finally starting to catch on.

When we met with the dietitian for the first time, she advised us to give our baby a high-fat diet for the rest of her life. She even suggested adding a chocolate Freddo Frog at the end of each meal to boost calories and fat as Kari got older. I was shocked and said, "But what about heart disease? Won't all that fat clog her arteries and lead to a heart attack?"

Her response floored me. "Oh, don't worry about that. She won't live long enough to develop heart disease."

CHAPTER FIVE

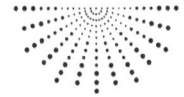

On the surface we appeared to be coping well, but anxiety constantly lurked in the background. How would we possibly be able to cope with all the demands of CF, along with the ever-present awareness that our baby girl would most likely not live past early adulthood? How would our happy-hearted baby deal with this heavy burden when she was old enough to become aware of the ticking time-bomb buried within her tiny body?

An especially difficult aspect of care for a young child with CF is avoiding coughs and colds that might lead to a chest infection, a stay in hospital on intravenous antibiotics, or even premature death. Kari was a very social child, so this was challenging. Friends and family learned to warn us or not visit if they or their children were unwell. Regardless, sometimes it was impossible to protect Kari and she did end up with a cough or cold, or worse.

Kari's first experience of a chest infection came quite early, at the age of five months. It started with a slight cough, so her paediatrician prescribed antibiotics as a precaution, which was standard practice in CF care. Unfortunately, she reacted to the antibiotic with vomiting. She'd been a chubby, healthy baby up until this point, but the weight started to drop off her quite drastically.

We visited the doctor, but our usual GP was on holidays and the locum seemed unconcerned. When Kari continued to be unwell and lose weight, I booked a paediatrician appointment. Regrettably, her usual paediatrician was also on holidays so we saw a doctor who didn't know us. He clearly didn't believe me when I told him how much weight Kari had lost and commented, "If she weighed that much before she got sick, she must have been gross." I was shocked, but he was the expert and he said she was fine. He sent us home, where her health continued to deteriorate.

Several days later, when her usual paediatrician returned, I went straight in with Kari. He examined her and told me to go directly across the road to the hospital where he started her immediately on intravenous fluids. She not only had pneumonia but was seriously dehydrated – a very dangerous combination for someone with CF.

From that time on, I was never afraid to stand up to any doctors who didn't take seriously Kari-Lee's condition or my instincts in relation to her health. I became the mama bear who fought for her cub, although I always tried to do so politely, at least initially.

The first hospital stay was always going to be traumatic. Seeing our tiny five-month-old baby enduring needlesticks and cannula insertions just broke my heart, but I'm a practical sort of person and knew it was necessary. I decided to always be by her side, comforting, reassuring and providing lots of fun experiences in amongst the trauma. Following a ten-day stay in hospital on intravenous antibiotics, and frequent chest physio sessions from the hospital physio, Kari was released and we headed off to enjoy her first Christmas in Adelaide with Peter's family.

We'd originally planned a road trip, but Kari's paediatrician strongly advised us to fly. The risks of dehydration caused by the heat of a twenty-hour drive through inland Australia were too high. This was our first indication of just how much CF could rule our decisions and our lives.

Kari-Lee continued to flourish and charmed everyone with her sweet nature and winning smile. She found pleasure in socialising, so we spent lots of time visiting and being visited. Things are different now, with parents often choosing to limit the number of people who have contact with a young baby, particularly one with cystic fibrosis, but that was not the way it was in 1990.

Kari's first year passed in a wonderful blur of sparkling days. To look at her, Kari was a picture of health, yet always in the background lurked the spectre of CF and the fact that any cold could become something much, much worse. We were diligent about her health needs, never missing physio sessions or medications and making sure she had a full and healthy diet.

Every six weeks we drove to the CF clinic at a children's hospital in Brisbane, where Kari saw CF specialists, including doctors, nurses, physiotherapists, pharmacists and dietitians. This was a huge time commitment, especially when combined with the daily requirements of chest physio and medications.

My wonderfully supportive mum would accompany me on these visits. It was so helpful to have an extra pair of hands and someone to entertain Kari-Lee through the long hours of waiting that were always involved with clinic. It made such a difference in practical ways, but more importantly with the whiplash of emotions that CF could cause, especially when the test results weren't great.

In the early days, we had something to look forward to during those long days in Brisbane: a "mothers and babies" group. This was in the days before awareness of the dangers of cross infection became so strong that children with CF were never allowed near each other. Before we had to face the doctors and other medical personnel, a group of five to eight mothers and our young babies with CF would gather in a small room and share stories, laughter and occasionally tears. This was a precious time, because we truly understood each other's lives in a way very few could comprehend. We were there to celebrate the milestones and victories and to offer support when one of our babies wasn't doing so well.

One family who stood out had twin boys. While they looked almost identical only Charles had CF, but both boys played with Kari-Lee. Unbeknown to us at that time, Charles would come to play a special part later in Kari's life.

Despite all the intrusions of CF, our lives were filled with peaceful days spent with our sweet girl as she grew into a delightful child. We became used to all the extra routines required by CF and incorporated them into our lives. Kari was a bright baby and toddler with a very inquisitive mind. She had a winning smile and an upbeat, easy-going personality with a great sense of humour, even at a young age.

~

Whenever Kari became unwell, we gathered all our faithful friends to fervently pray for her healing, not just of the current infection, but complete healing from cystic fibrosis. The elders of the church would come to anoint her with oil, as instructed in the Bible for anyone who is sick. Her name would be added to prayer lists in churches far and wide.

Sometimes, our prayers would be answered in the way that we hoped, but sometimes they wouldn't and the infection would progress to the point of needing hospitalisation. This was certainly a test of our faith and we also had to deal with the few people who believed Kari's lack of healing was caused by our lack of faith, or by some generational curse, or some unconfessed sin or unforgiveness on our part. This was a heavy burden to bear on top of the already huge emotional and physical load of living daily with CF.

I clung to the fact that Kari was our miracle child, sent from God. He loved her even more than I did. The issues and questions around different Christian teachings about healing remained a source of confusion, hurt and rumination, but I clung to my knowledge of a merciful and loving God who promised to be with us whatever we had to endure.

When Kari developed a moist cough at seventeen months, we did what we always did: called for prayer and increased her physio. When her health didn't improve, her paediatrician decided she needed hospitalisation. We assumed it would be a quick stay in the local hospital again. Her CF doctors had other plans. They wanted her admitted in Brisbane, which would mean me relocating to Brisbane with Kari for the duration of her ten-day hospital stay.

In our local hospital, Kari was always given a private room but in Brisbane she was put in a CF ward, a very old ward which was demolished soon after her stay. Cockroaches ran amok and some of the windows were low and unsafe for a toddler.

In this ward, beds lined both sides of the room and eight children with CF shared the room. All their meals were eaten together in a dining room where, in addition to a full meal, a giant bowl of calorie-laden hot chips was placed in the centre of the table. Everybody helped themselves, often coughing across the table towards each other as they chatted over their dinner. Cross infection was apparently never considered, although I did my best to keep Kari and her food separate from the other children, many of whom were teenagers.

The teenage girls doted on Kari-Lee with her ringlet curls, big eyes and engaging smile, and she enjoyed the attention. Often when I arrived in the morning, I'd find Kari sitting on one of their beds while they played with her. I couldn't know which bacteria lived in the lungs of these teenagers with CF and what was being unwittingly shared with Kari as they played, ate and coughed together.

I was unable to stop this. Any nurses I expressed my concerns to seemed unalarmed. It was difficult as a parent to express how vulnerable I felt my tiny girl was, when she was receiving what was considered the best medical care at the time.

One day, when Kari was receiving chest percussion from her very experienced CF physio, a doctor arrived with results from Kari's sputum test. Children with CF have different bacteria growing in their lungs and these require different antibiotics to treat them. The doctor reported that Kari-Lee had Pseudomonas aeruginosa growing in her lungs, the most common bacteria that affects people with CF.

The physio commented to me, "Well, at least it isn't cepacia."

"What's that?" I asked.

"Burkholderia cepacia are a family of bacteria that grow in the lungs of some people with CF." She added, sadly, "They're usually dead within a year."

I felt deeply sorry for those poor people with cepacia, but very relieved that wasn't what Kari had. A few days later, our ten days in hospital was finished and it was time to head home.

We were elated to be escaping the hospital environment with its smells and sounds and procedures that were no fun at all. As we reached the door of the ward, one of the junior doctors caught up with us and casually said, "Oh, by the way, some more tests came back, and Kari has cepacia growing in her lungs." And then he walked away.

Shock. Horror. Fear.

I turned to Peter and couldn't speak. He didn't grasp the significance of what had been said.

I hurried out of the ward before anyone could see my tears, my trauma, my trepidation. Once we got in the car, I broke down and explained to Peter that our precious baby, the chirpy, gurgling toddler in the back seat, had less than a year to live.

My nightmares were coming true. My Kari was dying, and soon.

I cried all the way home, trying not to upset Kari, who drifted off to sleep soon after we left the hospital. Peter tried to comfort me but I'd heard that life sentence of "less than a year" and I couldn't think about anything else. I wept for my beloved child and the suffering she'd already endured and for what was ahead.

I also wept for me and the end of my dreams, the loss of this most precious little person who had my whole heart.

CHAPTER SIX

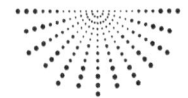

*I*magine waking up in the morning feeling physically exhausted and emotionally drained, but for the first few moments you're not quite sure why. Imagine spending hours every day forcing your cute toddler to lie upside down and thumping her as she begs you to let her go and play, just as any child would want to do. Imagine forcing her to eat more food than she could possibly want and teaching her to swallow whole capsules which many adults couldn't manage. Imagine making her miss out on play dates, birthday parties, or simply spending time with friends and family because one of them just might have a cold, because they sneezed twice the day before. Imagine having your ears so finely attuned to coughs and sneezes, even those of strangers at the shops, that your family and friends joke about your "cough-meter" going off. Imagine lying awake in the middle of the night listening to your child coughing, sometimes on and on and on to the point of vomiting, and not really being able to do anything about it. Imagine watching doctors find a vein as nurses hold your screaming toddler down yet again, so that they can insert a needle and cannula into her tiny little veins. Imagine knowing that this will forever be a part of her life and will only get worse, not better, despite all the medication pumped into her and the hours of physio and exercise you force on her.

This was our life after we left the hospital that December day in 1990. Of course, I'd contacted the doctors and was reassured that the form of cepacia bacteria found in Kari's lungs was only one type and was probably different from the one in Canada that often led to imminent death. The doctors believed that it could still be eradicated from her lungs with appropriate antibiotic therapy.

Despite their assurances, the reality of the life-shortening and fickle nature of CF was now firmly embedded in my psyche. The heart-breaking reality that Kari would probably have a shorter life than most, despite our best efforts, was now all too clear. We could do everything in our power and still there'd be totally unexpected factors, like bacteria that I'd never heard of, which would steal more of the years that I'd hoped and planned to have with my treasured child.

Despite all this, our lives were mostly contented. Kari-Lee was a big factor in this with her happy heart, helped of course by a complete lack of awareness at her young age of what cystic fibrosis really meant.

The burden was ours, not hers, at least in those idyllic early years where enjoying life in the moment was mostly easy. The dark shadow of CF kept its horrendous face hidden in the gloomy reaches of the night, where I cried countless tears into my pillow. I learned that there was a name for what I was experiencing – "chronic sorrow". It involves recurring, intense feelings of grief in the lives of the parents of children with severe, chronic health conditions. It's sometimes called a "living loss". While it stayed mostly in the background, any flare-ups could trigger profound sadness.

Kari's bright and friendly personality meant she had lots of friends. Because we needed to be so careful that she didn't catch colds and other illnesses, her social outings were mostly limited to people in our close circle of friends who understood the need to inform me if they or their child were unwell. Sunday school and our mum's group called GEMS were the main places where Kari had the best time with her little friends.

Our very best friends had four boys who were like brothers to Kari. We shared life together. Church friends were a huge support to us in the difficult early days as we tried to come to terms with Kari's diagnosis, especially those in our home group which met at the home of Kari's godparents, "Mr and Mrs Moon" as little Kari called them. Frequent prayers were offered for Kari to be healed from cystic fibrosis or at least for her to stay healthy enough for long enough for a cure to be found.

Other vital support came from our family. We were fortunate to have my parents living nearby. Kari-Lee absolutely loved spending time with them. Time at Nana and Pa's was always fun. Cows, chooks and ducks, cooking and sewing lessons, Shirley Temple movies from the 1930s and delicious old-fashioned food made the days special. Nana shared Kari's sunny disposition and positive approach to life and they developed a special bond.

My two sisters, who lived nearby, had plenty of children around Kari's age. Simple games like running through the sprinkler, jumping on the trampoline or digging in the sandpit were favourites. My brother was the only family member living far away – in Canberra, over a thousand kilometres away. In March 1992, Kari-Lee and I set off on a railway adventure to visit him. I knew Kari would be a good traveller, but it was a very long journey for a three-year-old, so I'd brought lots of things for her to do. These were more needed than I could have imagined because unexpected motion sickness virtually incapacitated me not far into the journey. I spent most of the trip lying down with my eyes closed, trying hard not to vomit. Kari was amazing. Aged just three, she entertained herself and cared for me for twelve hours on that train. She really was such a warm-hearted, capable child.

Peter's family were an important part of Kari's life too. His sister and her husband moved to Queensland from the USA in 1993, bringing two little daughters. Many people thought the older one, Rebekah, was Kari's twin. Not only were they born just days apart, but they shared the beautiful, big Venning eyes with distinctive eyebrows, along with adorable ringlets and cute heart-shaped faces. Photos of Rebekah giving her sister "chest physio", with Kari looking on, showed that it was just a natural part of life for them. Cute pictures of them reading their matching children's Bibles and wearing matching clothes, capture their closeness.

Peter's parents lived in Adelaide but came to Queensland for a month every winter around Kari-Lee's birthday in June. As a surprise when Kari was three, we'd taught her to recite Nan's favourite poem, called *Granny's Tale*, from the 1930s. The poem was thirty lines long and little Kari-Lee managed to learn the whole thing. During dinner on her birthday, we said, "Kari, can you say *Granny's Tale* for Nan?"

"No," said Kari, as three-year-olds are prone to do.

"Please," we said.

"No."

Finally, I resorted to a bit of bribery. "I'll give you a jellybean if you say it."

"Okay. Granny's Tale. There, I said it." Our cheeky daughter held out her chubby little hand for a jellybean.

At three, she was smart and funny, and that never changed.

At three, Kari already had a very genuine, childlike faith in a God who loved her. Of course, her understanding was only that of a young child, but, perhaps due to what she had already been through with her CF, she was wise beyond her years in some ways. She spoke of longing to go to Heaven to sit on Jesus' lap. Whenever she'd say this to me, I'd reply, "Yes, it'll be wonderful, but please not yet."

At three, Kari-Lee began dance lessons, which would lead to one of the greatest passions of her life. Initially, she learned ballet, but later that expanded to include many different forms of dance. She spent hours at home practising and making up her own dances. Kari once told me, "I'd die if there wasn't music and dance in the world."

At three, a special love in Kari-Lee's life was our sweet-natured border collie, Tessa. Many joyful hours were spent running around the backyard, chasing balls or butterflies. Stroking Tessa's soft hair or snuggling next to her, reading a book, helped Kari form a special bond with her only "sister" who'd been part of her life since birth.

AT THE AGE OF FOUR, Kari ended up in the local hospital again with a severe chest infection. Hospital was a dangerous place for a vulnerable child with CF and Kari caught rotavirus, a gastrointestinal virus leading to severe diarrhoea and vomiting. She was extremely unwell and lost a lot of weight, undoing months of our hard work keeping Kari at a good body weight, essential for a child with CF.

We struggled with thoughts of this being Kari's future life, in and out of hospital on a regular basis, battling constant chest infections and other complications. It wasn't the life we'd hoped and dreamed of for our cherished daughter.

CHAPTER SEVEN

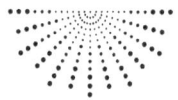

"You can't be serious? You might have another child who'll be a burden on society for the whole of her life. One child with CF is surely enough!"

This shocking yet understandable response from a family member caused us to reconsider our decision, even though we had not made it lightly. After much prayer and discussion we had decided we were prepared, despite the risks, for another baby. Our chances were three out of four to have a child without CF and we felt it was a reasonable decision. Not everyone agreed.

Because we believed that life came from God, if He chose to bless us with another child, with or without CF, that was in His hands. Of course we hoped our next baby wouldn't have to live life with CF, yet Kari-Lee was a happy and wonderful child despite the challenges of CF.

We prayed some more, sought counsel from wise friends, then decided to go ahead and leave the outcome up to God.

DESPITE HAVING BEEN through IVF before, there was little I could do to really prepare for the incredible emotional upheaval involved.

It was no better this time around. The drugs were just as potent, the waiting was just as traumatic, the emotional roller coaster ride was just as wild. In all, we went through six more rounds of IVF over the course of two years. All unsuccessful.

Having Kari in our lives helped somewhat with the devastation following each unsuccessful round, but it was still deeply and intensely painful. It's hard for others to understand the anguish, because to many it doesn't seem like a loss when you weren't really pregnant in the first place. It was a lonely road in many ways, despite caring friends praying for us and doing their best to support us.

Alongside the IVF process, we started on the long and intrusive path to adoption. Prior to Kari being born, we'd investigated adoption and had our names on three separate adoption lists: Australian adoption, special-needs adoption and international adoption. All adoptions in Australia go through the government, so once Kari was born we were ineligible for Australian adoption. While special-needs adoption appealed to us, we decided against it, due to Kari's significant health challenges and the time we needed to invest in her treatments. We chose to pursue international adoption.

I wonder if any government agency has asked you to describe how you learned about sex, or what you and your husband last argued about, or how you disciplined your child? We were required to answer these questions, and many more like them, in a twenty-page document. Once we'd satisfactorily completed that step, there were home visit assessments by social workers. Finally, after about a year of intense investigation into all areas of our lives involving police checks, health checks and character checks, we were allowed to apply for adoption.

Next was the huge decision of which country we wanted to adopt from. Once we committed we were required to stay with that country unless their programme closed. We chose Taiwan because their Christian adoption programme appealed to us greatly. The babies were very well cared for and, importantly to me, so were the relinquishing mothers.

At that time there were no children adopted from Taiwan in Queensland so I took a train trip interstate with my mum, travelling over two thousand kilometres for a weekend. We met with some adoptive families with children from Taiwan, which helped to seal our decision.

We were required to do an in-depth study of Taiwan and present an album of our work to demonstrate our commitment to teach our future child about the culture of their birth country. We also needed to make a book about our family to be shared with prospective parents. While both assignments were gratifying, I felt pressure to prove our worth as future parents. In no other circumstance that I'm aware of, are people required to demonstrate their suitability as parents. Gradually, we made our way through all the required steps until the auspicious moment came when our file was sent to the Christian Salvation Service (CSS) nursery in Taipei.

Kari blossomed as the waiting continued. She was thrilled about the prospect of a little brother or sister and looked forward with great anticipation to their imminent arrival.

Months passed and still we waited.

At CSS, the birth mother can choose the family her child will go to live with, from a selection of three or four families. We discovered that while our file was being shown to prospective parents, they weren't choosing us for some reason. This was both disheartening and distressing. It was posited by staff at the nursery that it might be related to Kari having CF, because in many cultures disability still had a powerful stigma attached to it. Cystic fibrosis was also virtually unknown in Taiwan as it primarily affects people of Northern European descent.

The staff suggested that we take a new set of photos which showed Kari-Lee running and climbing and playing to emphasise her health, which at the time was very good. We followed their advice and had some beautiful family photos taken which I treasure to this day.

These photos had the desired effect and just before Christmas 1994, we heard the wonderful news that an adorable baby girl had been allocated to our family.

We were sent the first photos of our baby at ten days old. They quickly became worn at the corners as we gazed repeatedly into her cute little face and proudly shared her photo with all our family and friends. Still, the waiting went on.

We heard tragic stories of babies who died before they could meet their family, and so many other things that could prevent this precious little girl making it to Australia to fulfil Kari's and our dream of a little sister. All we could do was wait and pray and trust and hope. Wait and enjoy our life with Kari.

∼

KARI-LEE STARTED PRE-SCHOOL. Standing at an easel painting on her first day, she became aware of the young girl painting next to her.

Kari said, "Want to be best friends forever?"

The girl, Rachel, smiled and said, "Sure."

And they would be.

Kari thrived in the school environment and found learning both enjoyable and enviably easy. She'd been reading since the age of three and was soon reading chapter books.

In 1995, Kari-Lee started Year One. Peter had taught at the same Christian school since before she was born, so it was a familiar, friendly place. Rachel was equally excited as they stood in the assembly hall waiting to join their new class and teacher.

Without proper preparation, school could be a dangerous place for a child with CF, so I'd made a chart for Kari's teacher to help her and the children in the class understand the main impacts of CF on Kari during a school day. Cystic fibrosis could be daunting, but I knew that having the teacher understand would be totally worth it for Kari to experience school with the least-negative impact on her health.

Each time she ate, Kari would need to take her enzyme capsules, called Pancrease. To make it easier, I calculated how many capsules needed to be swallowed with each item of food, wrapped the correct number of capsules in cling wrap and sticky-taped them to the item of food. She just had to swallow them when she ate that item of food. Simple.

Unfortunately, especially as she got older, this didn't always happen. Kari would "forget". Teachers would come up to Peter in the staff room with neatly wrapped packages of capsules that had been dropped or hidden around the playground. We went through seasons where Kari would have to eat her lunch with Peter in his classroom full of Year 7 students, to make sure she swallowed her capsules. This was so embarrassing for her that it usually led to Kari becoming much more responsible. For a time.

Dehydration is dangerous for children with CF, as they lose so much salt through their sweat glands. Kari needed to drink an electrolyte replacement drink called Glucolyte and take salt tablets if the weather was hot, which it frequently was in sub-tropical Queensland.

Kari-Lee's lunchbox was not the typical lunchbox of a child in Year One, being filled with items that had a much higher calorie count and fat content. During Year One, a student teacher was assigned to Kari's classroom and taught the children all about healthy food for their lunchbox.

That afternoon, Rachel ran crying to her mother. "Mummy, I'm sad because Kari-Lee's mummy doesn't love her."

"What? Of course she loves her. What are you talking about?" asked a puzzled Gaye.

"She gives her lots of unhealthy foods in her lunchbox. They're really bad for you," said Rachel.

Gaye and I had a quiet laugh when she told me, but it was hard to convince five-year-old Rachel that what the student teacher had taught her didn't apply in Kari-Lee's case.

Young kids at school haven't heard of social distancing. They have a great propensity for sharing germs – touching each other's belongings, holding hands, not covering their mouths when coughing or sneezing.

This led to us developing a strategy which we applied up until Kari was in Year Five. Once there were two or three children in Kari's class with a cold, I'd take her out of school and home-school her for the remainder of the winter. Kari was a fast and eager learner, so she usually finished all her work before lunch and we got to enjoy lots of fun mother-daughter activities for the rest of the day. In days to come I would be thankful for those years where we had so much extra time together, even though it was hard for Kari, who thrived on being at school with all her friends. It was yet another thing that CF stole from her, but she didn't complain.

As parents we felt so helpless. I thought constantly of what else I could be doing to keep Kari well for as long as possible, until a cure could be found. No matter how much work and how much prayer we put into keeping the insidious effects of CF at bay, it gradually invaded more and more of Kari's life.

CHAPTER EIGHT

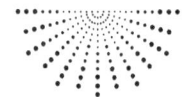

The piercing shriek of the alarm clock propelled me from a deep sleep, which had surely only started moments before. I remembered ironing my new outfit at midnight, then checking the nursery one more time, determined to get everything just right before falling into bed.

We were up bright and early for the special trip to the airport. Kari could barely sit still. Finally, it was time. We made our way to the observation deck to see the plane bringing our precious new baby, whom we'd named Tiana. Peter spotted it in the sky and began videoing the moment to share with Tiana in later years. Tears trickled down my cheeks as I thanked God for this precious gift, remembering everything we'd gone through to get to this point. It was an emotional moment.

That is, until Peter realised he'd been videoing the wrong plane.

We quickly diverted our attention to another plane – this one an EVA plane, which was the airline bringing Tiana to us.

The emotional moment had passed and by the time Tiana's plane touched down on Australian soil we were all laughing.

After what seemed hours more waiting, the doors of the arrivals lounge finally opened to reveal our escort holding a rather dopey-looking baby. Tiana stared at us uncomprehendingly with what would later become known as her "airport stare". We initially wondered if there might be something not quite right with this cute little girl. We soon discovered she'd been awake for the whole eight-hour overnight flight from Taiwan, a pattern that would continue in varying degrees throughout her life. She fell asleep soon after being placed in my arms and that was it – she was mine.

KARI BLOSSOMED AS A BIG SISTER. Feeding, bathing and playing with Tiana for hours brought great joy. One day, when Tiana was one year old, she was sitting in her high chair finishing her lunch. Peter was marking school papers at the table so I asked him to watch her while I did some housework.

A short time later, Kari came to find me with a funny smile on her face. "Come and see, Mummy. Tiana looks like a boy."

"In a minute, darling," I answered. She ran off but was soon back.

"Come and look, Mummy. Tiana has short hair."

This time I paid attention and ran out to the dining room. There was Tiana, her fringe (bangs) cut off almost back to her hairline, and there was Kari with my very sharp scissors in her hand. I'd left them within her reach when I trimmed Tiana's ever-growing fringe earlier. Kari thought she could improve on my work and managed to cut off Tiana's hair while Peter sat just inches away, completely oblivious, absorbed in his work.

DURING THESE EARLY SCHOOL YEARS, dance played a big part in Kari's life. Rachel joined her at ballet and jazz, but Kari's favourite was always tap-dancing. She had a natural rhythm and musicality. With her ringlets and cute smile, she could have passed for a young Shirley Temple as she tapped her way through *On the Good Ship Lollipop*. Together, she and Rachel took part in musicals, concerts and dance exams, and spent many lively hours making up their own dances.

Their other favourite activity was playing with Barbie dolls. Rachel would arrive on Saturday morning with her arms full of Barbie gear. They'd disappear into Kari's room to allocate who'd have which dolls, clothes, or accessories and what the storyline of the day would be. Little would be heard from them for hours, other than gleeful giggles. They'd surface for food, then head back to play.

Rachel's dad, Bruce, would arrive in the afternoon to take Rachel home, only to be met by looks of horror and cries of, "But we haven't even started playing yet, we're still setting up."

Tiana longed to join in the Barbie games, but when I suggested this to Kari she brushed it off, saying, "She doesn't know how to 'talk the Barbies' properly yet."

AT EIGHT, Kari had the honour of being flower girl when my brother Charlie was married in the lovely bush setting at our home. With a beaming smile, sparkling eyes and head held high, she led the wedding procession, wearing an enchanting pink dress which Nana had sewn for her. She looked adorable with her ringlets flowing down her back, a crown of flowers on her head.

What most wedding guests didn't realise was that underneath her beautiful bouquet of Australian native flowers was a bandage hiding an intravenous cannula. Kari had been in hospital right up to the morning of the wedding and would have to go back to hospital that night.

It didn't dampen her enthusiasm or dull her sunny smile. It was all part of living with CF. Kari-Lee had learned to take it in her stride and not let it stop her doing the things that mattered to her. This was a philosophy she would live by throughout her life.

A FEW DAYS later we boarded the Sunlander train to Cairns for the first leg of an incredible journey. Peter had three months' long service leave and we had decided to travel through the eastern states of Australia.

We spent a month in tropical North Queensland, exploring rainforests and waterfalls, snorkelling and cassowary-spotting, before heading back to Nambour to repack and head south. Our first stop on this leg was Adelaide, where we celebrated Peter's parents' fiftieth wedding anniversary with extended family and lots of friends. Kari had a great time with all her Venning cousins and was part of the family choir who sang Papa and Nan's favourite hymn *And Can It Be* at their celebration.

Back on the road again, we explored more of South Australia and Victoria, before arriving at Porepunkah, our base for a week in the snow. What an awesome time Kari-Lee had in the snow at Mount Buffalo. She tried her hand at skiing and soon proved she was way better at it than her old mum. She tobogganed with Tiana, laughing hysterically. I videoed Tiana coming down a steep hill in her toboggan and belatedly realised she was heading straight for a creek. I dropped my camera and ran, getting to her just in time. She and Kari thought it was a great joke.

A week circumnavigating Tasmania in a campervan was a great adventure, with two-year-old Tiana sitting up front between Peter and me. Kari had her own seat in the rear but could still communicate with us. She was able to do schoolwork as we drove along and thought it was the best sort of school ever.

After Tassie, we headed up through Victoria and New South Wales, stopping to visit my cousin on his sheep station near Narromine. Kari and Tiana bottle-fed baby lambs, watched the shearers at work and tramped down the wool.

Before we were ready, our trip was over and life went back to normal, but all the memories were ours to treasure forever.

Over the next few years, we did lots of travelling as a family, including two wonderful family holidays with Kari's Venning cousins. They savoured the freedom of swimming, playing, eating together and sleeping in each other's cabins. Whenever some sort of order was needed, perhaps for an ice-cream treat, Peter's brother would shout "order of age" and all twelve children would line up from oldest to youngest, a bit like the Von Trapp children in *The Sound of Music*.

These were wonderful times of innocent, playful fun, building memories for a lifetime.

At school, Kari continued to progress, with consistently positive reports from her teachers. I treasured comments such as these from her report cards:

"It's been a joy, privilege and blessing to teach Kari-Lee."

"Very sweet, loving nature. Sensitive, courteous, gentle, kind-hearted. Positive, happy attitude. Delightful."

"Meticulous worker. Shows considerable initiative. Always gives her best effort. Thoughtfully considers the needs of others. Excellent example. Encourages others."

"Kari-Lee has a profound effect on everyone who interacts with her."

Most of the time it was easy for people to forget Kari-Lee even had CF. Very few saw the tremendous amount of work that went on behind closed doors to give Kari this appearance of normality. Every single morning without fail, whether we were at home, on holidays or travelling, Kari would have an hour of chest clearance physiotherapy, several nebulisers and multiple tablets and capsules.

CF affected even her choice of hobbies. Kari learned to swim at a young age like most children in Australia, but for her it was a vital aspect of keeping her lungs strong and healthy. Every summer she spent hours at swim squad. She was always singing and for a time took lessons – great exercise for her lungs. She took drum lessons and became an accomplished drummer with a natural sense of rhythm. This kept her chest walls strong and flexible. She played drums at school and church – that is, until a boy's teasing comment: "Girls shouldn't be drummers, it's for boys."

Occasionally, CF led to unique opportunities. In 2000, Kari had the exciting privilege of running alongside Peter as he carried the torch for the Sydney Olympics through Nambour, representing people with CF and their families.

Kari rarely complained about or rebelled against what was an incredibly intrusive CF-related regime. She certainly didn't love it, but she tolerated it with a willing spirit.

She had several hospital admissions throughout her years in primary school, reminders that regardless of how well she looked on the outside it was a different story on the inside.

Each infection and hospital stay felt like a knife twisting in my heart, as I was fully aware that any one of these infections could spell the end for Kari. The cepacia bacteria, which was permanently in Kari's lungs, could sometimes take over the lungs of a patient with CF in a way that doctors couldn't treat. This was called "cepacia syndrome" and Kari was a candidate for it.

AT ELEVEN, Kari came face to face with the harshest reality of CF. Some years earlier in the local hospital, she had interacted with a boy with CF. It had been the first time since she was a toddler that Kari had met another patient with her condition. While they weren't allowed anywhere near each other due to the risks of cross infection, a friendship formed with friendly waves through the glass. The boy had a gift for drawing and one day he drew a cartoon especially for Kari, which she treasured.

When she read in the newspaper that he had passed away aged only fifteen she was deeply and profoundly affected. Her own mortality and likely shortened life were staring her in the face. While we reassured her that the same fate didn't necessarily await her, it was obvious for weeks afterwards that her mind was preoccupied with processing his death and all its ramifications. She stuck his drawing and newspaper cuttings on her bedroom door and wrote a piece about him in a school autobiography assignment.

So many prayers were offered for Kari's healing and safekeeping throughout all her life. I knew I had to trust her to God, but it was so hard. Thankfully, Kari had her own quiet but strong faith. She believed that God loved her, her life was in His hands and she could trust Him. Unlike many children of her age, she knew that this life was not all rosy, but that God was with her through whatever she had to face.

My mother-heart ached with longing to take this burden from her, to find a way to keep her safe forever, to let her live a normal life like her friends, but sadly I didn't have that power.

CHAPTER NINE

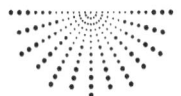

*L*ively Irish music and loud tapping filled the air as colourfully-dressed children jigged on a makeshift stage with the stunning vista of Mooloolaba Beach spread behind them. It was Saint Patrick's Day 2001 and Kari was part of a group performing at the Surf Club.

One of the mums, watching with me, leant across and whispered, "I guess her limbs will become stiffer and weaker as she gets older and she won't be able to dance anymore?"

My mind turned somersaults trying to understand what she meant, but finally I realised that she thought Kari had CP (cerebral palsy) rather than CF (cystic fibrosis).

It's one of many times over the years that I've had to explain CF. Despite being the most common life-shortening genetic condition in Australia, most people had never heard of CF.

While having an "invisible" condition had its advantages, there were also downfalls. Sometimes, when she needed extra understanding or support, it wasn't there. Few people had any idea of what Kari-Lee went through, or how incredibly hard we all worked to keep her well.

As Kari matured and made new friends in high school, she started choosing not to tell people that she had CF. She didn't want to be pitied or treated differently. Because of the invisibility of her CF, she was able to share details with only those she chose.

This led to an interesting situation when Cystic Fibrosis Queensland decided to make a short fundraising segment for television.

Kari-Lee was invited to be the teenage representative and to demonstrate how the digestive enzymes needed to be taken each time she ate. By now, she was on a stronger enzyme than Pancrease, this one called Creon.

The setting was nearby Sunshine Plaza where a camera crew met Kari and several of her friends.

Kari's only stipulation was that she didn't want to be the teenager with CF. She volunteered her willing friend Rachel for the part. So, the girls were filmed chatting and laughing on the boardwalk, shopping, then eating their snacks, with Rachel swallowing the digestive enzymes and Kari looking on as one of her non-affected friends. They both thought it was a great joke.

Another development which made it easier for Kari to keep her CF private was the change in chest physio techniques.

The days of pummelling her for over an hour each day changed to a less invasive system called PEP (positive expiratory pressure) when Kari was around twelve years old. PEP involved Kari blowing long, slow breaths into a mouthpiece attached to a tube. This tube connected to a machine that provided pressure which could be graded according to her needs. The mucous that was loosened then needed to be "huffed" to the larger vessels of her lungs where it could be coughed out.

PEP was often done simultaneously with one of her many nebulisers: Ventolin to open her airways or hypertonic saline to help with viscosity of mucous. PEP was very new at the time, so when she was unwell, we still added chest percussion to make sure her lungs were cleared. In the US a vibrating vest was often used, but that wasn't common in Australia.

As she grew older, another more difficult technique was introduced. This was called Autogenic Drainage (AD) and used Kari's breathing speed and depth to clear mucous from her lungs.

AD required a high level of skill. Kari needed to draw in a very deep breath, hold it, then let it out all the way. Once her lungs were completely empty, she had to take in a very small breath and continue breathing only in that lower part of her lungs until she felt the mucous start to move there. She then needed to increase her breaths gradually to "collect" the mucous and bring it up to the point where she could cough it out. This was repeated at each "level" of her lungs until all the excess mucous from all parts of her lungs had been expelled. This usually took around forty minutes.

When I tried it myself, I felt like I was suffocating and was unable to continue. Yet Kari learned AD when she was relatively young and her physios assured me that she was very good at it. It gave her much greater freedom because she could do it anywhere and anytime, with no equipment needed.

While this was wonderful for Kari-Lee, it was difficult for me. No longer could I tell if she was doing her chest clearance. She would often be sitting at the computer chatting to friends on Myspace and I would say, "Time to do your chest clearance, Kari."

She'd respond, "I'm doing it now."

Was she? I couldn't tell. I had to trust her.

That might sound like a minor thing, but it was huge for me. When Kari was a small child I'd had almost complete control over her chest clearance, diet, medications, and everything else that went towards keeping her as well as possible for as long as possible.

My mission in life was to ensure that Kari-Lee survived in the best achievable health until a cure for CF could be found. Now I was having to relinquish most of that control into the hands of a teenager. A teenager with a "she'll be right" attitude towards life. While Kari was a responsible girl, she was much more relaxed about life than I was.

It was a difficult time. I loved her so deeply and longed to keep her safe, but she wanted to spread her wings and be a normal teenager. While there were definitely some power tussles involved, thankfully our relationship survived the shift of control and she became her own primary carer in high school, with frequent reminders (which she might have called nagging) from me.

∽

No matter how much Kari chose to keep her CF private, its impact on her life couldn't be denied.

In Year Ten, Kari was admitted to hospital with an ongoing chest infection. It developed following surgery to remove nasal polyps, another unwelcome side-effect of CF which haunted Kari over the years.

This time, the antibiotics and increased chest physio weren't having the usual desired effect. This time, Kari kept getting sicker and sicker, with raised temperatures and increasingly virulent sputum production. This time, the doctors seemed concerned at her lack of improvement.

There were whispered references to cepacia syndrome and I feared that my nightmare, tucked away when she was a toddler, might now be coming true. Eventually, the infection came under control and Kari recovered to her usual state of health. It was a frightening time and a stark reminder that her life was always in the balance.

Just over a year later, the increased pressures of Year Twelve added so much stress to Kari's body that she ended up spending four stays of three weeks each in hospital. Twelve weeks in total. Away from school. Away from home. Away from friends and family.

Such an intrusion into the life of a happy teenager.

The last of these stays led to an interesting situation, frightening at the time, but a great story in years to come. It happened at one of her last clinic visits before transitioning to adult services at a different hospital. Peter and I were away, so Kari caught the train to Brisbane and successfully got herself to clinic. Staff made Kari comfortable in one of the consulting rooms and each of the professionals came to see her there. This system was designed to reduce the risk of cross-infection because of the virulent bacteria that continued to live in Kari's lungs.

Unfortunately, this time the system led to a disconcerting mix-up. The doctors decided that Kari needed to be admitted for a "tune-up" before her upcoming sinus surgery. They left her waiting in the consulting room with assurances that someone would be along soon to take her to a ward. She waited. And waited. And waited. Nobody came. It was hard to know how much time was passing, but when Kari finally peeked out the door, all was dark and quiet. The clinic had finished and she'd somehow been forgotten.

She managed to locate a staff member, only to be told that there were no beds available and she'd have to come back in the morning.

It was now night-time and she had no way of getting back to Nambour. She rang us in a panic, but we were hundreds of kilometres away. Thankfully, some dear friends who lived on the other side of Brisbane came to her rescue and took her back to their place for the night. They provided her with clean underwear, toiletries, and a change of clothes, then transported her back to be admitted the following day. In true laid-back Kari form, she had chosen to ignore her mother's sage advice to pack an overnight bag just in case she was admitted.

When Kari-Lee's care was moved to an adult hospital, we expected our connection to the children's hospital to be over – but we unexpectedly found ourselves back there with Tiana. For over a year, she'd been suffering increasing pain in her right ankle and foot. Initially, we thought the problem was tendonitis or a stress fracture from her heavy load of calisthenics, after winning the State Duo Championships in 2005, the State Solo Championships in 2006 and competing at the Nationals.

An MRI finally revealed a large venous malformation stretching from under her foot, entwined in all the muscles of her calf, up to behind her knee. She was referred to a vascular clinic, where unfortunately there was little to offer other than a compression garment which eased the pain and swelling to some extent, along with ever-increasing doses of painkillers. Amputation was discussed as a future option, certainly not something Tiana wanted to contemplate at the age of twelve.

While Kari loved sharing many things with Tiana, having a lifelong medical problem necessitating frequent regular visits to the hospital was not one of them. It was a good reminder for Kari-Lee that a lot of other people suffered like her, but in different ways that were not always visible to an observer.

Cystic fibrosis affected almost every aspect of Kari-Lee's life, yet she determined at a young age that she would not let CF stop her living to the full. She would not "suffer from" CF. She would not "battle against" CF. She would live with CF and she would live an amazing life.

Once, when I asked Kari if she wished she'd been born without CF, she thought for a moment and said, "I'm not sure. I don't think I'd be the person I am today if I hadn't been born with CF."

CHAPTER TEN

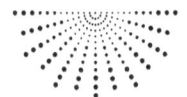

Soft corkscrew curls tumbled from her loose ponytail. Luminescent green eyes gazed out between long, thick lashes. A sweet smile played on plump, rosy lips as Kari-Lee shyly posed for photos prior to her semi-formal dinner – the culmination of Junior High School. She was the picture of girlhood morphing into womanhood.

From my vantage point near the kitchen doorway, the sight caused a tug in my heart. My little girl was growing up.

CF had not stopped Kari blossoming into a beautiful young woman.

This wonderful end to her junior high years was capped by her birthday party a week after the semi-formal. Kari had been born in the middle of winter but always longed for a pool party. In 2003, she decided it was time. She declared she'd have a fourteen-and-a-half birthday party in the middle of summer, her first party where boys were invited. This allowed her the chance, when she thought I wasn't watching, to shyly sit on the knee of a boy who'd said he liked her. What glorious fun she had, her glowing smile a testament to the joy radiating from her.

CF did not stop Kari living a life filled with hobbies and interests.

Like me, Kari had always loved horses. She'd even contemplated using her Make-A-Wish to ask for a horse of her own, but after considering all the time and commitment involved in owning a horse, she decided to wait and choose a different wish when she was older. Instead, she channelled her love of horses into learning how to ride well and how to care for a horse.

Her swimming ability also developed after joining the local swimming club, where she won a trophy for most improved in her first year. Great excitement accompanied the building of a pool in our backyard. The biggest advantage of having our own pool was that Kari could swim laps any time she wanted, knowing the pool was always clean and available.

During the holidays, a short course in surf skills ignited a passion which led to her training as a surf lifesaver. Once qualified, she proudly patrolled as a fully-fledged surf lifesaver for several years at Alexandra Headland Surf Club. She excelled in the first-aid component, which was her favourite part of the training and many years later would lead to her future career path.

CF did not stop Kari experiencing other losses in life.

Sadness engulfed our family when our beloved border collie, Tessa, who'd been a part of every day of Kari and Tiana's life, succumbed to paralysis ticks. As Peter gently carried her lifeless body out to the backyard for burial, tears ran unchecked down his face. It was probably the first time the girls saw their dad cry, broken by the loss of his treasured furry friend. They learned the hard lesson that death is a part of life.

Our next puppy, Loolah, was Kari's special dog, a responsibility and privilege that she took seriously. Sadly, after several years with us, it became evident that backyard life didn't suit this boisterous Houdini-like border collie. After repeatedly finding her escaped from whatever modifications Peter had made to our fencing, we had to make the sad decision that she wasn't safe at our home. A friend with ample acreage and animals on her farm took her in and Loolah lived long and happily. For Kari, though, it was another loss. Saying goodbye to her special friend was gut-wrenching.

CF did not stop Kari caring for children.

Kari loved babies and enjoyed babysitting for families in the church. She longed to have her own baby, a yearning I was all too familiar with. I prayed that cystic fibrosis would not rob her of that blessing. Carrying a child held extra challenges and dangers for someone living with CF, but Kari looked forward to it with great excitement. She was determined that CF would not interfere with her dreams.

When twin girls arrived for Uncle Charlie and his wife, Kari's love of babies prompted her to ask if she could be their nanny-helper during her school holidays. Permission was granted, preparations made, excitement mounted, culminating in a September flight to Canberra. Two weeks of cuddling, feeding and bathing babies was a dream come true for fourteen-year-old Kari. Entertaining their two-year-old sister added another layer of fun to the mix.

Over the years Kari-Lee took on some wonderful babysitting challenges: a family with seven children, a young girl with Down syndrome, and nannying three boys under four years old while attending university.

CF did not stop Kari chasing her dreams.

In Year Eleven, Kari was excited to study film and television, with the first semester dedicated to photography. This led to unexpected recognition when Kari won first prize in the student section of the Maroochy Shire Council photographic awards, with a photo of Tiana leaping high in the air on a local beach. Bolstered by her win, Kari went on to enter the Queensland Premier's Multicultural Photographic Awards and was shortlisted as one of twelve photographers in the student category for two years in a row. The seed of a possible career path in photography was planted in her mind.

CF did not stop Kari getting a job.

At fourteen, she started her first official job at a donut shop in Nambour. One of the perks was being able to bring home leftover donuts at the end of the day. While this was great for Kari-Lee and her need for a high-calorie, high-fat diet, it led to great temptation for the rest of the family.

CF did not stop Kari pursuing her passions.

Kari's passion for dance, which began when she was a young child, grew and flourished. She studied dance as a senior school subject and revelled in being part of the dance chorus in the school musical.

When her love for Irish dance began to wane after five years, her dance teacher suggested she try Latin dance. A group from Brisbane, called Rio Rhythmics, were holding Brazilian dance classes in a nearby storage shed. From the very beginning she was captivated, starting with one class a week, quickly progressing to two and soon squeezing in as many classes as she could. She was the youngest in the group, with most being adults, but she soon found a place in their hearts and they all looked out for her.

Later, when she had her driver's licence, Kari took every opportunity to drive to Brisbane to take part in more advanced classes, until she reached the stage where she was an assistant student teacher in some classes.

CF did not stop Kari-Lee excelling at school.

While Kari achieved wonderful results academically, even more important to us was the development of her character. She won awards for academic excellence, but also for Scripture memorisation, citizenship (being a blessing to others and building community) and culture (through dance and drama). Her schoolteachers continued to sing her praises with comments like:

> "Kari-Lee is an asset to the school because of her admirable qualities. She always has a kind word for everyone. She's well-loved and a joy to have in the class."

> "Kari-Lee produces consistently excellent work, is extremely creative and talented, with a keen sense of humour. She's a perfect student who has stood out as an example to others."

Our hearts swelled with pride when Kari-Lee was awarded the prestigious Clem Davies Young Achievers Trophy for Overcomers in Year Nine, an award not based on academic achievements, but attitude and perseverance.

CF did not stop Kari's sense of adventure and love of travel.

As a family, we loved to explore Australia, near and far. Holidays at beaches all along Queensland's vast coastline and regular road trips to my brother in Canberra and Peter's parents in Adelaide made the girls seasoned travellers. Hours spent together in the car built bonds of love and laughter (and a bit of jostling for space in the back seat).

An exhilarating family holiday in Western Australia was a highlight. White sandy beaches stretched for miles. Spectacular sunsets over turquoise water blended into cobalt depths. Best of all were the simple pleasures of being together as a family. Long, winding drives through peaceful countryside, unexpected adventures, family games nights. Riding the famous Indian Pacific train two thousand kilometres across the Nullabor Plain was a great shared experience.

Memories to lock away in the recesses of my mind, to treasure and hold onto when times might get tough.

CF did not stop Kari stepping out of her comfort zone.

Mud. Neck-deep mud. Kari-Lee covered in mud. The leadership-training and team-building camp set the tone for Kari's final years of school. Character traits like courage, mateship, perseverance and resilience were exemplified and enhanced through challenges based on historical events Australians have faced. In the Kokoda Trail exercise, each group carried one member on a stretcher through a mud-filled gully.

It would have made sense for Kari to volunteer as the casualty on the stretcher, out of harm's way of dangerous bacteria and infections which might lurk in the mud. But no. No way. That wasn't Kari's way. She was in the thick of it all, covered in mud, living life to the full, meeting challenges head on, never letting CF hold her back from all she wanted to accomplish in life.

CF did not stop Kari inspiring others.

As she started Senior High School, one of her new teachers wrote, "You're an inspiration to us, Kari-Lee, with your eagerness to always do your best, to persevere with joy in your heart, a smile on your face and encouragement for the whole class. Keep on being a blessing." What more could a mother's heart desire in her child?

She didn't just tackle Year Twelve, which was demanding enough without the extra challenges of CF. She took on two university-level subjects in Computer-Based Art and Design to get a head start on her future degree. She bloomed in the university environment.

CF did not stop Kari making us proud.

During dinner at the end-of-school formal (prom), everyone grew quiet as the MC stepped up to the microphone. One honoured student was to be named "Spirit of the College". Nobody knew who it would be. This esteemed accolade was based on character, not academic achievement. A hush descended over the whole ballroom.

"This student displays the qualities that epitomise our college," announced the MC. "They have lived out the values of excellence and Christian character, while fostering a sense of social responsibility. The 2006 recipient has been described as a person who possesses the following characteristics and qualities: diligent in all tasks; reliable and responsible; an amazing human being; never gives up; polite, respectful and courteous; sweet and kind; displays integrity; is not self-seeking; a strong Christian faith; a role model; always positive; loves God.

"The recipient of the 2006 Spirit of the College Award is…

Kari-Lee Venning."

Surprise then delight and gratitude filled my heart and yes, even a little pride, that other people saw all these wonderful qualities that my beloved girl shared so cheerfully with the world. A treasured mother-heart moment indeed.

CHAPTER ELEVEN

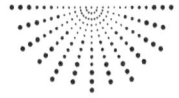

*T*he high school years and ordinary life were left behind, replaced by sheer exhilaration aboard a catamaran as it sliced effortlessly through pristine waters teeming with a kaleidoscope of colourful sea life. Kari-Lee had escaped to relaxed freedom in a remote slice of paradise called the Whitsunday Islands to celebrate Schoolies.

"Schoolies" is a traditional Australian graduation celebration where school leavers take a holiday after final exams. The thrill of adventure on this Scripture Union getaway called Backflip was a well-earned reward for the grinding effort of Kari's final school years. Living on yachts and exploring the green serenity ashore on remote islands made the ten days pass in a blur of fun and friendship.

A week later we waited in the arrivals lounge as fresh-faced, wind-tousled youths tumbled through the door, laughingly jumbled together in a mishmash of salty sun-kissed bodies.

This was a fitting end to five years of high school, where Kari had consistently worked hard, but derived the most enjoyment from the social side of school. When asked to name her favourite subject at school, the answer was usually "lunch time".

Kari's love of photography led to her studying a Diploma of Photography at TAFE (Technical and Further Education) alongside a Bachelor of Arts majoring in Computer-Based Art and Design at the University of the Sunshine Coast (USC).

Two years later, Kari shyly but proudly escorted us to view her photographic display in the graduating class exhibition, the culmination of her Diploma of Photography. We admired her talent as she laughed and bantered with friends she'd made during the intense and challenging years of study and assignments.

A fortnight later we gathered to witness her graduation from TAFE, complete with pomp and ceremony, caps, gowns, and well-earned congratulations. Her studies at university would continue for another year with a slightly different focus. Kari had discovered Italian and loved it so much she changed her major to Italian.

Small groups of people gathered on the pebbly banks of a bubbling creek as Kari-Lee and her friend, who called each other "twinnie" because of their matching curly hair and body shape, made their way to a deeper pool. Their matching T-shirts read: "There is always hope."

Peter waded in next to Kari, with our pastor on the other side. Kari's voice rang out, clear and strong, declaring her faith in Jesus Christ and her willingness to follow Him in the waters of baptism.

Peter supported her as he tipped her backwards under the chilly water and raised her up dripping, but triumphant.

Several of Kari's closest friends from church were finishing high school a year later than her. One of their mothers arranged a trip to Vanuatu to help at a mission base, serving lots of children. Kari-Lee was excited to be included as it combined three of her great loves – small children, mission trips and tropical islands.

Spending their days in small, poor villages, the girls presented the Christmas story through songs, puppet plays and skits. Sometimes they taught kindy classes and helped with whatever was needed. In the evenings they relaxed and played guitar with the team from the base, or helped with "community night" where all the local children gathered for songs and games.

This mission trip was a natural progression from two that Kari had been part of during her high school years. Together with twelve young friends, and three adults, mostly from our church, Kari had headed to Western Queensland on two mission trips called Beach to Bush. The teenagers shared the Christmas story with schoolchildren in remote areas, in similar ways to the Vanuatu trip. It was a great adventure, travelling long distances in a minibus and camping in tents. Deep and abiding friendships developed during many hours on outback roads, nights dodging thunderstorms in their tents and days performing and sharing with hundreds of children at different schools.

These mission trips started a slow-burning desire in Kari's heart to do more mission work with children. She began to contemplate volunteering in Africa, perhaps at a Watoto village. She started sponsoring a child through Compassion and dreamed of making a difference in the lives of children living in poverty around the world.

IN THE DISTANCE, a necklace of twinkling lights defined the coastline of the exotic island of Tahiti as our plane floated gently down towards the dark ocean and the fruition of Kari-Lee's Make-A-Wish. As we entered the airport to the accompaniment of ukuleles, garlands of tiaré flowers were placed around our necks in welcome. Kari's face radiated utter joy, her eyes sparkling as she basked in the perfect fulfilment of her dream.

Jagged peaks, silhouetted against a pure cerulean sky, poked their way up from within the vast green swathes of palm trees covering the island of Moorea as we chugged ever closer in the catamaran ferry. Kari and Tiana were fizzing with eagerness to settle into their own private bungalow and flop onto the huge king-sized bed. Within minutes, they'd changed into swimmers and jumped from their wooden balcony into a turquoise lagoon.

The water that lapped under their hut was teeming with colourful fish.

With frangipani or tiaré flowers tucked behind our ears, we made our way to dinner each evening, where exotic dishes like whole lobster or chocolate shells filled with fresh mango mousse made Tiana's eyes pop. Breakfasts were buffets fit for a king, with delectable tropical treats in abundance.

Once we dragged ourselves away from the scrumptious food, there was a whole island to explore. Pushbikes took us to the nearby village for homemade ice-cream, while the dolphin sanctuary just down from our bungalow provided lots of entertainment.

Adventures abounded.

One day we hired a motorbike and a go-kart (allowed on the road in Moorea) and circumnavigated the island, taking the whole day to discover all that we could about this fascinating place. Road rules seemed chaotic. When Peter pulled out with Tiana on the back, and automatically started driving the motorbike on the left side of the road as we do in Australia, Kari and I panicked. In Tahiti they drive on the right. Thankfully they met no oncoming vehicles and we were able to catch their attention by repeatedly beeping our horn and waving frantically.

A day of kayaking almost ended in disaster when Peter attempted to cross the strong current to the nearby motu (tiny island), but capsized, losing Kari's thongs and his sunglasses to the hungry ocean. Thankfully, he survived and we enjoyed exploring the island from an ocean perspective.

Kari's favourite time came in the evenings, when we frequented every possible Tahitian dance show we could find. As a dancer herself, Kari fully appreciated the amazing skill and grace of the women. Their hips could gyrate at an astonishing pace or could slowly and gracefully sway, as they told traditional stories with their hands and bodies. At every show we attended, the professional dancers would choose a few members of the audience to join with them for one dance. At every show we attended, Kari-Lee was chosen. Her face glowed with an incandescent smile, the joy within unable to be contained.

For the entire week, filled with magical, unforgettable moments, Kari floated on a cloud of pure happiness.

∼

ON OUR RETURN, we travelled (metaphorically) from tropical Tahiti to captivating South America for Kari-Lee's eighteenth birthday party.

Brightly coloured tablecloths, exotic dishes and lively Brazilian music set the mood, as Kari's friends and family gathered to celebrate her officially reaching adulthood. After enjoying the meal, speeches and cake-cutting, Kari enticed friends onto the dance floor for the promised Latin dance lesson. Her infectious giggles at the amusing attempts of some of her friends transformed into delight as she danced the night away with anyone willing to let themselves go and savour the fun.

A slideshow of treasured moments skated through my mind's eye as I gazed at my precious daughter, now on the brink of adulthood.

There'd been times when we'd been terrified that she wouldn't survive her childhood years, times when we'd been devastated by the burden of CF that she carried, times when we'd wept at the unfairness of life.

There'd been times when she'd made us double up with laughter, times when she'd made us incredibly proud, times when the joy that she brought into our lives made our hearts swell and overflow with gratitude.

Through it all, her happy heart shone, her sparkling presence blessed us and we looked forward to watching the unfolding adventures of her adult life.

CHAPTER TWELVE

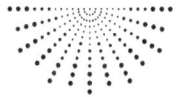

Sitting on the side of the highway, smoke billowing from our car engine, trucks and cars flying past. This was not the way we'd planned to begin our long-awaited 2009 holiday to Taiwan. After being towed to safety we finally made it onto the plane for our eight-hour flight to Taipei.

We landed in another world. People, people everywhere. Very few of them looked like us. Noise, horns honking, voices clamouring, most of them in a language we couldn't understand. Smells – unfamiliar, sometimes unpleasant smells – assaulting our nostrils with fatty beef, stinky tofu and wafts of sewage.

This trip was the realisation of years of planning, wanting to explore Tiana's birth country with her. Now she was fourteen the time had finally come. Our first few days in central Taipei were spent in luxury at the Cosmos Hotel, where the buffet breakfasts made the girls' jaws drop in awe and delight.

We visited the CSS nursery, which was basically the same as when Tiana spent her first five months there, but now housed in a different building. After handing over the suitcase full of gifts and provisions we'd brought from Australia, the girls were invited to hold some of the delightful babies awaiting adoption. As usual, Kari-Lee relished any opportunity to snuggle a baby, but Tiana's eagerness to interact with these babies, who were living the life she'd once lived, brought tears to our eyes. The girls each chose one special baby who they would have liked to take home. We then had the special privilege of meeting some of the staff who'd looked after Tiana when she was a baby and who still worked in the nursery.

Taipei offered us a wealth of unique experiences. Ancient Buddhist temples with incredibly intricate stonework and clouds of incense. Night markets packed with teeming humanity and carts of fried chicken feet. Taipei 101, the tallest building in the world until 2009, which the girls excitedly summited while Peter and I enjoyed coffee with our feet firmly on the ground. Three levels of underground shops beneath the nearby Taipei Main Station provided hours of amusement for Kari-Lee and Tiana. It was a new experience for Tiana to be the one who blended in while Peter, Kari and I stood out – sometimes literally, as we towered over most of the local people.

For the following two weeks we travelled by bus, taxi, van and train, discovering remote mountain villages, spectacular waterfalls, giant cypress trees and hot springs tucked away in quaint mountain villages. We marvelled at the sheer magnificence and raw beauty of Taroko Gorge, where marble cliffs dropped dramatically to the river far below, a stark contrast to the serene beauty of Sun Moon Lake. We discovered that Taiwan has impressive surf beaches, picturesque mountains, and caves with hanging water curtains.

Exploring the countryside, we tried to be friendly, often greeting people with our limited Mandarin vocabulary: "Ni Hao" meaning "hello". Encouraged by our seeming grasp of their language, they would respond with long sentences which made no sense to us. When we'd reply with, "Sorry, English," they'd look disappointed and turn to Tiana, spouting a torrent of Mandarin. Their astonishment at her unexpected response of, "Sorry, English," had to be seen to be believed. They obviously and understandably assumed she was our tour guide. It caused great amusement among our family.

We experienced a traditional tea ceremony, shaved ice treats, and stir-fried bird's nest fern, but decided that red bean ice-creams weren't our favourites. At the end of our three weeks, I asked everyone to share their memories of the trip. Kari and Tiana both agreed their funniest memories were of me falling off my bike into an irrigation ditch during our forty-kilometre bike ride and me being dumped by a wave at the surf beach and being tumbled on top of Tiana. I was glad to provide them with such amusing entertainment.

～

No sooner had we returned from our amazing adventures in Taiwan than Kari-Lee was offered an astounding opportunity to study in Italy for a semester, commencing in September. She decided to explore Europe for a month before her studies, so it was action-stations getting her ready for departure in early August. While I was incredibly excited for her, I had concerns about her ability to manage her health. Yes, she was twenty years old and a responsible sort of girl, but she always played down her CF.

In recent years I'd been gradually handing over the control to her. It was sometimes hard to watch her have a more laissez-faire attitude to things. Did she actually do her AD chest clearance exercise? I didn't know. Did she actually swallow her digestive enzymes with each meal? I didn't know. Did she take all of her other medications every day? I didn't know.

The stringent control I'd once wielded to ensure she stayed as well as possible was difficult to relinquish. There was only so much reminding (nagging) she would tolerate before she got annoyed with me. I had to remind myself that this was Kari-Lee's life and she needed to live it the way she wanted, so I hid my fears and encouraged her to chase her dreams.

In my diary I listed some of my fears related to her trip to Italy: plane crash, swine flu, serious infection, earthquake, abduction, rape, mugging, getting lost, travelling alone, not coming home.

On August seventh, Kari took off on her adventure of a lifetime, but only two days into her trip one of my fears was realised. Kari ended up in a hospital emergency room outside London, unable to walk, with a dreadfully painful, hugely swollen, purple ankle and foot. Many hours and many tests later, doctors were still unsure what was wrong, but decided it was an infection, possibly enthesitis, which can affect people with CF. Two days rest and antibiotics saw Kari back on track, but it was a worrying start for her already tense mother on the other side of the world.

Of course, Kari didn't let a little thing like that hold her back, but set off exploring all the highlights of London, including Buckingham Palace where she caused a guard to break the rule of keeping his eyes straight ahead. He turned to gaze at her and her friend snapped a photo.

The day before joining a Topdeck bus tour of Europe, Kari and her friend went to the West End musical *We Will Rock You*, then danced at a salsa club until 3.00 am. Still, they were up early to catch the ferry from Dover to Calais with their group, arriving in Paris for a walking tour followed by the Eiffel Tower by night.

Amazing experiences piled one on top of the other: the awe-inspiring scenery of Switzerland, the history and romance of Italy, cruising the Rhine in Germany, bike rides in the Netherlands, filling Kari's days with indelible memories to treasure. The whole group bonded in a very special way.

All too soon, they returned to London where sad goodbyes made way for a new adventure for Kari as she flew off to Athens. After a few days alone seeing "a million marble statues", Kari-Lee joined another tour to the Greek Islands, where she quickly made new friends. Sailing, swimming, exploring and dancing made for idyllic days which blended into fun-filled evenings heralded by stunning sunsets, displaying a kaleidoscopic palette of colours. Kari climbed a volcano, rode a donkey up a mountain and had a mud mask in a hot spring.

As their ferry chugged back to Athens, Kari looked forward to her next season, studying in Italy. Unfortunately, it suddenly occurred to her that she didn't have her passport. She'd left it in the safe of the hotel on Mykonos. She was supposed to leave on a ferry to Italy the next day – impossible without a passport. Panicked phone calls back to Australia resulted in her staying for a few days with friends of Tiana who lived in Athens. They generously showed her around the city and looked after her until her passport caught up.

Her eventual twenty-two-hour ferry ride to Italy was an experience, sleeping alone in an isolated bunk below-deck on a huge cruise ship. She was unable to detect any other people nearby, which made her feel vulnerable, but she arrived safely in Italy and caught the train for the last leg of her long journey to Urbino.

Urbino is a walled town in the Marche region of Italy, in the foothills of the Northern Apennine mountains. Entering Urbino is like stepping back hundreds of years in time, with mostly medieval buildings and cobbled streets. The area is classed medium-high risk for earthquakes, so my fears were not entirely unfounded. Kari soon discovered how hilly it was. She posted on Facebook, a social network she had recently discovered: "I'm definitely going to get fit here, so many hills!"

Most of the population of 24,000 were students studying at the university. Kari's room, shared with an Italian girl, was quite basic, with a single bed each, a bookshelf and a desk. A "kitchen", comprising a bar fridge with a one-burner hotplate on top, took up one corner, while there was a separate bathroom with shower, toilet and bidet. This last caused much hilarity to Kari-Lee, not being used to such contraptions. It ended up being used to store toiletries, rather than its intended use. While the room was initially stark and bare, Kari soon stamped her personality with a colourful bedspread, curtains, photos, books and a poster of a tropical island.

She quickly made friends in the Italian language classes that preceded her full-time university course, which would be taught completely in Italian. She posted, "Learning another language is hard. Learning a complicated subject IN another language is REALLY hard."

These friends, including one student from the Sunshine Coast and others from all over the world, would remain her "gang" during her time in Urbino. Kari's subjects included Dance Education, Muscle Strengthening and Fashion Design, all fun subjects, but way more difficult when taught and tested in another language.

Kari settled in well, quickly acquiring a solid grasp of the language, becoming accustomed to the Italian way of life and enjoying a full social calendar with her many friends. Far away on the other side of the world, we were grateful for the relatively modern invention of Skype. When the time difference allowed, it enabled us to make contact via the old-fashioned landline phone hanging on the wall in Kari's room. Catching her in her room was a challenge because, in typical Kari-Lee fashion, she was out living her life to the full at every possible opportunity, not wanting to miss a single moment of this sensational experience.

Back home, we missed her cheerful presence deeply.

CHAPTER THIRTEEN

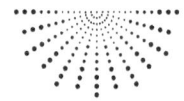

*B*oom-boom…boom-boom…boom-boom. The beat of my heart thundered in my ears. As my train approached the station, my stomach turned somersaults as I craned my neck to catch a glimpse of the platform. Despite the freezing temperature, a wash of heat spread from my face down my neck as the moment I'd been anticipating for so long drew near. I spotted a lone figure huddled in a grey overcoat and my lips parted in an uncontrollable smile. There she was. My Kari-Lee.

I leapt out of the train dragging my reluctant, heavy suitcase and enveloped her in a fierce mama-bear hug which spoke of the months of aching, of longing, of missing her.

The exhaustion of my days-long journey of flights and cross-country trains melted away as I gazed at Kari's beloved face.

"Let's get something to eat," she said in true Kari style.

My dream holiday was underway. Together we enjoyed the thickest, richest, creamiest hot chocolate I've ever tasted before catching the bus to Urbino, arriving in time for dinner. That evening we rugged up warmly and joined the fun at a night market in the town square. It was bone-chillingly cold and I was glad to snuggle into my sleeping bag for an early night.

Kari had one more week of university lectures before holidays, so my days were spent taking long walks, helping with cooking and getting to know Kari's many friends. On my third day in Urbino it snowed and kept snowing for the rest of the week, turning an already beautiful setting into a magical winter fairyland.

∼

On our last day in Urbino we packed our suitcases before the girls' final class. In high spirits, Kari headed out at midnight for a farewell celebration with her friends.

I waited up until 4.00 am but finally snuggled into my sleeping bag, only to be awoken by strange noises at 5.00 am. Hysterical giggles and hooting laughter gradually resolved into Kari-Lee and her friend, slowly making their way up the snow-laden hill. It sounded like Kari was doing a commendable imitation of a drunk person, but as I looked out the window to join their laughter, I saw her stumbling along, repeatedly falling over in the snow. I realised this was no jovial imitation. Kari was drunk.

My shock and disappointment were intense. I'd never seen her drunk, didn't know she'd ever been drunk. I pulled myself together enough to support Kari as they bumbled up the steps, then helped her undress and climb into her sleeping bag.

I didn't sleep well. Such a disappointing start to our much-anticipated two weeks travelling together.

The morning brought little improvement. Kari woke late, vomited, took the bus with me on the winding road to Pesaro, vomited again and made it to the station to catch our train across Italy. Kari's befuddled brain caused us to miss our train, so we arrived at La Spezia later than planned.

Kari's adamant assertions that she'd only had three drinks didn't help. I wasn't a happy mother, but I knew I needed to stop feeling disgruntled. This wasn't how I'd imagined our special mother-daughter trip but, thankfully, the hotel's lights beckoned to us across the road from the station. We gladly showered and fell into bed.

In the morning, everything was new. I was able to put my disillusionment behind me and we had a great day exploring. The pretty scenery in the Bay of Poets was enhanced by the recent unseasonal fall of deep snow, but unfortunately the public transport system was unable to cope. We struggled to find a bus back to the hotel, waiting hours and finally climbing a huge hill to flag down a lone passing bus. Thankfully, we were able to see it all as part of the adventure.

Arriving back at our hotel just in time to grab our suitcase and race to the station, we discovered that trains were also affected by the snow. Eventually, we arrived in Levanto on the edge of the Cinque Terre coast in darkness, to find that no taxis or buses were running because of the snow.

Quite willing to walk, we asked for directions to our hotel, but nobody had heard of it or even the street it was in. Some friendly locals directed us in what turned out to be the wrong direction and we became hopelessly lost. It was snowing, cold and dark and we were dragging a heavy suitcase on wheels through foot-deep snow. Fortunately, we'd regained our sense of humour and camaraderie, so we were able to laugh even while struggling. Finally, another local led us to the hotel lights shining in the dark. When the tiny lift bearing us and our suitcase became stuck between the two floors we giggled at the absurdity of our day, before finally being released to tumble into bed.

We spent the next two days exploring the breathtaking treasures of Cinque Terre, renowned for its fragile beauty. Five tiny villages perched on the edge of steep hills plunging down to the ocean, accessible only by boat, train, or on foot. Snow and heavy rain had affected some tracks but we were able to walk between three villages and catch the train to the others. Kari kept me entertained with jokes and commentary in Italian. Back in our cosy hotel, we enjoyed a log fire in the comfy lounge area, complete with hot chocolate by the Christmas tree.

Next day we had a complicated train journey to Nice, patching together our journey amongst delayed and cancelled trains interspersed with long, cold waits on deserted station platforms. We arrived in darkness and pouring rain and foolishly decided to walk the relatively short distance to our quaint pensione. By the time we arrived, we were completely drenched along with everything in our backpacks and suitcase. Seeing the humour in our continuing mishaps, we gaily hung everything around the room, turned the heater on full and went to bed.

A 4.00 am start took us from Nice to Avignon to Montpellier to Barcelona, with the last leg on a rattly, slow old train, providing ample opportunity to drink in the scenery rolling past our windows and enjoy each other's company. Our Barcelona taxi dropped us at a modern complex where we discovered the unexpected luxury of a huge two-bedroom apartment. This led Kari to post, "I LOVE Barcelona! It's the awesomest thing ever!"

Exploring Barcelona on Christmas Eve culminated in an evening visit on a packed metro to the Magic Fountain, which had featured in one of Kari's favourite childhood books. A stunning display of lights, music and a spectacular changing fountain kept us mesmerised for hours.

We made it back to the apartment to discover that Kari's camera had been stolen from her handbag. The camera was replaceable but the photos were not. All the precious photos of our trip so far were gone. I was inconsolable – and angry at Kari, who'd ignored and laughed at my advice to be more careful with her handbag security. I went to bed and cried, feeling that our special Christmas was ruined.

I woke with a better attitude, managed to put my angst aside and headed out for an early morning walk. On my return, Kari-Lee and I cooked and enjoyed a Christmas feast. This was the only time we'd ever been alone on Christmas Day and while it felt a little strange, I appreciated the unique privilege.

In the evening, we arrived at our booked flamenco show only to discover it wasn't on. Unimpressed, but determined to celebrate Christmas, we wandered the famous Las Ramblas boulevard, enjoying street performers, charming market stalls and eye-catching Christmas light extravaganzas.

Next morning, another train trip disrupted by weather eventually brought us to Avignon, Provence, where our rabbit-warren hotel overlooked the pretty town-square markets. Kari posted: "A magical night in Avignon, with Christmas markets, European waffles, fairy floss and a wander round the little town."

I realised just how much I simply enjoyed Kari's company. She'd grown into an adult I loved to spend time with.

After a morning exploring – and laughing at each other's French – we jumped on the train for our return journey to Nice. Kari posted: "A beautiful day by the sea in Nice. Castles, fudge, baguettes and crepes." Interesting how often food featured in her posts.

After three days exploring, it was time for our return trip to Rome. As usual, things didn't go according to plan. Our train from Milan to Rome was repeatedly delayed, then cancelled without warning due to snow. Finally, we boarded the luxurious Eurostar instead and made it to Rome in time to meet my two sisters who'd just flown in from Australia.

New Year's Eve in Rome was the stuff dreams are made of. Kari, now familiar with the layout, the metro and the sights of the city, was our guide. After hitting some of the unmissable highlights of Rome, we headed home for dinner amidst thunder, lightning and heavy rain, then out again in light drizzle to the Trevi Fountain, where we threw our coins over our shoulders.

This was when her legendary pink umbrella first came to the fore. Due to the consistently inclement weather, we spent much of our time in Italy holding umbrellas high, Kari's a bright hot pink. Amongst the sea of black umbrellas, hers stood out like a beacon, making it easy for us to follow her through the hordes of people milling around Rome. She acted as an invaluable tour guide, speaking Italian fluently and understanding the ways and customs of the locals.

After discovering Kari's favourite gelato shop closed, we ducked out of the ever-increasing rain to enjoy an Italian hot chocolate. As we made our way towards Piazza Navona, the ancient public square where Kari-Lee had planned to dance the New Year in, lightning and thunder increased as the rain got heavier. We surrendered, headed home and dried off, but all around us we could hear a cacophony of fireworks.

Finally, Kari and I could resist no longer. We ran laughing down the steps and out into the street, where we watched dazzling fireworks whizzing through the sky over the Colosseum. It truly was a pinch-me moment.

On New Year's Day at the Colosseum, a tour gave us great insight into this spectacular structure, but Kari stole the show when some "Roman guards" persuaded her to pose with them and I was able to take priceless photos.

Next morning, a three-hour bus trip to Naples followed by a brief city tour led to the phenomenal highlight of Pompeii. Later, a slow and at times frightening trip on the edge of a precipice transported us to Sorrento, a coastal town with sweeping water views, perched atop cliffs.

We woke to the rare sight of sunshine streaming through the windows and made the most of our day with an excursion to the Isle of Capri. Rough seas had prevented boat trips for the past few days so our journey was quite bouncy, but the alluring blue of the ocean distracted us from our queasy stomachs. A chairlift to the top of Mount Solaro offered us spectacular, postcard-worthy views. Exploring the island occupied most of the day before dinner back in Sorrento, where Kari daringly went on a date with our flirtatious Italian waiter.

We relocated to the idyllic setting of Amalfi the following day in the usual drizzle, but still managed to investigate the extraordinary striped cathedral. Next morning, sunshine inspired us to catch a bus to Ravello, up a very winding, very scenic road on the very edge of a cliff. This iconic cliffside town high above Amalfi offered unparalleled, panoramic views which mesmerised us before our hair-raising return journey.

We chose to get off at Positano, a picturesque town cradled between crystalline, turquoise waters and rugged rocky mountains. We made our way down past colourful, cliffside villas onto the wide beach where we found a restaurant for lunch, located right on the black sand. Kari couldn't believe we were dining where movie stars dined.

Back to Rome, days of fun and exploration in Florence and Pisa before a long train trip brought us to Urbino, Kari's hometown. She took pleasure in sharing the highlights of her new home before joining us on the last leg of our memory-making trip, back to Rome.

It was so hard to say goodbye to Kari-Lee, even knowing she'd be coming home in just a few months. Her absence in our lives at home left such a void. My fears for her safety threatened to rise afresh.

Yet, what was the point of a life if not to live it to the full? That was Kari's attitude and I had to admire it. She wasn't content with a safe, cotton-wool-wrapped existence. She wanted to celebrate every moment, finding and spreading joy, living a life that was worthwhile.

I hugged her tightly, drank in the sight of her precious face one more time, then turned to walk away. Time to go home.

CHAPTER FOURTEEN

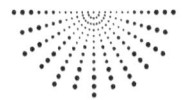

*K*ari's Italian adventure continued but so did the cold winter. She posted in January 2010: "Tempted to wear my Havaianas in the snow today for Australia Day but think I'll pass on the frostbite." Still, she made the most of it: "Epic-est snow fight! My fingers are SO COLD! And I'm all wet, but so happy."

Our summer-loving girl missed the warmth of the sun, so she and two friends hatched a plan to escape to Egypt once their exams were over. Kari had hankered to visit ancient Egypt since childhood. Back in Australia my fears escalated, considering recent bombings in Egypt directed at tourist towns where Kari would be staying. Yet how could I possibly deprive her of this dreamt-of experience? (Not that I had any say in the matter.)

"HAVING THE BEST TIME!!! I LOOOOOOVE EGYPT!!!!"

I don't think Kari could have expressed it any more clearly. Mind-blowing experiences formed a mental scrapbook for her of exceptional, enduring memories. Visiting the pyramids of Giza, the Sphinx and the tombs of ancient pharaohs and queens fulfilled Kari's childhood imaginings.

She belly-danced with locals on the banks of the Nile beside a campfire, rode a camel to dinner in a Nubian village, quad-biked in the desert and dined in a remote Bedouin tent camp. Starlit nights sleeping on the deck of a felucca as it drifted down the Nile contrasted with sunny days snorkelling in a huge coral garden filled with rainbow-coloured fish in the Blue Hole, near Dahab on the Red Sea. Dahab also provided plenty of opportunities for dancing, a vital part of any holiday for Kari.

A deeply meaningful highlight for her was climbing Mount Sinai, which she had heard about all her life as the place where Moses received the stones bearing the Ten Commandments. Leaving at midnight, they climbed in darkness and freezing cold, reaching the summit at 6.00 am to watch the sunrise.

Returning to zero degrees in Rome was a rude shock, followed by the sad task of packing up her life in Urbino and farewelling her many friends. A few days in Milan, Berlin and London capped off Kari's European adventure before the long flight home to Australia.

She barely had time to catch her breath because excited preparations were underway. Peter and I were leaving for New Zealand in three days, to be followed three weeks later by Kari and Tiana. Peter and I had an awesome time exploring the North Island, before flying to Christchurch where we'd arranged accommodation through Christian House Swaps.

We met the girls at the airport and our family adventure began. Our week in Christchurch offered bike rides through the pretty city, picnics by the river, hours soaking in thermal pools, bushwalks through lush rainforest and hanging out with blue penguins at the International Antarctic Centre. Leaving Christchurch, we travelled west across the expansive Canterbury Plains before the road started winding up into foothills. Driving through jaw-dropping alpine scenery we arrived at breathtaking Arthur's Pass, then wound our way down to the wild west coast. At Franz Josef Glacier Park, an hour of walking brought us close to the terminal face. Back at our motel, we soaked in the hot pool and laughed as freezing rain tumbled onto our uplifted faces.

"I think I can, I think I can, I think I can." With my face pressed into a vertical wall of icy snow, I pushed myself up the 867 steps cut into the side of the mountain bordering Fox Glacier. Finally making it to the top, we were rewarded with a far-reaching view of untamed natural wilderness against a stunning mountain backdrop.

The girls relished the thrilling experience of walking on a glacier, even when Kari slipped and dropped her camera. She posted: "I'm the clumsiest person I know. I have no luck with cameras. Face-planting in the ice isn't fun. Why are the epic falls always mine? At least when I do things, I do them well."

Stopping at awe-inspiring lakes and mountain views, we made our way to the picture-perfect town of Wanaka, where trees in jewelled autumn colours formed a bold display. While picnicking by the lake we were thrilled to witness part of "Warbirds over Wanaka," a biennial air show. Planes darted and looped in the sky above us, ducks paddled tranquilly by, our family laughed and chattered together. I seared these pictures into my mind, precious family moments to treasure always.

Adventure-filled Queenstown held multiple highlights for Kari-Lee: the Skyline Gondola and fast-paced luge rides high above Lake Wakatipu, followed by jet-boat rides on the Shotover River. She posted: "Shotover Jet Boat today. GREAT fun! Once again reminded how breathtaking and beautiful this earth is."

High on Kari's to-do list was a drive through Glenorchy to Paradise, viewing secluded locations used in two of her favourite book and movie series, *Chronicles of Narnia* and *Lord of the Rings*. Soon we were plunging through multiple creek crossings, admiring hidden sanctuaries and untouched wonders. After a day at idyllic Milford Sound, we headed for Dunedin.

"The Cadbury Chocolate factory was like being in Willy Wonka's factory. Pipes full of chocolate running overhead and all. It's going to take me a long time to get through all my freebies!" posted Kari.

Dunedin and the Otago Peninsular provided days of scenic drives accompanied by the *Mamma Mia* soundtrack, songs which will forever transport me back to those carefree days, travelling with our family of four, windows wound down, wind blowing in my face, singing our hearts out. All too soon it was time to drive the girls back to Christchurch to catch their flight home. Even then, I didn't underestimate the immense privilege it was to have my grown-up daughters happily share a holiday with their potentially boring and embarrassing parents.

Peter and I spent another six days in Dunedin, building up our bike-riding fitness in preparation for our epic two-hundred-kilometre ride along the Old Otago Rail Trail. This had been the catalyst for the whole trip to New Zealand, a fundraiser for Cystic Fibrosis Queensland, supporting the people who supported Kari-Lee.

The next five days involved miles and miles of riding along gravel tracks for hours on end, through beautiful, big-sky country dotted with quaint towns. Sore bottoms and sore hands were a small price to pay for the privilege of joining this ride through striking colours and epic scenery.

And then home, back to our girls and back to reality.

CHAPTER FIFTEEN

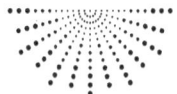

Kari-Lee's return heralded the start of a relationship with a lovely young Christian man who'd been attending our church while Kari was in Italy. Many boys had previously tried to win her heart, but she'd always chosen to be good friends instead. This time she was caught up in a whirlwind romance and it appeared that he was too, although he chose not to make the relationship public.

After several months, he asked to meet Kari for a private chat. She thought he was going to suggest taking their relationship to a more serious level. Instead, he broke up with her.

Kari was blind-sided, devastated, shattered, crushed. I'd never seen her so upset. She came home and cried for days, not eating, not going out. I ran her warm bubble baths, made soothing cups of tea and pampered her in any way I could. Gradually she emerged from her clouds of grief, but it seemed she never really trusted Christian guys in the same way afterwards.

Soon after this, Kari-Lee celebrated her twenty-first birthday with a campfire party in the backyard. It was a cold, bleak day so everyone ended up inside, but that didn't dampen Kari's spirits. Photos of the day show her surrounded by friends and smiling brightly, wearing a gorgeous polka-dotted dress, looking every bit the beautiful young woman she'd become.

While her health mostly remained good in those "golden years" following high school, CF intruded with another sinus operation. Then the painful swollen ankle condition returned sporadically and we all hoped it wasn't going to become an ongoing CF-related issue.

August was a big month for Kari. She was gradually realising she'd like to do something different with her life and decided to train as a paramedic. On-road training, where learning is done in a practical hands-on manner while accompanying actual paramedics, was still available. This option was Kari's preference, rather than completing another university degree. After impatiently waiting many weeks for paperwork from Italy and from previous employers, she filled out all her forms and excitedly sent them in.

Frustratingly, she received a reply saying that applications had closed just days before but would open again in the future and she should reapply. In the meantime she landed a job, not in photography, but at a mobile phone shop, which provided her with an income and more independence. That allowed her to buy her own car in September, a cute yellow Toyota Yaris with the numberplate LLI, leading to the nickname "Lillie", also the name of my beloved Nana.

When the phone rings in the middle of the night, it's rarely good news. That's how we learned that Peter's parents had died together in a car accident, returning from a funeral interstate.

The initial shock gave way to trauma, sorrow and grief, as we mourned these two who'd been so special to our whole family. Kari posted: "To my beautiful grandparents, friends from kindy and married for over sixty years. I love you both so much and will miss you. May you rest in peace together."

Our certain knowledge that they were now celebrating with Jesus eased our grief somewhat. Nan had prophetically said in a phone message earlier on the day she died, "We're all just a breath from eternity."

Their Queensland funeral brought many relatives from interstate. It was Kari and Tiana's first funeral, followed a few days later by a replica memorial service in Adelaide for relatives who couldn't fly to Queensland.

It became a memorable week for the girls, with eighteen cousins together, some of whom rarely saw each other. Despite the sad occasion, they enjoyed each other's company so much that one suggested they have a reunion in ten years.

I quietly commented to Kari's cousin, who also had CF, "Kari's not expected to live that long." Her predicted life expectancy was thirty years.

"Neither am I," he said, then shared that information with the group.

Somewhat taken aback, as CF was rarely acknowledged, they said, "Let's make it five years then. We'll get together in 2015."

∽

TRAVEL, driving long distances, flying and photography. Four of Kari's passions came together in a new job working for a photography franchise.

This involved travelling with a hair and makeup artist to towns all over Australia, photographing groups of people who'd been booked by company agents. Kari-Lee worked in out-of-the-way and varied places like Broken Hill, Dubbo, Armidale, Mackay, Shellharbour, Mildura, Airlie Beach, Whyalla, and Esperance, four-thousand kilometres away.

She loved aspects of the job and it provided her with plenty of adventures. In early 2011 when she was twenty-one, her photography income enabled her to achieve her goal of moving out of home into a shared house with friends from church. Riotous nights of fun and laughter as well as deep meaningful conversations forged close bonds of friendship that lasted a lifetime.

A RANDOM INCIDENT while dancing in Brisbane led to Kari's car being impounded, which led to a chance meeting, which led Kari into a new and secret relationship. Kari kept this relationship from me because the man was not a follower of Jesus.

I realise many people might wonder why that was a problem. Spending four years myself during university in a deeply committed relationship with a non-believer had caused me to do some serious grappling with aspects of my faith and to ultimately make the heartbreaking, deeply painful decision to end the relationship. It was one of the hardest things I'd ever had to do.

I finally realised that my faith in Jesus was fundamentally central to my life. It undergirded everything I believed and how I lived, infiltrated all my thought processes, and determined how I reacted to things that happened in my life.

Marrying someone who didn't share that could never bring the deep and unbreakable union I desired. I'd hoped to spare Kari similar angst. Once I discovered the relationship, she listened tearfully to my concerns and basically agreed with them, but by then her feelings were too involved for her to follow my advice.

It became a point of contention between us, although we didn't let it spoil our relationship.

AFTER ALMOST A YEAR, Kari-Lee decided to leave her photography job, disagreeing morally with the company's principle of charging people what she felt were exorbitant amounts of money for photography packages they'd spend months paying off. She found a job as a barista, working in the café at the school she'd attended, where Peter still worked.

So many changes: new job, new home, new car, new man. But more life-changing events were yet to come.

CHAPTER SIXTEEN

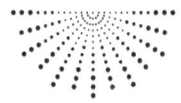

"Air Pacific Flight 810 take-off has been delayed."
"Air Pacific Flight 810 has been further delayed."
"Air Pacific Flight 810 has been cancelled."

A frustrating start to the culmination of months of planning and dreaming for Kari-Lee. Through dance, Kari had come to love the culture and country of Brazil, so when the opportunity came to travel there in 2012, she leapt at the chance. First planned stop: New Year's Eve in Fiji, followed by New Year's Eve on Santa Monica beach, made possible by the time difference.

Sadly, due to mechanical problems with the plane, Kari and her friend, Kristal, instead arrived New Year's Day. They didn't let it dull their enthusiasm but enjoyed a whirlwind few days at Disneyland and other Los Angeles highlights before flying to Cancun, Mexico.

This beachside paradise was a step on the way to what Kari called "my number one destination for ages! CUBA!" Eight days exploring and dancing, in the home of salsa, was the realisation of a dream.

Back to Mexico for eleven days backpacking with a bus pass through Mexico, Guatemala and Belize. Relaxing in a hammock strung between two palm trees at their shack right on the white sand beach, overlooking turquoise ocean on Mexico's Yucatan Peninsula, was Kari's idea of paradise on earth. Exploring Mayan ruins at nearby Chichen Itza provided some cultural and historical education before they caught the ferry to the small Caribbean Island of Caye Caulker.

"I'm on this little island off the coast of Belize, chillin' in the palm trees, casually riding my bike around, reggae music pumping out of all the shacks, thinking to myself, 'Could life get any better?'" posted Kari.

A jungle hut in Guatemala was next, followed by climbing an active volcano, then: "Went to explore Mayan ruins in Guatemala today. Saw pyramids, temples, monkeys, a toucan and patted a wild tarantula!"

Joining a backpackers' tour through Honduras, Nicaragua, El Salvador and Costa Rica led to Kari's usual array of mishaps: "It's been an eventful few days. My camera was stolen along with all my photos and the next day we had a massive accident in the minibus! But all good, we spent the last few days in a tiny untouched surf village in El Salvador, so life is good." There were also unexpected highlights, like when she saw Will Smith filming in Costa Rica.

Ring-ring! Late afternoon in Nambour, but one in the morning in Costa Rica, so why was Kari calling me?

She was alone in a hotel in San Jose, because, in typical laid-back Kari style, she hadn't organised her Brazil visa in time to travel to São Paolo with Kristal. While she waited a few days, her friendly guide had been showing her around. He was due to collect her at 7.00 pm but didn't arrive. He rang Kari at midnight to say he'd been kidnapped at knifepoint and driven around to ATMs for hours in an attempt to steal money from his accounts. Kari-Lee shared that story with me, then wondered why I worried when she travelled.

Eventually she made it safely to Brazil, via Peru, and the essence of her holiday began. "Words seriously cannot describe my current situation. All day and night, people partying in the streets, samba music, colourful costumes everywhere. Tonight, we dance in the Rio de Janeiro Carnival in the Sambadrome!"

This pinnacle was followed by dune-buggy rides in Natal and visiting Salvadore, "the best, coolest place in the world which has all my favourite things in one place", before heading off to "our tree-top hotel in the Amazon. I'm finally living my dream in a tree-house in the jungle."

Kari-Lee continued to enthuse: "Yesterday my breakfast was eaten out of my hand by a cheeky monkey, I went bush-bashing in the Amazon rainforest, ate a coconut maggot, went piranha fishing (and caught one), then danced half the night. Gotta love life in the Amazon." Swimming with pink dolphins and visiting the thunderous Iguaçu Falls topped off her month-long Brazilian experience.

Flying home to Australia via Buenos Aires in Argentina gave Kari the opportunity to experience tango dancing. Naturally, Kari had a bit of "a scary experience. Sick and completely lost at midnight in Buenos Aires by myself," but she soon recovered to "visit the street markets when a samba band came my way".

RETURNING to her old life in Australia in March couldn't compare to the exhilarating adventures of South America. Perhaps that was part of the reason Kari agreed to join our family holiday to Central Australia in June. Perhaps she was excited to explore an iconic part of Australia that few Australians get to see. Perhaps she had fond memories of all our family holidays through the years. Whatever the reason, I'll always be grateful.

Before our holiday began, Kari was invited to be part of an exciting new drug trial which promised amazing benefits for people with CF. This was the first drug designed to treat the underlying CF defect in the chloride channel of each cell, which caused the drastic effects on multiple organs in the body. There were strict criteria to be included in the trial and we were immensely grateful when Kari was accepted. As it was a double-blind randomised trial, it was possible that Kari-Lee would be receiving a potentially life-changing new medication. We looked forward to the study starting later in the year.

A THREE-HOUR FLIGHT over increasingly-dry land brought us into Alice Springs, where we had a day of hilarious family fun at the annual Beanie Festival, trying on outlandish beanies and taking ridiculous photos.

Next day, a long drive west through the very heart of Australia took us past red desert sands and spinifex. As the iconic sight of Uluru came into view, Kari coined the phrase of the trip, repeatedly exclaiming, "It's so BIIIIG! I can't believe how BIG it is!"

For those who don't know, Uluru is a giant rock, 3.6 km long and taller than the Eiffel Tower. Blissful family days were spent exploring and learning about this majestic monolith and the nearby Kata Tjuta, a group of massive domed rock formations.

Next stop: Kings Canyon. We laced up our hiking boots and headed to the canyon. Kari and Peter tackled the challenging Rim Walk on towering 300-metre-high red rock cliffs. Tiana and I enjoyed a more sedate pace on the Kings Creek Walk below. Wandering through palm trees, native plants, creeks and lots of wildlife, occasionally we were able to wave to Kari and Peter far above us. Their strenuous walk, starting with five hundred steps up the hillside, rewarded them with spectacular panoramic views along with peaceful, cool waterholes for well-deserved rest breaks.

After reuniting to watch the sunset together, we luxuriated in a well-earned soak in our room's spa bath.

A week investigating the multitude of natural wonders of the MacDonnell Ranges and countryside surrounding Alice Springs took us to awe-inspiring chasms, gorges and waterholes, each one worthy of paragraphs of glowing descriptors.

I was quietly overwhelmed with gratitude – for days filled with family adventure, family laughter and family bonding. Of course, there were times when minor clashes occurred – when I took one too many photos of them, when someone was tired and hot, when we all needed a little space from each other – but generally it was a harmonious and peaceable time, with endless fun, oceans of laughter and silly poses galore.

CHAPTER SEVENTEEN

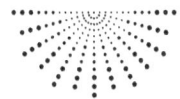

Back at home, things changed drastically. Our family was shattered and blindsided by Peter suffering a complete breakdown.

He'd been struggling for some time with his teaching role, feeling immensely stressed and unsupported at school. Pressure had been building inside as each small thing stacked up to create an internal time bomb. A seemingly minor occurrence soon after returning from school holidays traumatised him, causing a complete unravelling.

He packed a bag and left home one day while I was at work, leaving a note indicating he wouldn't be returning and implying he intended to end his life. Beside myself with worry, I involved the police who tracked him down and eventually returned him to my care.

He took the whole term off on sick leave, receiving treatment, counselling and medication after being diagnosed with severe, chronic depression. When he'd left initially he'd been driving to Cairns, so after several weeks I encouraged him to join me on a month-long road trip to Cairns together instead.

He bought a ute and campervan and we set off, stopping at picturesque spots along the east coast of Queensland until we arrived in Cairns. There he received love and support from our friends, Janine and Cam, before we headed further north to Port Douglas and Cooktown.

Along the way, Bible study and working through a devotional book with challenging insights helped bind us together, starting to mend some of the fractures that had resulted from recent happenings.

∼

In August, Kari caught influenza and was quite sick for a short time. Although she recovered well, the most devastating effect was that it precluded her from the trial of the new Vertex CF drug. It was shattering news, but there was nothing we could do to change it. We hoped another opportunity would open soon.

She was working at a new coffee shop, right on the beachfront at Mooloolaba. It was an idyllic setting for beach-lover Kari, who often spent her lunch breaks sitting on the beach, gazing out over her beloved ocean. The owners, who had two sons younger than Kari-Lee, loved her so much they often joked about Kari marrying one of their boys. I didn't mind who Kari's future husband might be as long as he was a follower of Jesus. Kari was still in contact with her friend who wasn't a believer. He'd moved to New Zealand, but I wasn't sure how their relationship stood. I prayed fervently that God would bring a Christian man into Kari's life.

In October, Tiana was turning eighteen, entering adulthood. A garden party beside Nana and Pa's picturesque dam was planned, but Kari also took Tiana out to celebrate. Kari invited the elder brother from the café, I'll call him Nic. One of his friends, who also happened to be the brother of Kari's friend Rachel, came too.

Partway through the evening, Tiana noticed Kari dancing cosily with Nic but she didn't mention it to us.

Two weeks later, Peter and I were at the café, planning to meet Kari for lunch, when I was startled to see her coming from the carpark holding hands with Nic. They dropped their grip before reaching us, but I'd seen enough. When I mentioned it later, Kari didn't deny it and the romance blossomed from there.

PETER RETURNED to work at the beginning of October thinking he was recovered. He lasted less than three weeks. The stresses of teaching in this environment were too great for him and he attempted to overdose.

More sick leave led to an application for Workcover (insurance for injuries, both physical and mental, sustained at work), which was rigorously fought by his employers. Most of the documents and submissions were handled by me, as Peter's mental state prevented him from being of much assistance. Depression took over his life and I was constantly on edge fearing he would try to harm himself.

Then Tiana had to move to a new restaurant to continue her school-based apprenticeship as a chef, due to ongoing issues (not of her making) at her original placement. She was also struggling with depression and very unhappy at school.

At the same time, Kari was becoming increasingly unwell – although she hid the extent of it from me. As she and Nic became more involved, I heard about Nic's recent nickname, "Sleeping Nic". He would fall asleep anywhere, anytime. Kari started to join him. She was so tired that she stopped dancing and exercising. She also started to lose her appetite.

As she didn't live at home, it took some time for me to notice the decline in Kari's health. She'd always tried to keep any negative health issues from me as she wanted to be independent. I was so focused on Peter's mental health challenges, writing letters to Workcover, and keeping Tiana safe that I wasn't paying the close attention to Kari's health that I normally would.

In early November, Kari was admitted to hospital with pneumonia. This was the first time Nic became aware that Kari was living with CF. She hadn't mentioned it previously, because when she was well she chose to keep that information to herself, afraid it might cause people to treat her differently. After many years of practice, she was able to surreptitiously take her enzymes so that nobody would notice. Or she'd just not take them with company.

We described all her other symptoms to her doctors and further tests were run, including one for glandular fever (mononucleosis).

All results came back negative, so doctors continued to treat her as usual for a CF-related lung infection.

Just a week after being released from hospital, with her doctor's agreement Kari jetted off with Tiana for two weeks in New Zealand.

To celebrate her high-school graduation, rather than join a typical Schoolies event Tiana had chosen to explore the North Island of New Zealand with Kari-Lee.

I had concerns, many concerns. I didn't feel Kari was well enough to be travelling. I was also concerned about Kari reconnecting with her past boyfriend who now lived in New Zealand. I felt that my prayers asking God to send a Christian man had been answered in Nic, but I knew the power this past relationship had over Kari.

I was concerned about Tiana too and some of the choices she'd been making.

In the end, after voicing my concerns I just had to entrust them to God and pray fervently for their safety.

They had a marvellous time together despite Kari's energy levels being nowhere near normal. She posted: "Exhausted after a big day. Hiked to Cathedral Cove and walked where William Moseley walked in the Narnia movie. Lay on Hot Water Beach in the sunshine. Thankful for beautiful weather."

It was very cold in New Zealand, probably not helpful to Kari's health challenges, but she and Tiana arrived back full of exciting stories about white-water rafting, dodging a tornado (uncommon in New Zealand), visiting Hobbiton and generally having an awesome time together.

These golden years after Kari-Lee finished high school had been adventure-filled and free from sickness. The slight blip of pneumonia in November was soon put behind her, as she delighted in her growing relationship with Nic. He was invited to join our exuberant extended-family Christmas celebration on Boxing Day, a sure sign that things were getting serious.

I was grateful to see Kari-Lee so happy with Nic. Although her health hadn't returned to its normal level, Christmas was a joyful time. Nic blended in with the family and Kari's radiant smile spoke of deep contentment. The future looked bright and full of potential.

CHAPTER EIGHTEEN

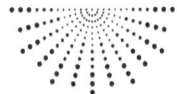

"First day of Paramedics. I'm gonna save the world!" The new year started on a high when Kari-Lee was accepted into Paramedic Science at the University of the Sunshine Coast (USC).

Her budding romance with Nic blossomed and they started attending church regularly together. She was enjoying her café work overlooking iconic Mooloolaba beach. Life was great, apart from the niggling problem of her health.

Other family members were having a more difficult time. Peter's struggle with depression continued, along with frustrating legal and administrative issues around his Workcover claim. During the holidays, his position had been made redundant while he was on sick leave. Much of my time was occupied with letter writing related to this, while accompanying Peter to appointments and doing my best to support him.

Tiana was now working full time in her chef apprenticeship, but she wasn't happy with what she saw as our controlling restraints on the lifestyle she wanted to live.

I felt like I was balancing multiple plates on fragile, skinny sticks, any of which could crash to the ground with catastrophic consequences.

It was a shock for us all when Kari's lung function didn't bounce back to pre-November levels, but instead hovered around fifty percent of what it should be. Her debilitating fatigue continued.

I was extremely concerned, but when we went to CF clinic in January, for some reason her name wasn't on the patient list. We waited for hours in the hope that someone would see Kari-Lee, because she obviously wasn't as well as usual. We phoned the CF nurses and left messages for them to ring us, but had no response, as they were probably busy at clinic.

In the end, rather than make a fuss we left, a decision I will always regret.

EVENTUALLY, Nic was diagnosed with glandular fever and, soon after, so was Kari. She hid how unwell she was, because that had always been her tactic to live as normal a life as possible. This time, it didn't work.

Her Facebook post near the end of March told the true story: "I just want to sleep. Forever. I'm constantly tired, no matter how much sleep I get."

At CF clinic three days later, a shocking lung function of just thirty-two percent, the lowest it had ever been in her life, saw her admitted straight to hospital. She was extremely unwell with pneumonia and glandular fever. Her doctors were so concerned they admitted her to the High Dependency Unit (HDU), one step down from ICU.

On the surface, we took this in our stride. I went into "practical problem-solver" mode and Kari continued to smile and joke with her nurses and visitors.

Underneath, it was a different story. After years of Kari's CF lying relatively dormant, it had dramatically reared its ugly and frightening head. Once again, we were reminded that Kari lived every day of her life with a severe, life-threatening condition. Once again, we were reminded that despite our best efforts CF could claim her life at any time.

Once again, we were reminded that her life was completely in God's hands.

After seventeen days in hospital, Kari was well enough to be discharged to administer her own intravenous (IV) antibiotics. This was something I'd done for many years, but now she was living away from home Kari took full responsibility.

Expecting the usual gradual improvement in health, we were all aghast when Kari deteriorated rapidly, needing hospitalisation in HDU just twelve days later. Her lung function had plummeted again to thirty-four percent.

This was not how life worked. You got sick, you went to hospital, you had treatment, you got better. It was jarring to realise that the pattern wasn't holding, that Kari's doctors were concerned, that the usual fixers weren't fixing things.

After a frightening week in HDU, followed by two more in her normal ward, Kari-Lee was released, again, on home IVs.

We were all cautiously relieved but decided to augment the medical treatment with natural supplements to boost Kari's ability to fight infection and hopefully ward off any recurrence. Tests had shown the cepacia bacteria, which usually lay dormant in Kari's lungs, had been stirred up. The debilitating effects of the glandular fever on her previously strong body had paved the way for the bacteria to flourish, multiply and take over her lungs, causing pneumonia. She would need every possible arsenal in her weaponry to fight this insidious and powerful bacteria.

I spent weeks researching natural supplements to boost immunity, reduce inflammation and ward off infection. Kari, mostly willingly, subjected herself to the administration of all these new treatments along with the myriad she already endured, in a tenacious bid to get her health back on track.

Imagine how shockingly appalled we were when, despite our increased efforts, it happened again just thirteen days later with another crash to thirty-four percent lung function.

An admission to hospital, while a common event in Kari's life, was still an involved ordeal. Firstly, she'd need a PICC line (peripherally inserted central catheter) to dispense intravenous antibiotics. A long thin tube would be inserted through a vein in her arm and passed up near her shoulder to the larger veins near her heart. Careful monitoring was needed for complications like infection and blood clots, both of which Kari experienced at some point. Often the PICC needed to be inserted with ultrasound guidance and sometimes had to be done in theatre by an anaesthetist.

Admission involved blood tests, lung function tests, blood pressure, temperature and weight checks. Settling into a hospital room for weeks at a time meant bringing items from home to make the space her own, even though it never felt like home. Adapting to hospital food was a major challenge for Kari, who'd been subjected to it for most of her life. The often-unappetising meals caused problems for Kari, who needed premium nutrition to maintain her weight and health even when well. While fighting an infection, it was paramount.

Probably the most difficult aspect for Kari was the social isolation. While I endeavoured to spend most of my non-working time with her in Brisbane, few others made the hundred-kilometre journey.

Thankfully, in 2013 her friend Rachel lived in Brisbane so she was able to visit more frequently, but Kari was cut off from many social interactions, her dancing, her work, her studies, her multitude of friends. Of course, now that Nic was on the scene he was a frequent visitor, as much as his work allowed. Many nights he drove home very late and very tired, causing an anxious two hours for Kari till he arrived safely.

"I've arranged a meeting with the lung transplant team." These words from Kari's CF doctor hit us like a lightning bolt.

It was impossible for us to believe we were at that point. He tried to soften the blow by explaining it was a precautionary measure, but Kari and I were overwhelmed at this breath-robbing news.

In our wildest imaginings we hadn't expected to be thinking about transplant for at least another ten years, and hopefully never.

A lot of friends couldn't understand our reticence for transplant; they saw it as the permanent solution to CF. What they didn't realise was that even if you survived the dangerous surgery, statistically just over half of lung-transplant recipients are alive after five years. Life expectancy after lung transplant was said to be ten years. We were definitely not ready to limit Kari's future to ten years.

∼

WE INTENSIFIED our efforts to get Kari-Lee well and avoid the need for transplant. I'd already put out repeated calls for prayers for her healing, but now we called for a day of prayer and fasting, with many willing participants.

Next day, Kari went to a meeting with a well-known local with a healing ministry. He'd prayed for her previously, mostly when she was a child. In recent years she'd either been well enough not to be actively seeking healing or too embarrassed as a teenager to go forward. This time, just like every other time, there was no evidence of change, but we were encouraged to continue believing as change might take some time to become noticeable.

At the same time, Kari's CF doctors started her on a radical new antibiotic, chloramphenicol, which had potentially dangerous side effects. This indicated how desperate things were becoming and after two weeks suffering debilitating side effects the drug was stopped.

Kari's world and mine shrank to a laser focus on beating the invasive cepacia bacteria.

For a time, it was looking better, as Kari drew upon reserves she didn't even know she had and fought to get better. For a time, things seemed to be stabilising, with lung functions hovering around forty-five percent, even when they finally removed her PICC and stopped IV antibiotics after a month. For a time, as friends far and wide rallied in prayer, we dared to hope that Kari's health had turned the corner.

It was not to be. In early July, when her lung function once again dropped into the thirties, Kari was devastated to be readmitted to hospital. Just before she was readmitted, we managed to get Kari to a meeting with a gentle older man with an international healing ministry. Despite his heartfelt, faith-filled prayers, along with those of hundreds of others, Kari continued to deteriorate and began coughing up blood.

This time, she had to make the heart-breaking call to cancel her university enrolment on the instruction of her doctors. This was another crushing blow, after having to give up work in March.

CHAPTER NINETEEN

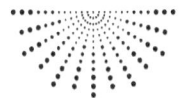

I watched a young woman, full of life, with a promising career ahead and a tender love story in its infancy.

I watched her suddenly have no energy, after travelling the world and experiencing countless thrilling adventures.

I watched her doing absolutely everything the doctors told her and way more, yet continually getting worse instead of better.

I watched her being trapped for weeks in a barren hospital room, far from home, friends, family, hobbies and fun.

I watched and was helpless to change it.

2012 became a year of revolving doors, in and out of the hospital. Kari was in hospital every month of the year from March onwards.

During her second admission in August, we were forced to face the inevitable. Kari-Lee needed a double-lung transplant. Meetings with the transplant team confirmed what we already knew. In most ways Kari-Lee wasn't sick enough for a transplant. Her lung function wasn't low enough, her weight wasn't low enough, her exercise tolerance wasn't low enough. She'd never even been on oxygen in her whole life.

But the inescapable fact was that her body was unable to fight off the infection caused by the nasty bacteria residing in her lungs.

While she was on intravenous antibiotics she gradually improved, but as soon as they stopped her lung function plummeted, her inflammatory markers skyrocketed and her body began to shut down. This frustrating roundabout was literally sucking the life out of Kari.

As a mother, as a doer, as her carer for all her life, the powerlessness I felt was indescribable.

I'd done everything humanly possible. I'd rallied all my believing friends to pray. I'd called upon all the supernatural powers of Heaven to heal her. Nothing I did or said or prayed seemed to make the difference.

All her life I'd been aware that Kari's life was in God's hands, ever since He'd asked me to give her back before she was even born. That didn't make this any easier. I loved this child of mine with all my being and I'd move Heaven and earth to see her well. My helplessness was stupefying.

What a blessing it was, considering all this, for Kari to remain out of hospital for the entire month of September. Not only did she avoid hospital but she was well enough to attend an extended-family gathering in Melbourne.

Kari and Nic flew down together and Nic was able to meet everybody, gaining a secret tick of approval from all. All the cousins except Tiana were there. She couldn't get time off her new job, having recently made the decision to move to Brisbane to live with her boyfriend's family and continue her apprenticeship there.

October arrived, and with it another hospital admission. Although Kari's health was relatively stable, her CF doctor likened it to treading water. She wasn't drowning, but she was working arduously to keep her head above water. He strongly recommended Kari put her name on the transplant list, but she wasn't ready to give up hope of recovering without such drastic intervention.

Always an optimist, Kari's resilience was being sorely tested. She needed a miracle and she needed it soon.

Breaking through the cloud of exasperation and frustration surrounding Kari came a bright burst of delight.

On a rare evening out of hospital, Nic took Kari for a romantic dinner. They were strolling in the moonlight on Kari-Lee's favourite beach near Coolum when Nic handed Kari one of the towels he'd been carrying.

In her usual exuberant style, Kari flapped the towel open to sit on it, not realising that hidden within its folds was the engagement ring Nic had been nervously carrying around for weeks, since asking Peter's blessing to marry Kari.

Up into the air flew the ring – thankfully in a velvet box – before landing somewhere in the dark on the sand. Scrabbling around together, falling about laughing, finally resulted in Nic on one knee, then a sparkling ring on Kari's finger.

A wedding planned for April followed by a honeymoon in Bali gave Kari even greater incentive to get better.

Painfully, November brought more trials. In preparation for the seemingly-inevitable placing of her name on the transplant list, Kari had to have all four wisdom teeth removed, along with fillings, to prevent any potential bacteria from her mouth affecting the outcome.

She endured an overnight oxygen trial, a painful blood gases test, a gynae biopsy without anaesthetic, and multiple blood tests. On top of that, she had to give up her ticket to a Beyonce concert and sacrifice her dream Bali honeymoon on doctor's orders.

Ongoing and irremediable gagging and nausea led to an endoscopy, which the gastro team, in their fear for Kari's fragile lungs, decided to perform without any sedation. Kari described it as one of the worst experiences of her life.

Then, a massive hailstorm destroyed the asbestos roof of Kari-Lee's share house. We moved all her belongings out while wearing protective disposable overalls, boots, masks and gloves. Kari moved home to our granny flat, where we were able to care for her more easily.

IT SEEMED nothing was going right, but when the doctors told Kari to hurry up and get married as she might not survive until her planned wedding in April, we picked ourselves up and determined to give Nic and Kari a magical wedding.

We threw ourselves into preparations to turn her engagement party, planned for five weeks' time, into a surprise wedding – so her name could be on the transplant list before Christmas.

CHAPTER TWENTY

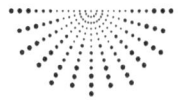

From within the dark forest of fear and suffering, of uncertainty and disappointment, yes, even at times of despair, there appeared a glimmer of light, of hope. A wedding. A day of joy, and anticipation of a future together.

From the moment she woke that day, Kari was radiant. Her sparkling smile lit up the very air around her and touched anyone who looked at her. She floated on a cloud of happiness, untouched by minor details of weather, arrangements, or last-minute cancellations.

After a lazy morning, Tiana, still unaware that the day was anything more than an engagement party, treated her adored sister to a special foot spa and pedicure. Rachel, also unaware, arrived to keep Kari company, freeing Peter and me to spend the day finalising all of the many preparations needed to carry off the surprise wedding picnic.

Working with Nic's parents and a few faithful friends and family, tents and gazebos were erected, a mobile cool-room trucked in for the food, a portaloo installed. Blackboard signs were posted, decorations arranged, picnic rugs and baskets scattered around the edge of the dam. With paper lanterns and fairy lights strung through the trees, a wonderland was created.

As the starting time of 2.00 pm drew nearer, friends arrived to help with the "engagement party". Several assisted in the kitchen, creating fruit platters surrounding palm trees made from pineapples, arranging dainty sandwiches and quiches made by Nic's parents and their team, loading specially made drinks in bottles with their own "Nic and Kari-Lee" labels.

Others helped outside, with balloons, setting up badminton and bocce and a wheelbarrow filled with drinks. An instant photo station was created alongside a special table for signing the register, with an antique suitcase for cards and string lines for photos.

Every small detail was attended to in our effort to make the day magical for our girl who had suffered so much, lost so much, and had to give up the wedding of her past dreams.

At last, the cars began rolling in. People strolled across the yard, past the dam and the house, to the grassy area near the trees. An atmosphere of joy and fun enveloped all the different groups who arrived to share in this special day. Choosing a picnic rug, they gathered, chatted and laughed, enjoyed the sunshine, the peaceful setting and the giggles of children running and playing.

Everyone was overjoyed for Kari and Nic, for the love and joy they'd found in each other in spite of the horrendous circumstances. Today was a day to put that behind them and focus on a wonderful future together.

Kari looked gorgeous in a colourful, flower-sprinkled sundress, a gift from Tiana for this special day. Her hair and makeup had been beautifully done by a hairdresser friend, who was in on the secret and ready to do minor adjustments and add flowers later. A photographer friend was on hand to capture all the special moments. Another special friend from childhood was primed and ready to start the music when it was time for the ceremony to begin.

Our pastor arrived and chatted with the guests. The beaming couple mingled, looking relaxed and thoroughly enjoying their party. Kari-Lee especially was thrilled to be out of hospital and to catch up with so many friends and family whom she'd not been able to see for so long.

After an hour, it was time for the real purpose of the day to begin. Kari-Lee, Peter and I snuck away to the house to change Kari into her dress and add beautiful orchids to her hair. I hurried back and let Pastor Tim and the now very nervous bridegroom, Nic, know that the bride was ready. The music started and the sound of John Legend singing *All of Me*, floated across the dam. The song's words of commitment and dedication of their whole selves to each other brought tears to my eyes.

Kari appeared in the distance, at the house, looking fragile, but breathtakingly beautiful in a white lace wedding dress, on the arm of her proud Dad. They left the house and slowly made their way past the dam, across the grass to where the guests had assembled. Peter managed to safely support Kari, with only a few tears giving away the intense emotion of the moment.

Nic shared months later, "That moment when you stepped outside Nana and Pa's house and John Legend started playing, all the dreams that I could possibly imagine came true. When you were walking across from the house I was thinking 'Could this get any better?' Yes. And it did. You looked so beautiful and as I wiped away my own few tears, I knew it was right. It couldn't have been more perfect. It was the best day of my life and as we recited our vows and anticipated those sought-after words – 'You may kiss the bride' – nothing could have made it more perfect."

Quite a few guests still didn't realise that they were attending a surprise wedding and one was heard to comment, "That's a bit over the top for an engagement party, isn't it?"

As Kari drew nearer, whispers of, "It's a wedding," could be heard as family and friends gathered close to witness this joyful and momentous ceremony. Kari and Nic gazed at each other as the pastor joked with the crowd about how they'd been given "a special invitation, but maybe under false pretences". The ceremony was poignantly beautiful. Nic's quavering yet determined "I do" followed by Kari's quiet, confident echo. Two young people with aching uncertainty in their future circumstances, but with no uncertainty at all in their love for one another and their pledges to each other. Never had the words "For better, for worse, in sickness and in health, till death separates us" had such depth of meaning for all those watching on.

Tears trickled down my face as the pastor prayed, "Father

Almighty, You have known Nic and Kari from birth until this moment and You know the days ahead. We commit Nic and Kari into Your hands and into Your keeping."

Were they tears of jubilation, that Kari had found the one whom her soul loved? Were they tears of fear and uncertainty for what lay ahead? Were they tears of hope and trust, that the future would indeed be bright for these two young people who deserved it so much? My emotions were a tangled ball, tightly ravelled together so that it was impossible to feel where the joy ended and the trepidation started, where the hope blended into foreboding at the unpredictability of the future.

Kari-Lee continued to sparkle and shine throughout the whole ceremony, her smile lighting up the afternoon as she pledged her love and commitment to Nic. She seemed on another plane, above the mundane, in a dimension where joy was the air she breathed. Nic blushed and stammered through his vows, like a schoolboy who couldn't quite believe he'd won the ultimate prize. Heartstrings were tugged, quiet tears were wiped, happiness infused the air surrounding all who witnessed these unforgettable moments. Their union was soaked in prayer and drenched in laughter. Their kiss incited loud cheers and clapping, the exchange of rings led to the usual moments of doubt whether the right sizes had been bought, and Kari's trademark face-pulling made an appearance.

At the close of the ceremony, it was time for the official paperwork. No bridesmaids, no groomsmen – who would co-sign? Subtle signals with pointing and beckoning fingers to those who'd been previously chosen and asked to fill these roles in the intended April wedding led to Nic's cousin and Rachel stepping up. Laughter replaced tears as jokes were exchanged, followed by a triumphant raising of clasped hands by the new couple.

In the background, one of Kari's favourite songs, *Never Knew I Needed* by Ne-Yo, captured the moment perfectly. In recent years, Kari-Lee had decided she didn't want to get married, or, if she did, it would be to a man of Polynesian or Islander ethnicity as she "didn't feel attracted to white guys". She'd even made a hundred dollar bet with Nic's dad at work that she wouldn't ever marry a white man. And now, at the end of her wedding to not only a "white guy" but her boss's son, she handed over a $100 bill with a huge smile on her face. She'd realised that Nic was, in fact, the man she never knew she needed.

Everyone hurried to surround Nic and Kari in enthusiastic hugs and wholehearted congratulations, with a bit of ribbing thrown in about the sneaky surprise.

Next it was time for speeches. First Peter gave his well-prepared and well-presented father-of-the-bride speech. He spoke of his precious "Parbi", the name Kari called herself when she was too young to pronounce Kari properly. It had always been his nickname for her. He shared how precious she was and what a blessing she'd always been to us. He joked with Nic about the fact that when Peter was Nic's sports teacher at school, neither of them would ever have dreamt he'd marry Mr Venning's daughter.

Then it was my turn. I'd written a beautiful speech but unfortunately in the rush that morning I'd left it at home. I was able to remember the important bits, sharing with those gathered about how God had His hand on Kari-Lee even before she was born. I said, "I really honestly believe that Nic is God's answer to my prayer and that Nic and Kari are meant to be together." I was honest about my early reservations about how young Nic was and what little life experience he had compared to Kari, but that I was now convinced he was a "man of true character and a blessing to Kari and to us".

With Nic's parents speaking next, we had all of the usual speeches, followed by an open invitation for anyone who'd like to share.

To the front they came, one after the other, many in tears. Everyone wanted to bless and honour this special couple on this incredibly significant day of their lives. So many beautiful stories, heartfelt thanks and funny anecdotes. An opportunity to speak out the thoughts and feelings we often keep tucked away, saved for a funeral, when the recipients are unable to appreciate and be uplifted by them.

Kari's friend and housemate tearily spoke directly to Kari, saying, "You're the most amazing girl I've ever met. So generous and kind-hearted, who loves everyone unconditionally. It's just God shining out of you."

Nic's friend felt that Nic and Kari's union was "a love of the ages, to love so wholeheartedly despite all uncertainty. Just to love and to give over to love completely."

Rachel talked about her many joyful memories of the years she and Kari spent playing together, including make-believe weddings, "and it just makes me so happy that you got your fairy-tale".

Kari's uncle described Kari-Lee as "an absolute blessing from Heaven, not only for your parents, but for the rest of us". To Nic he said, "You have no idea who you have in your hands, she is a gift from God."

So many people wanted to share their love and admiration for Kari and Nic that the light faded, the fairy lights came on and the stars began to twinkle as we all listened, mesmerised.

We'd intended to share an ice-cream creation station for dessert. Instead, the cold air began creeping across the flat from the dam, causing shivering and a general rustling among the crowd. Family photos were abandoned due to the lack of light and instead we moved to the excitement of the wedding cake cutting. A stunning two-tier cake decorated in Kari's favourite multi-hued ocean colours had been lovingly prepared by Nic's mum. It comprised one layer of carrot cake, Nic's favourite, and one layer of hummingbird cake, Kari's favourite.

As Kari and Nic joined hands on the knife that Peter and I had used to cut our own wedding cake, it was the culmination of five frantic weeks of planning. Everyone sampled their cake before farewelling the jubilant couple, who left for Brisbane ahead of their flight to Cairns for a romantic tropical honeymoon. As I watched the tail-lights disappear in the distance, I felt at peace, knowing that we had indeed done the very best we could to give Kari a wedding day to treasure, to look back on in the hard days ahead and to remember for the rest of her life.

KARI AND NIC's honeymoon in tropical North Queensland had a great start, with champagne and a signed take-home bottle of wine from the Qantas crew. "We should get married all the time!" Kari posted.

Her disappointment over having to forgo their planned honeymoon in Bali was forgotten as she revelled in sharing new adventures with Nic. "Today was Nic's first time on a boat in the ocean and first-time snorkelling! Was a beautiful day out on the reef, lots of pretty fish and coral. And we found NEMO!!"

Her enthusiasm couldn't even be dampened by an allergic reaction caused by exposure to sunlight interacting with one of her antibiotics, which made her face swollen and eyes misshapen. "So, I woke up today and I look like an avatar… and it's not going away. Maybe I'm adjusting to the tropical rainforest a bit too well?"

Evening tapas, cocktails by the beach, fancy dinner at a classy restaurant, relaxing by the pool and sleeping in a huge comfortable bed instead of a hard hospital bed all contributed to an awesome honeymoon, briefly erasing the spectre of hospital and transplants.

CHAPTER TWENTY-ONE

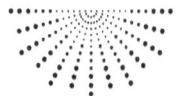

*R*eality hit like a sledgehammer when Kari was readmitted to hospital just a day after their return. Four days after that, she was listed for transplant. Our Facebook posts reflected our very mixed feelings.

Kari: "Massive day today. I'm now officially on the waiting list for a double-lung transplant. Even though I really don't feel sick enough at all, and to look at me you wouldn't think me different from anyone else, the doctors say it's the best thing. Was a massive decision and it makes me feel a bit ill…"

Me: "I'm so not ready for this… but it's going to happen anyway. I need to get my head in the right space. I need to hand it all over to God (I'm trying) and trust Him to work out timing and details. It's just not something you ever think you're going to face. It's very hard to prepare for. Of course, I realise it's even harder for Kari, as well as the future donor and their family. I need prayers for peace, but mostly that God will bless Kari with an amazing outcome. As always, her life's in His hands. It just becomes more real at times like these."

THREE DAYS later our dreams and nightmares collided. Kari was woken in her hospital bed in the middle of the night to prepare for transplant. She'd been deeply asleep. She was all alone in Brisbane. Nic and I were at home on the Sunshine Coast. None of her familiar nurses were working.

She started to panic – crying, shaking and vomiting. Very unlike Kari, but completely understandable. She didn't phone me because she didn't want me to worry, especially as she knew it mightn't go ahead. Two people are called for each set of donor lungs and whoever is sickest or matches the lungs best is chosen. Thankfully, Kari found Rachel's brother awake on Facebook and was able to chat with him to calm her nerves.

In the end, the other, much sicker person received the transplant. This experience made Kari realise she wasn't ready to be on the list. She asked to be removed until after Christmas, for which I was relieved. While the transplant team was satisfied with her decision, the CF doctors were not. They felt her need was urgent. It was extremely stressful and confusing for her.

CHRISTMAS DAY WAS WONDERFUL. Kari had been released from hospital and we spent the day sharing love, laughter and food with Nic's parents and grandparents, Tiana and her friend. The following day, Boxing Day, we celebrated Nana's birthday with my extended family. Photos of Kari-Lee from the day show an upbeat, healthy-looking young woman snuggling with her new husband, enjoying the antics of Pearl the poodle and relaxing with her family.

On the last day of 2013, Kari and I drove to the CF clinic, where her lung function continued to hover at only thirty-one percent of what it should be. She reluctantly but hopefully put her name back on the transplant list and we headed home.

An hour later, Kari was contacted by the transplant team, who'd removed her name until they could reassess her, including her psychological readiness for transplant. We didn't know when that assessment might happen, but we had to trust God's timing.

Kari posted: "Many people have been saying that 2013 has been the worst year. I have to agree. What a life-changing, emotional, HECTIC year! My life's been completely turned upside down in the last twelve months. At the same time, I've been super blessed by love and support from people I love and I've been given the greatest joy of a wonderful husband. (Still sounds weird.) This year's taught me to make the most of small joys and never take a good thing for granted, because you never know when it can change in a flash!"

Just two days later, she wasn't feeling so upbeat: "So here's the decision I have to make… Fade away and die in the next few months, or get my body hacked open and my organs ripped out. Thanks life. Thanks a lot."

Even our positive Kari was struggling with the huge life decisions facing her, along with the burden of putting absolutely all her effort, prayers, determination and hope into getting better, but instead continuing to decline uncontrollably.

A SUNBEAM of joy poked its way through these grey times in the shape of an adorable chocolate Labrador puppy. Kari had longed for a puppy for years, but her housing situations and frequent travel meant the time wasn't right. Until now.

Maloo Sheniqua moved into Kari's home and heart. Trips to the beach lifted everyone's spirits and Maloo soon proved she'd be the beach dog Kari had dreamed of. "All you need is music, sunshine, beach, nice lunch with good friends, and a run with a cute puppy to make you feel great about life."

FEBRUARY 2014 BROUGHT a wonderful development when Kari's lung function improved: "Smashed the 40%!!!! (First time since September) And added another kilogram in a week. Great motivation to keep fighting."

We were all full of hope that her recovery was on the way. She'd managed to stay out of hospital since December, a marvellous achievement. Even more exciting, the doctors stopped her three IV antibiotics for the first time since her honeymoon. No more PICC in her arm. Kari made the most of the last days of summer with lots of fun times with friends.

"Watching a little old Italian couple playing in the waves and having the best time. Possibly the cutest thing I've seen all week. It's those little things."

There was a tiny flicker of hope that transplant might not be needed. The CF doctors were very wary, but the transplant doctors didn't want to see her for two whole months.

∽

In late February, Kari was admitted to hospital with severe cramps, very high temperatures and high blood pressure.

Then she developed a blood clot near her new PICC line which caused her arm to discolour and swell up. "The doctor had four goes to get a PICC line in my other arm so I could go home today. No luck, so I'm in for another night."

∽

In March, Kari posted: "Flipped my calendar and this is the saying: 'I've decided to be happy, because it's good for my health.' Pretty perfectly appropriate."

Her days were filled with being a wife in their little granny flat, beach time with Maloo, cafe dates with Nic and picnics by the river. To top it all off she attended her first Zumba class in over a year and lasted the whole hour straight. "It feels sooo good!"

More excitement for Kari when three close friends all had babies in one weekend. Motherhood was something Kari longed to experience because she adored babies. Unfortunately, there were great risks involved in pregnancy with CF. Childbearing following double-lung transplant was even more risky and rarely achieved.

However, Kari was determined. This fuelled her motivation to continue her intense efforts to improve her lung health and reduce inflammation to avoid the need for transplant.

She was still living by her own mantra of enjoying the little things in life: "There truly is so much beauty in this world. The curious voice of a little kid, an old man helping his wife sit down, a mother holding her tiny baby close to her chest, the sun on our back, the breeze in our face. Life's little joys are hidden in every day."

Unfortunately, Kari's health continued to deteriorate. She fought hard to stay out of hospital, posting: "Sometimes life just isn't fair. At all."

For the first time Nic joined our special family tradition of watching the sun rise on Easter Sunday, reading Bible passages and singing Resurrection songs, followed by hot cross buns and Milo. It was such a special time and I drank in the vision of Kari, swaddled in blankets, her beautiful face lifted to the rising sun, a glow on her cheeks.

It was becoming clear that she was very sick, but she really wanted to enjoy Easter with Nic before heading for hospital. After a special birthday morning tea for Peter, where Kari lay limply on a chair, we drove directly to the hospital. This time, even she acknowledged it was where she needed to be.

Kari was extremely unwell. I asked on Facebook for prayer as she wasn't improving. High temperature, racing pulse, extremely high inflammatory markers and not-great oxygen saturation. It was all too scary for me. She suffered more trauma when a new doctor tried to insert another PICC. After many attempts due to all the scar tissue in Kari's arm, and close to twenty X-rays to check the position, it was finally in.

Kari posted: "Life was so much easier when I was invincible."

Finally, the antibiotics brought the raging infection under some control. She posted on April 30th, 2014: "Hey everyone. So, it's time. I've fought as hard as I could and done everything possible to try and get myself back to health, but for some reason it hasn't worked. So, I have to go back on the waiting list for double-lung transplant, probably by tomorrow. As the list is currently short and I'll be high priority, it most likely will be happening fast. I'd love to catch up with everyone because I won't be seeing people for a while, but time just doesn't allow, so I want to say thank you to everyone for their continuous support over the last year. I couldn't have done it without the positive, encouraging words from friends and family.

Hopefully I'll see you all on the other side when I can get on with living life!!!!"

～

Kari was out of hospital in early May, but now an oxygen tank sat beside her bed at home, a frightening sign of her deteriorating health. She bemoaned the fact that there was another tube to get tangled in while sleeping, along with her IV tubes, but it was definitely needed.

She could no longer do ordinary tasks like dressing herself, hanging washing, making her bed, doing the dishes, going outside at night, or walking one hundred metres without having a coughing fit, vomiting or lying down. Often all of those together.

Still, her spirit was strong. "How boring would life be if I was 'normal'? This journey I'm on, it's an adventure. Moulding me and making me a more patient, grateful, passionate person."

For the transplant to go ahead, someone had to commit to three months' leave to care for Kari. I chose that role so Nic could keep working and have an income. I applied for leave and explained I couldn't nominate dates yet, as we'd only have two hours' notice that the transplant was happening. I arranged a locum for my position who was willing to operate on those terms, but my boss just couldn't get his head around the situation. He kept returning my leave form and asking me to fill in the dates.

When I repeatedly explained why that wasn't possible he continued to question me. "Why do you need so much leave? She might get better faster than that. Can't someone else do it? Doesn't she have a husband?" Finally, I just gave up and left the form with him, hoping it would all work out when the time came.

My Mother's Day card from Kari was filled with heartfelt, meaningful words, something I'll always cherish. She and Tiana went to great effort to cook me a beautiful meal. It was so good to sit down as a family and enjoy the simple yet so very precious – and now rare – experience of being together for a meal at home.

The end of May brought some much-needed fun when Kari and Nic decided to escape to the Gold Coast for a special weekend. A

PICC in her arm and IV antibiotics couldn't wipe the smile from Kari's face. A huge bed in a fancy hotel room, a drive-in theatre movie, a day at Sea World, ice-creams at the beach and special dinners provided memories to sustain them through the hard hospital times ahead.

∼

On May 31ST, Kari received the call for her transplant.

We raced down to Brisbane, full of hope, but after a short wait it was decided that the donor lungs weren't viable.

How much longer could Kari survive without new lungs? When would the next call come?

∼

Only two days later she was back in hospital, this time with liver trouble. She was in a catch-22 situation. The liver problems were caused by the copious, endless antibiotics she was on, yet every time these were stopped the infection overwhelmed her body again. The only long-term treatment was a lung transplant, but that was dangerous while her liver was so inflamed.

We prayed for a way out of the corner she seemed to have been backed into.

No matter how sick she was, Kari never lost her sense of humour. "Help, they've got me locked up again and already tried to feed me fake egg omelette," she posted on her first day back in hospital in June.

While she was trapped in hospital, we decided to surprise Kari with an early superhero-themed party for her upcoming twenty-fifth birthday. Kari had a fondness for superhero movies and we wanted to honour her as our own superhero.

We arranged to meet at a friend's house and told Kari she was being brought there for a short break from hospital to have a massage. When she arrived with Nic, we all jumped out. "Surprise!"

Her friends had gone all-out with their costumes and Kari had a great time catching up with people she hadn't seen for weeks. Nic's mum fulfilled a dream of Kari's with a croquembouche birthday cake.

As I watched her laughing and chatting with friends, knowing how terribly unwell she really was, even I didn't realise how thankful we'd be in just a few days that we'd decided to have this early birthday party.

She returned to hospital a blessed but still very unwell girl.

As the doctors promised, Kari was released the day before her birthday on 19 June. I joined in Kari's happiness at heading home yet worry gnawed at my insides as I looked at the fragile shadow of her vibrant self she'd become. If a donor didn't come soon, I feared we could lose her.

Transplant was something we'd tried so hard to avoid because the dangers were significant, but it was becoming increasingly obvious that it was the only possible way she would survive.

CHAPTER TWENTY-TWO

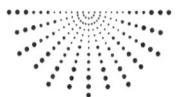

Kari-Lee was delighted to be home in the granny flat with Nic and Maloo the evening before her birthday. She'd dreamt of sleeping in her own bed.

Peter and Nic settled down to watch the first State of Origin football match, a big event in the sporting calendar. Kari and I relaxed with a cup of tea, a simple thing which made us appreciate being away from the hospital at last.

Suddenly into this peaceful existence intruded the unwelcome sound of our landline telephone ringing. Usually, we ignored it as only telemarketers used that number, but for some reason I felt compelled to answer.

I could barely believe what I heard. Donor lungs had been found for Kari! In stunned astonishment, I hung up the phone. When I told Kari her face reflected the tumult of emotions tumbling through me: excitement, fear, disbelief, anxiety, relief. We raced into the lounge room, to share our news with the boys.

"Oh sure," they said, laughing. "Good joke. Lucky it's half time and you're not interrupting the game."

They took quite some convincing to believe it was true. Once it sank in, everyone sprang into action. We had two hours to get to the hospital and it was a ninety-minute drive. After quickly packing, we piled into the car and made it to Emergency in time.

A long, long night of waiting followed. Peter, Nic and Tiana dozed in chairs or on the floor, but nobody got much sleep.

Kari was involved in lots of preparation. Being cannulated. Having multiple blood tests. Being shaved. Repeated nurses' observations. Having a surgical shower and chest X-ray. At times, I caught her off-guard, looking serious and pensive, as she contemplated the enormity of what was ahead. One of her favourite nurses removed her nail polish. The transplant nurse arrived around 1.00 am.

Even with all this preparation, there was no certainty that the transplant would go ahead. While Kari was being prepared, the donor lungs were undergoing rigorous testing to ensure they were viable and an excellent match for Kari. We thought about the donor's family who, in their darkest hour, had the strength and generosity to choose organ donation amidst their own stupefying grief.

At 6.00 am on Kari's twenty-fifth birthday, we were told that everything looked good. We all walked down with her to the doors of the operating theatre. This was a hard goodbye. While there was good reason to hope, there was no certainty that Kari-Lee would survive this major surgery. I knew of several people with CF who died during their transplant operation.

Kari's heart would be stopped, her lungs removed. For a time she'd be technically dead. All other options had been exhausted and we had to trust that this was the way forward. The surgeon was someone we'd never met or even heard of, but we trusted he knew what he was doing.

Kari looked so incredibly small and vulnerable. It just wasn't fair that she should have to endure this. She sat bravely, looking forward and stoically receiving hugs from each of us. I prayerfully committed her into God's hands, but couldn't help the few tears that leaked from my eyes as the doors closed behind her.

We knew it would be a long wait. The surgery would take six or seven hours. There was nothing we could do to hurry things up. It just had to be endured.

We dispersed to Tiana's Brisbane flat and to Rose Cottage – a house near the hospital provided by Cystic Fibrosis Queensland for families who came from outside the Brisbane region – to try to sleep. It was very difficult to relax, knowing what Kari was going through, but I managed an hour's sleep and felt better for it.

After filling the hours as best we could, we headed back to the Intensive Care Unit (ICU) waiting room, where Peter's sister and husband were waiting. Kari's long-time friend Rachel, her husband Winston, Rachel's mum Gaye, who was also my friend, and Gaye's husband, Bruce, came to join us after waiting at home became too much for them.

Around 1.00 pm, seven hours after we'd farewelled Kari, the surgeon came to tell us that the surgery had been successful. Kari now had beautiful, shiny, new lungs.

CHAPTER TWENTY-THREE

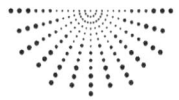

*I*n an open cubicle, surrounded by countless beeping and flashing machines, lay our precious Kari, eyes closed, looking peaceful. At 6.00 pm we had finally been allowed in to see her. I went first, with Peter, having some idea of the sight that awaited me.

Tubes snaked everywhere, including a ventilator breathing for her which puffed and hissed quietly on each breath. A central line entered her jugular vein. Four tubes leading into it delivered strong pain medication and antibiotics to prevent infection. A PICC line in her forearm provided more antibiotic coverage. A naso-enteric tube was taped into her nose to provide nutrition while she was unconscious. A large bag hung on the side of the bed, draining blood and fluid via four thick tubes coming through her chest wall from her new lungs. A catheter drained urine into a bag. An oximeter was clamped onto her finger and a blood pressure cuff around her upper arm constantly monitored her status.

I stroked her forehead and sat down, holding her hand, whispering to her.

She'd survived this incredibly traumatic surgery but the road to recovery would be long and difficult. Deep down, I knew my Kari and I knew she'd be up for the challenge. She loved life so much that she'd do everything in her power to be the best she possibly could.

Only two people at a time were allowed into the ICU. Because Nic was a little wary of what he might see, I escorted him to see Kari-Lee. I walked up to Kari's bed thinking Nic was right behind me, and started explaining the machines to him. When I turned around, his pasty, blood-drained face, wide eyes and shaking hands told me that none of my words had adequately prepared him for the sight of his sweet Kari lying helpless and surrounded by frightening-looking apparatus. I quickly grabbed a chair for him, until he recovered.

Our pastor called in to visit us and pray for Kari. Tiana went in with him and told me later that the sight of Kari lying there "looking dead" was incredibly confronting and traumatic. She felt very awkward having only the pastor with her. I had been unaware, thinking she was used to seeing Kari unwell, but later regretted my insensitivity.

As the evening progressed, Kari had visits from some close family and friends.

AROUND 9.00 PM Kari became restless and was fighting the ventilator tube in her throat. This was one of the things she'd been dreading. For some reason, the thought of this tube down her throat worried her more than many other things which seemed more distressing to me.

The nurses thought she wasn't awake enough to extubate, as she had her eyes closed most of the time. They tested by asking her to open her eyes, which she did briefly. When they asked her to wiggle her toes, she kicked her legs up and down. She definitely wanted to convince them that she was awake.

Once the tube was removed – a gagging, eye-watering procedure – Kari was much more settled and started to open her eyes and speak a little.

Amazingly, next morning, just hours after a double lung transplant, the physios came to take Kari for a walk. This was a complicated procedure as she was hooked up to so many machines. They connected them all to a huge mobile walker device, which Kari pushed along in front of her.

Minutes before they helped her to stand she was fast asleep due to all the strong painkillers circulating in her body, but up she got and walked around the ICU with their help. She did the same in the afternoon, even while drowsy and having trouble keeping her eyes open.

During the day she ate three meals. The large incision down the front of her chest made it extremely painful for Kari to cough, yet she needed to, so that her new lungs would stay free from secretions. The physios taught her to hold a rolled-up towel firmly against the incision whenever a cough was needed.

On Saturday, two days after transplant, the central line was removed from Kari's neck and replaced with a PICC line. The four chest drains were removed. She had two assisted walks, with a longer one in the afternoon.

There was great excitement when it was decided that Kari was well enough to leave the ICU. She was transferred to a surgical ward at three o'clock. She posted on Facebook: "I'm alive!! All my chest drains are out and I'm out of ICU. Still a bit tired and sore but eating like a hungry racoon and on the uphill climb."

More visitors were now allowed, including Nic's cousin, a tall, solidly-built guy. He asked Kari lots of questions about a double-lung transplant.

Kari supplied brief details. "They cut you open, saw through your sternum, prise apart your ribs, disconnect your bronchi and trachea to remove the old lungs, then reconnect everything, wire up your sternum and sew you back up."

That was all too much for this big, tough guy. He fainted, taking the adjustable table and physio equipment with him as he fell. Kari's nurse wanted him to be checked over in Emergency. He was too embarrassed, saying his friend would drive him home.

As he started to leave, he fainted again and was carted off unceremoniously to Emergency in a wheelchair. He sent Kari a photo of himself lying on the bed in his purple hospital gown, which matched hers. It gave her a good laugh.

∽

AFTER ALL THE WONDERFUL PROGRESS, Sunday was a hard day. At midnight I was woken in my bed at Rose Cottage by a phone call from Kari to say they were taking her back to ICU to have a chest drain reinserted because she was breathless.

I rushed up to be with her, but nothing happened for a long time. We were left waiting for hours.

Eventually, a cardiothoracic registrar arrived and gave Kari a painful local anaesthetic in her side. Then followed a traumatic experience involving lots of hard pushing and a loud pop as the drain penetrated her chest wall.

Because it wasn't bubbling or oscillating as it should an X-ray was ordered, which found the tube was kinked into the wrong position. They had to pull it out and put Kari through the ordeal again. We were awake until 6.00 am, then managed a short hour's nap. Nic arrived at nine, completely unaware of the night's traumatic events.

∽

ON MONDAY, Kari managed to walk half a kilometre with the physio. I was amazed and impressed. What a fighter. She was overjoyed when the doctors removed her catheter, which was uncomfortable and restricted her movement.

The next day Peter returned after spending time at home caring for Maloo, Kari's dog.

Different friends blessed her in different ways. Her Urbino friends came with a thoughtful care package complete with fluffy socks, soothing body cream and tasty snacks.

Kari's cousin, living in Japan, started sending her origami paper cranes. This stemmed from a Japanese legend that if one thousand origami cranes are folded in one year, that person's wish will come true. While we weren't sure about the basis of that, the cranes made pretty decorations, hanging in strands from the ceiling in Kari's otherwise bland hospital room.

On Wednesday, Kari exceeded all expectations with a one kilometre walk in the morning and gym session in the afternoon. Sometimes it was easy to forget that she'd had a double-lung transplant just five days earlier. Her recovery was marvellous.

Nic's parents arrived with lots of home-cooked meals, something Kari really appreciated. It was important for her to eat well to aid her recovery, and home-made meals were a huge help.

In the afternoon, Kari had the first of many intensive education sessions with the transplant coordinator.

THURSDAY STARTED WELL, with the removal of the remaining chest drain followed by visits from Kristal with her baby, then Gaye and Bruce with a basket of goodies from their church.

Unfortunately, just hours later, there was drama again. A chest X-ray revealed a pneumothorax – air in the space between the lungs and chest wall. Doctors started Kari on oxygen again while we all prayed. Two hours later, another X-ray showed no improvement. "Please, not another chest drain to be punched in," she said.

Alongside all this drama, Kari was undergoing desensitisation to Bactrim, a medication required after transplant but which she was allergic to. This involved gradually increasing hourly doses for five hours, with close monitoring and tests every fifteen minutes.

Along with physio and transplant education sessions, it wasn't a relaxing day. While Kari remained positive, tension was high the next morning as she went off for a bronchoscopy under general anaesthetic, followed by an X-ray. Thankfully the results were good, with no pneumothorax apparent.

THE BUSY DAYS progressed with ever-increasing education sessions involving transplant coordinators, pharmacists, dietitians, diabetes nurses, physiotherapists and occupational therapists.

Regular morning walks of increasing length, involving hills and steps, and an afternoon gym session of increasing intensity kept Kari sleeping well most nights despite the pain.

Daily injections of clexane to prevent blood clots, and insulin for post-transplant diabetes – a very common complication – became part of life, along with multiple nebulisers including one cytotoxic drug which required us all to vacate the room.

Kari, as usual, took it all in her stride and continued to sparkle. Most days there were visitors, often the faithful regulars, but sometimes welcome surprises. Kari continued to impress all the staff with her amazing physical recovery and her ability to absorb the plethora of information needed to manage life after a lung transplant.

EXACTLY TWO WEEKS after Kari received the life-saving gift of a double-lung transplant, it was time to put her new lungs to the test in the respiratory laboratory. FEV1 is 'forced expiratory volume' – a test that calculates the amount of air a person can force out of their lungs in 1 second. Prior to transplant Kari's FEV1 had dropped below thirty percent. Now she blew at seventy-five percent capacity, an awesome improvement.

She repeated the six-minute walk test, which physios use to assess cardiovascular fitness. More impressive improvement.

While her results for leg strength and step-ups were lower than before transplant, this was entirely expected as leg strength is drastically affected by transplant. Kari's continued hard work would soon reverse that.

All these outstanding results led to a splendid outcome. Kari could go home in the morning, provided the doctors were convinced by the results of her bronchoscopy.

Anticipation bubbled inside us, tinged with a touch of anxiety, as we waited impatiently for the results following her trip to theatre for the bronchoscopy. At last, four hours later, Kari got the go-ahead to leave the hospital. Her glowing face and beaming smile endured, even through the painfully slow wait at pharmacy for her shopping trolley overflowing with post-transplant medications.

As we finally accelerated onto the motorway, Kari posted on Facebook: "I'm on my way HOME!!! Home to my own bed and my puppy and my new life!!"

CHAPTER TWENTY-FOUR

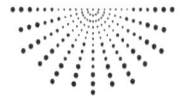

Sensational. Awe-inspiring. Spectacular.

Kari's recovery from transplant was a joy to behold. Like a butterfly emerging from a dark cocoon, she gradually blossomed, spread her wings and started to fly again.

On her first day home she attended a wedding. Nic was a groomsman and left home early. Kari dressed in a beautiful lace dress which made a great impression on Nic. Months later he shared, "My favourite memory was at my friend's wedding. I was performing my groomsman duties when I looked outside the little church window and there you were. Two weeks after having a double-lung transplant and just out of hospital, in the most beautiful blue dress I'd ever seen. I could not have imagined it any better. It was as though time stopped when I looked at you."

After a weekend filled with fun family gatherings, Monday morning was time for me to take Kari back to the transplant clinic for a check-up. We followed the usual routine of blood tests, X-ray, breathing function – with great results and an improved FEV1 of eighty percent. Next was a meeting with doctors, physios, dietitians and transplant nurse coordinators, something we would become very used to over the coming months.

At last, we escaped the hospital and took the opportunity to meet Tiana for lunch and some shopping. Normal life. We would never again take such things for granted.

The next day we designated as Kari's twenty-fifth birthday at home, as she'd missed out on all the usual celebrations due to being unconscious in surgery. We woke Nic and Kari with a rousing rendition of the birthday song, then sat on their bed as she opened twenty-five presents.

Nic cooked pancakes for us all, wearing Kari's new teal apron. It was a beautiful sunny day, so we had a picnic by the beach at Cotton Tree to celebrate. Kari was still full of energy, so she and Nic headed to Sunshine Plaza shopping centre, while I went home for a long sleep.

It was so exciting to see Kari full of life and able to keep going for hours and hours. Just a few short weeks earlier we'd wondered if she'd even be alive by her birthday. I was so incredibly grateful to have her home, cheerful and on her way to being healthy. She was certainly making the most of the new life she'd been given.

Wednesday was an epic day for Kari-Lee. She lunched with friends, then followed it with a four kilometre walk along the Maroochy River with Peter and Maloo. Four kilometres, less than three weeks after having a double-lung transplant.

Kari's recovery was a miracle to watch. Even that walk didn't tire her out. She still had plenty of energy for a Mexican dinner at Nana and Pa's followed by watching the second State of Origin football match. So much had changed since the previous match. Her life, which had been ebbing away as her lungs deteriorated, was now restored with new vitality and effervescence. Kari was coming back!

Thursday meant another trip to Brisbane for transplant clinic. As well as the usual assessments where she recorded an FEV1 of eighty-one percent, Kari had a gastric emptying study. This involved swallowing a radioactive egg which was then tracked through her digestive system. For some reason Kari found this exciting, particularly as it didn't taste as bad as she'd anticipated. During the two hours we had to wait for it to reach her stomach, we managed a bit of fun with a quick shopping trip to Chermside and lunch with Tiana. The results wouldn't be known for some time and in fact I have no memory of what was found. At the time it didn't seem too important.

Once we arrived home to the Sunshine Coast, Kari went dancing with friends at a Brazilian night. Her energy was boundless and she wasn't going to waste a moment.

The weekend brought more fun with a "Gangsters and Glitter" Latin Ball. Kari and Nic dressed up and danced the night away. Somehow, the next day she still had energy to go for a walk and swim with Maloo at Chambers Island.

So many of Kari's favourite things that she'd been deprived of for so long were now possible again. She was determined not to miss any of it. Maloo played a big role in Kari's recovery, providing lots of laughter with her entertaining antics as well as encouraging Kari to go for walks and spend time at the beach, a favourite place for both.

I was relieved that the issues with my leave had been sorted out and I was free to have this special time with Kari. She needed my help with tasks she couldn't yet manage such as washing clothes, making her bed, washing her hair, but most of all she needed me for driving. She found it frustrating not to be independent in this area, but the doctors were very strict, so she had to rely on me.

The bonus for me was that I was blessed with extra time with Kari. As an adult, she'd been very independent and had spent lots of time away from the Sunshine Coast, travelling around Australia with her photography job and travelling overseas as much as she could squeeze into her life. Even when she was nearby, she had such a full life with all her friends that I didn't get to see her as much as I would have liked. So, while I would never in a million years have wished for her to be sick enough to need a transplant, even that had its silver lining for me.

I soaked in the irreplaceable moments and locked away the memories made during these precious days, treasuring them in my heart.

The second Monday out of hospital meant yet another two-hour trip to transplant clinic in Brisbane. This time, as well as further improvement in lung function to eighty-seven percent, the doctors told Kari that her clinic visits could drop to once weekly instead of twice.

Hospital was gradually releasing its hold on Kari's life.

~

Post-transplant life still meant unrelenting dedication to important routines to ensure an ongoing recovery.

What many people didn't realise was that a transplant is not a one-time event and then everything's fine. It's a lifelong adjustment involving scores of medications, dietary restrictions, activity requirements and precautions.

Every single day, Kari had to weigh herself, take her temperature, measure her FEV1, swallow copious amounts of tablets, have an insulin injection, a clexane injection, administer intravenous antibiotics three times a day, get sufficient cardiovascular exercise and follow the post-transplant diet rules.

She was only allowed to drink triple-filtered water and had to follow a "pregnancy diet" avoiding buffets, soft cheeses, deli meats, sushi and fruit juice. This diet aimed to reduce the chance of vomiting or diarrhoea, which would upset the delicate balance of her anti-rejection medications.

She needed to eat enough calories for her CF requirements and for recovery from major surgery. Although her lungs no longer had cystic fibrosis the rest of her body did, so the high calorie requirements were still important.

~

Lots of trips to the beach with Maloo helped to meet the requirements for exercise, as well as providing sunshine, fresh air and heaps of fun and laughs.

There were social events with dance friends, birthday dinners and catch-ups with other friends who Kari had been missing while spending so much time in hospital. At her next weekly visit to transplant clinic, Kari posted on Facebook: "So, health update for the week… 93%!!!! And I've put on 3 kg in a week."

During this time, Kari spent lots of time, effort and money planning and coordinating Nic's twenty-first birthday party. They chose a

Great Gatsby theme and had fun finding costumes and themed decorations for the celebration.

Everyone got into the spirit of the night: fringed frocks, feathered headbands and fedoras. Kari looked stunning in a pale-blue lace dress, with a pearl headband and long beaded necklace. Her smile lit up the room and although a PICC line still poked out from a bandage on her arm, everyone was excited to see her looking so well. She posted on Facebook July 26: "Happy 21st birthday to Mr Nic!! Not to be biased or anything, but he's a pretty good guy. Thanks for sticking by me through the last years."

It was hard to return to hospital just a few days later for her first bronchoscopy since her release. On Facebook, Kari posted: "Sitting in a hospital waiting room, wishing I was where I was yesterday."

The following morning at clinic, although there was a hint of bad news with some of the cepacia bacteria found in fluid in her new lungs, it was mostly good news. The doctors were not worried by the findings and allowed her to cease intravenous antibiotics, so that she was free to swim and surf and enjoy life even more. She wrote on Facebook on July 31: "IV-free for the first time since our honeymoon eight months ago! And even that was only for ten days."

Kari appreciated simple pleasures like cooking for Nic in their little granny flat that was home for the time being. She was saving their wedding presents for when they could set up a real home together, but she still found joy in creating a cosy nest for the two of them.

She went out for lots of meals with different friends – celebrating first birthdays and thirtieth birthdays, breakfasts, coffee dates, dinners and brunches.

A local newspaper wanted to write a follow-up article about her awesome recovery, which made Kari feel quite overwhelmed. That feeling changed to embarrassment when their photographer arrived unexpectedly one morning before she had showered or washed her hair. She bravely pulled herself together and posed for some photos which would become very special to me.

Then, the Cystic Fibrosis Queensland newsletter, Winter 2014 edition, featured a double page spread with Kari's story and photos. She was becoming quite the celebrity.

The following week brought a new challenge with four days of vomiting. Apart from feeling terribly unwell, Kari needed to avoid vomiting if possible following transplant, so this added an extra layer of anxiety. Still, Kari's sunshine nature shone through. The first day she started to feel better, she posted: "What a beautiful gift from nature flowers are. A small reminder that life's not so bad and to smile and be happy."

Kari decided it was time to find a way to express her deep gratitude to the CF and transplant teams who'd cared for her so well throughout the most difficult and darkest days of her life.

In her favourite hospital room, Room 9, a large canvas of pink frangipani on the wall had always lifted her spirits when she was stuck in a bland hospital room for weeks on end. Being a photographer, she decided to brighten someone else's life by enlarging two of her favourite bright and cheerful photographs onto large canvases for the wards. She chose a beautiful sunset from her holiday in Tahiti and a colourful macaw from her time in Brazil.

We also ordered a huge canvas of one of my favourite photos of Kari and Nic walking on the beach during their engagement photoshoot. We added the text: "We don't know what tomorrow holds, but we know who holds tomorrow." It seemed appropriate.

While we were waiting for these to arrive there was one more clinic visit. Kari received the great news she'd been waiting for: "I CAN DRIVE!! The doctor gave me the ok today!! Hoorah! Oh and 95% and chucked on another kilo or two."

THE FOLLOWING week marked two months since the life-changing telephone call telling us that new lungs had been found for Kari. So much had changed. It was starting to feel like normal life again.

Kari returned to her paramedic studies at uni, went dancing with friends, and was driving again. Kari and Nic enrolled in a budgeting course, looking forward to being like any other newlyweds. It was so exciting for them to anticipate a future life together, something which had looked unlikely not long ago.

In late August, Kari joined the dance gang to celebrate her friend

Kristal's thirtieth birthday. In photos from the night she looked carefree and healthy, grinning and chatting with all her dance friends, snuggling with Nic, making the most of her new life.

I took the opportunity to attend a weekend scrapbook retreat because Kari didn't need my constant attention and monitoring any more. I was gratified to share her story and photos with friends who'd been following her frightening decline over the past two years and her recent amazing recovery.

Life was so good, and I was deeply thankful.

CHAPTER TWENTY-FIVE

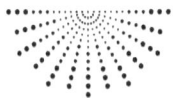

The newly risen sun shone brightly from a clear winter sky. Not a single cloud blotted the perfect blue canopy. The winter air was as crisp and fresh as a sweet red apple. The trilling of magpies and the cackling of kookaburras provided the soundtrack as Kari and I prepared for our drive to Brisbane.

Shivering in the cold and rubbing our hands together, we loaded the two large canvases into "Lillie", her cute yellow car. With Kari's favourite accompaniment of Brazilian music blaring from the speakers, we set off, discussing how we could avoid traffic for the Ekka – the Brisbane show. Laughing and chatting, we made the most of our time together, taking pleasure in the freedom of Kari not needing to spend the whole trip injecting strong intravenous antibiotics into a PICC line in her arm, as was usual on these trips. Life was good and at last things were looking up for Kari.

As we walked through the all-too-familiar doors of the hospital, I thought back to the long, painful weeks, months and years that Kari had endured in this place. That was behind us now.

We congratulated ourselves on deciding to go to X-ray before "breathers", where Kari's lung function was measured. This put us ahead in the queue, all part of our plan for a quick getaway to better things. After visiting the blood-test lab, it was time to see the transplant specialist, our last appointment for the day.

Pleased to see it was Dr Hopkins, who was always very positive, we took our seats in his office to find out the results of all today's tests. Everything was looking good and most exciting of all was the continuing improvement in Kari's lung function.

"These results look great. With the type of bacteria that was in your old lungs, transplants can go two ways," Dr Hopkins told us. "It's usually either a complete catastrophe or a tremendous result, with not much middle ground. Everything's pointing to a great outcome for you and a wonderful life ahead."

As he turned to his computer to check the X-ray images coming through, Kari and I snuck a cheeky thumbs-up and grinned at each other.

Abruptly, our attention was gripped by a long, drawn-out "Ohhhhhh……" escaping from his mouth. I felt like I was falling through space from a great height. On that one word, the world turned more slowly and the room faded into blurry darkness as I realised that everything in our lives was about to change, again.

There on the screen showing the X-ray of Kari's lungs was a dark shadow, visible to all of us. It obviously wasn't good.

Kari had mentioned to Dr Hopkins a few minutes earlier that she had a small, niggly pain in her side. She hadn't told me about it, which was typical of Kari who never liked to make a fuss about anything. He hadn't seemed at all concerned and said it was probably just adhesions from her surgery.

Now, his demeanour was completely transformed.

We all knew that this was extremely serious and could have dire consequences. He immediately booked an urgent CT scan to find out what was going on inside. We pulled ourselves together and made our way to Radiology, trying to grapple with the way life had changed so drastically in a matter of moments.

We attempted to maintain a hopeful attitude and prayed fervently that the CT would find something innocuous, but weren't surprised when the results came back showing an area the size of a tennis ball which looked like infection.

I booked myself into Rose Cottage. Tiana and Nic came to join me.

Kari was immediately booked for a bronchoscopy and admitted to her usual ward.

∼

I struggled to understand why this could be happening. Hadn't God provided a miracle through the transplant?

Kari-Lee had been through so much already and her life was just getting back on track. She was the "star" who made such an amazing recovery. Why now? Why her?

I tried so hard to maintain a calm and positive demeanour, but inside I was screaming. "NOOOOOOO… Please don't let this be happening. Please let it be a mistake. Please let it be something simple that can be fixed, so Kari can get back to her life again. Please God. Please God. Please…"

The nightmare was beginning all over again and all we could do was hang on to God, hang on to hope, just hang on.

∼

My diary shows the situation decomposing as I struggled to hold onto any semblance of a normal life for Kari:

> **Tuesday 26th August**: Transplant doctor very concerned. Thinks it's the old bacteria in Kari's new lungs. Terrible news. Kari depressed about being in hospital again.
>
> **Wednesday**: No further news. Took Kari for a walk to nearby café to cheer her up. CF team came. Keen to treat this infection aggressively, but transplant team concerned about effects of new drugs on Kari's kidneys.
>
> **Thursday**: Gaye came and spent the day with Kari and me.

Weeks later, my friend Gaye would tell me that God spoke clearly to her, telling her to be with me through what was ahead.

Another form of support emerged when Tiana started chatting to a young man in the cafeteria called Charlie. She found out he had CF and his room was just down the hall from Kari. We worked out that he was the same Charles who used to play with Kari-Lee on the floor when they were both babies. Kari found him on Facebook and they boosted each other's spirits by sharing stories and jokes about the hospital food.

> **Friday**: Kari's struggling with the whole hospital experience, which she thought was behind her, so we took her to Tiana's flat nearby for morning tea. Nic left work early and came down to surprise her.
>
> The Nurse Unit Manager brought a new fold-out chair-bed into Kari's room for Nic to sleep on. The staff want him to be able to stay in Kari's room as they've only been married for eight months and miss each other terribly.

By now, Kari was on a punishing regime of four different intravenous drugs as well as several oral drugs, on top of all her usual transplant medication. It meant she couldn't leave the hospital too often or for too long.

I drove home to collect more things for a longer stay in Brisbane, as I'd originally expected to be coming home straight after clinic. On Saturday morning, Kari rang and told me the transplant doctor had discussed the unlikely possibility of surgery in the future, to remove the infected area of her new lungs if the antibiotics couldn't clear up the infection.

Kari had more blood tests and IV antibiotics and was then released for a brief trip to the Sunshine Coast for her budgeting course with Nic. Afterwards, they came to our house, had some fun with Maloo, then lunch with Peter, before Nic left to play in another soccer final. Kari and I packed some of her things for a longer hospital stay, went to visit Nana and Pa, then drove to watch Nic at soccer.

Reluctantly, Kari and I then had to head back to hospital in Brisbane for the next IV drugs.

Sunday: A couple of good signs, medically, so I asked the doctor about Kari getting out on Wednesday afternoon to attend her uni lecture. That's when he dropped the bombshell that they're considering surgery THIS Wednesday, if things haven't improved dramatically by then. It will be a lobectomy where they remove one of the five lobes of her new lungs, hoping to remove the infection.

We were shell shocked and escaped to Tiana's for tea and pancakes. Nic arrived soon after. He'd run the Sunshine Coast half-marathon that morning.

The first day of spring brought Dr Peter Hopkins back to the wards. He said Kari would definitely have surgery on Wednesday unless both bloods and X-ray showed improvement. He started her on new IV antibiotics – ciprofloxacin, fosfomycin and taurolidine.

We were told that the last one was an experimental IV drug, usually used to wash out the thoracic cavity before surgery. I was told that Kari would be the first person in Australia to have it intravenously. It was super expensive and being brought in from overseas. It had to be warmed in a blood-warming machine before it went into her veins, and was given so slowly that it basically ran continuously.

The nurses were all having to learn new things so they were often playing catch-up, under pressure from the doctors who were concerned that we only had thirty-six hours on these new drugs to turn things around.

Monday 1st September: Blood tests and X-ray. Both worse. Inflammatory marker up to 98 from 66 on Thursday and 33 last Monday [normal is less than 5]. This is devastating. People have been praying and we were expecting improvement.

I've requested prayer. Heaps of people praying. Bruce [Gaye's husband] came to pray and anoint Kari with oil. He gave us an encouraging talk about faith versus fear. Nic drove him home to the Sunshine Coast.

Later, Gaye posted a blog about standing, based on Ephesians 6:10-17. This passage speaks about putting on the full armour of God, which consists of the belt of truth, the shield of faith, the helmet of salvation, the sword of the Spirit and the shoes of the gospel of peace. This armour enables us to stand firm against evil, to stand firm in our faith in God and not be swayed by circumstances.

Tuesday: A day of waiting, standing in faith and telling doubt to go. At times it was hard, but better than dwelling on negatives. Lots of people are praying and we'll wait on God. Lots of visitors today.

On Wednesday morning, Nic and I walked down with Kari for a very early blood test and X-ray. Then we had to wait for the results to show whether she needed surgery.

Wednesday: Heaps of people praying. Managed to stand in faith for most of waiting time. Doctor came to let us know inflammatory markers down to 62. Later a message saying X-ray looked better, so no surgery today. Yay! Thank you, God. We found out the infected area had reduced from 38 mm to 33 mm. Wonderful answer to prayer.

We all spent the day in Kari's room just chilling and enjoying the fact she didn't need surgery. So relieved things have turned around, but we know we're not out of the woods yet.

Thursday: Nic left early. Kari will miss him. When Kari's feeling down Nic sometimes whistles and pulls a very funny face, which makes her laugh. She needs reasons to laugh now.

Kari and I had a quiet day studying physiology for uni. The Endocrine System. Went for a walk with the drip stand to a nearby café, then to Rose Cottage where I cooked her lunch. Kari's feeling happier.

Friday: What a morning! X-ray and blood tests repeated. We expected good results, as Kari's feeling better. Kari's breakfast arrived at 7.45 am, but before she could start it the nurse came and said the doctors wanted her fasting. They also wanted her Clexane injection (blood thinner) withheld due to possible surgery. It seemed the results must be bad and they were preparing Kari for surgery. Devastating news. Not what we expected at all.

Fear set in. I continued to battle between fear and faith as time ticked away and the doctors still didn't come. We'd just sent out messages for extra prayer around nine when the doctors arrived to say everything looked good on the tests. All tests would be repeated on Monday, so this roller coaster was not over yet but the doctors were hopeful.

Spirits rising again. Hope blossoming. Things might be okay. A collective sigh of relief filled the room.

Soon after the doctors left, a nurse came in with a theatre pack to shave and prepare Kari for surgery. Had the doctors changed their minds again? No, the doctors just hadn't told the nurses that Kari didn't need surgery today.

I noticed Room 9 (Kari's favourite) was empty and asked if she could change rooms. We all pitched in and got her settled in her favourite room. Everyone's feeling much more positive and hopeful. A cheerful night.

On Saturday, I went to the hospital early and studied physiology with Kari. She was tired and unmotivated. After an evening walk outside, I left at 8.45 pm so she could have an early night. Then I had a call from Tiana to say she had fresh pizza to cheer Kari. I raced back to the hospital to get in before the doors locked at nine. Kari really appreciated it.

On Sunday, the nightmare worsened. I slept in until 8.30 am and when I rang Kari, she said she had a temperature when she woke up and the doctors were concerned.

I hurried to her room. Blood test showed inflammatory markers down even further to 25, but X-ray looked worse and temperature still unstable, so ordered a CT scan, which is more accurate.

It showed the infection had spread, so surgery is scheduled for tomorrow. The surgery we thought we'd avoided.

I couldn't believe we were here, facing major, life-threatening surgery again. The past two weeks had been like a wild, out-of-control roller coaster taking our hearts and hopes diving to the depths of despair and then flinging us up on high mountains of hope and answered prayers, before tossing us around unexpected curves and U-turns.

All the doctors had made it clear that the surgery would be very dangerous and very painful. It was only being attempted as a last-hope option. Kari was understandably afraid, although she hid it well for Nic's sake.

In my diary I wrote: "Don't think I'll sleep tonight, but I need to try so I'm able to support Kari and Nic tomorrow. I can't allow myself to dwell on what the outcome could be. Will I still have my precious girl this time tomorrow?"

CHAPTER TWENTY-SIX

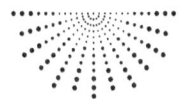

Monday 8th September: Surgery Day: Waiting for surgery, with no idea of time. Lots of people praying and sending messages.

Peter brought Maloo down from the Sunshine Coast so Kari could go outside to play with her. After an interminable yet all-too-short time of waiting, Nic, Tiana and I walked Kari-Lee to theatre at 12.30 pm. We delivered her into the caring hands of one of her favourite nurses, who would stay with her throughout the surgery.

We found out later that Kari needed an epidural, which she wasn't expecting. It really upset our brave Kari, so I'm thankful her nurse was there to calm and reassure her and hold her hand as the needle went into her spine.

Then the waiting. It was almost unbearable.

They'd told us three hours, but that passed with no word from anyone. On and on the time went while my mind swirled with horrific scenarios. Would they come to tell us it was time to say goodbye? Had Kari already died? We tried to bolster each other's spirits, praying and chatting, but the fear was there in everyone's eyes and the long silences were filled with thoughts we just couldn't share out loud.

The surgeon finally rang Nic around 6.00 pm to say surgery had finished, but it was a very difficult operation. They took out both her middle and lower lobes because they were stuck together. She was in recovery. They were trying to extubate her so she could go to the ward, not ICU.

Tiana, Rachel and Rachel's parents had sat with us for most of the day but when they left around 9.30 pm, Kari still wasn't back from recovery. Nic and I were finally allowed to see Kari around 10.00 pm.

She looked incredibly pale and was sleeping the whole time, although she'd respond if we asked her to. Nurses were very understanding and worked around us, letting us stay until eleven.

On Tuesday, she was moved to a single room once the surgeon was convinced she didn't need constant monitoring.

Kari managed to stand at her bedside morning and afternoon, doing careful marching on the spot with physio. She's barely eating. Managed one small custard all day. She's very nauseated with some vomiting. She looks very unwell and has no Kari-spark about her at all.

Some of Kari's friends came to visit. I was so impressed by my work friends who drove from the Sunshine Coast to support me. This happened a couple of times and meant so much to me. It was easy to feel forgotten in Brisbane, as few people made the long drive.

The whole experience we were living through was so devastating, so traumatising, so lonely. I knew that lots of people were praying, but sometimes I needed "God with skin on".

Every morning in Rose Cottage before I headed up to the hospital to see Kari, I got up early and spent time reading my Bible and praying. I wrote out passages that particularly spoke to me. It reminded me that God was with Kari and with me. He saw what was happening and He cared.

We needed a miracle that only God could provide, because medically things continued to be precarious.

Wednesday: Kari now has anaemia. Haemoglobin 74 (normal 120–140). Epidural removed, but chest drain still in. Bought a big butterfly balloon to brighten Kari's room and made a smoothie for her with heaps of calories and nutrition. She's hardly eating anything. Nic went home to Nambour.

On Thursday, the doctors seemed pleased and Kari felt a bit better despite increased pain and continuing nausea. Peter brought Maloo to a grassy area below so Kari could look out the window and see her. She was given a special IV stand from ICU as too many drugs were being pumped for a normal stand. Her catheter was removed, and her chest drain taken out, which significantly reduced her pain.

Saturday: I've started a Daniel fast: only fruit, vegetables, grain and water. I want to do everything possible to open the door for God to heal Kari. "This kind only comes out with prayer and fasting." [Matthew 17:21 paraphrase]

I got to the ward in time to see Dr Hopkins and the surgeon, who were satisfied but guarded about future infection.
Removal of the wound dressing exposed heaps of staples. Kari was feeling very, very tired. Her haemoglobin was 78. She still had a long way to go and was still nauseated. She had a short walk but slept most of the day. She was moved to Room 12 in her usual ward and felt happier with familiar nurses.

Sunday: Quiet day. Kari sleeping a lot. Nic's back. Popkins (Kari's special name for Dr Hopkins) came and apologised for putting Kari through everything with the intense drugs she's on. He's such a caring and kind-hearted doctor.

On Monday, we saw Popkins and another transplant doctor who

would be our consultant for the week ahead. Popkins was going overseas for a family holiday.

Kari's nausea and pain were still very bad. New nausea medication didn't make much difference. She had lost a kilo since the previous day. Kari wasn't coping well with visitors and just wanted to sleep.

We were shocked when Popkins said he was aiming to get Kari home in two weeks if all went well. Such unexpected good news. I'd been so worried, thinking that everything was on a downward spiral. Obviously, he had a different perspective. Our spirits rose again with hope for the future.

On Tuesday, Kari was looking a bit brighter so she tried some breakfast but it all came back up. She waited a bit and tried again with a dry cracker, then some smoothie, and up it all came again.

> Asked for prayer for nausea because she's losing weight and needs nutrition to fight infection and recover from surgery. Doctors started her on new anti-nausea medication called cyclizine. Kari took it at lunch time and managed to keep down a whole potato, three crackers, a little corn, a bowl of peaches and custard. It's the most she's eaten in days. Wonderful. This new drug seems to be working.

After a short sleep, they took out the stitches in her side around the chest drain and the twenty-one staples in her back. After a bit more sleep the physio took her for a long walk. She did some sit-to-stands and step-ups. Then another big sleep. She kept her dinner down too. I wrote in my diary, "So thankful for small progress. Things are looking better. Thank you, Jesus."

It didn't last…

> **Wednesday**: Nightmare goes to new level. The bacteria is back. Kari's temp 37.3. Rising all morning. X-ray and CT showed infection in upper right and lower left lobe. A disaster. Change of medications.
>
> Trying hard to stay in faith. Gaye came to be with me. Peter

> came down with Maloo. Inflammatory marker up again to 50. Kari very sleepy.
>
> Doctors have told us they're not sure they can save her but trying hard.

I couldn't believe it had come to this. How could this be happening? Only two days before, there was talk of getting her home. My mind and heart couldn't keep up with the wild unpredictability. The extremes left us teetering on the brink of a precipice. Were we about to fall off and plummet to destruction? Or were we about to step back from the edge and be saved? The fickleness of life was intolerable.

Our life had become a battle to save Kari. All our efforts, and those of staff, were focused on finding ways to help Kari-Lee beat this incredibly aggressive and resistant bacteria that continued to invade her lungs. Our impassioned prayers, along with literally thousands of Kari's friends and family around the world, joined in a constant stream rising Heaven-ward, beseeching the One who could save her to have mercy and heal her body.

ON THURSDAY, Kari's nausea improved and she was able to eat a little more. Her temperature was still erratically rising and falling, along with her inflammatory marker (up to 160).

> A transplant doctor had a very serious talk with us and asked Kari if she wanted to stop antibiotics and just go home to die. Kari was shocked and said, "Absolutely not!"
>
> I had a session with the social worker. So many things to try to sort out. Income protection, Centrelink, withdrawing from uni and even filling out an Advanced Health Care Directive for Kari.
>
> Lots of family visitors today. We all anointed Kari with oil and prayed again for her to be healed.

On Saturday, after normal temperatures overnight, the doctor was much chirpier. Kari's inflammatory markers and blood tests looked better, but her haemoglobin was down to 75. Kari was offered a transfusion but she said: not yet.

She had lots of visitors, including my brother and his family who had driven up from Canberra, as well as the CF team.

Kari's CF doctor informed us that further testing showed the bacteria in Kari's lungs was not actually cepacia, but in fact a type unique to Kari. They joked about naming it after Kari-Lee. It was unclear whether this uniqueness was making the infection more difficult to treat.

A former pastor from Nic's church came and anointed Kari and prayed. He told Kari she wasn't going to die.

Kari slept most of the day. Nic's mum cooked a special dinner at Kari's request. She kept it down.

But she had now developed a mystery tremor.

Sunday: Inflammatory marker up to 190! Absolutely terrible news. Dr said all Kari's sleeping could be due to TOXIC levels of tacrolimus [an immunosuppressant]. This could account for tremor and aching toes. Kari was given a unit of blood as haemoglobin very low. Visits from friends, including one who brought her six-week-old baby. This cheered Kari a little, even in her tremendously sick state.

On Monday, Kari slept a lot. Her temperature rose and fell and then rose and rose. Her weight had started climbing, which made no sense as she wasn't eating much.

Desperate to find something which might help Kari, I'd been researching experimental treatments and discovered a new type of therapy called bacteriophages. These were naturally occurring viruses that had evolved to attack bacteria. They could be designed to attack specific bacteria, so one could potentially be designed to attack Kari's own unique bacteria. This might circumvent the antibiotic resistance of the bacterial infection in Kari's lungs.

It was a relatively new science and there didn't seem to be anything in Australia. I found a doctor in Canada and sent him an email.

Tuesday: Very traumatic experience today. A blood clot developed in Kari's left arm so PICC was removed and central line put into the jugular vein in her neck. She had to go to ICU for the procedure. She was covered in sterile drapes, even over her face, and had an oxygen mask and lots of local anaesthetic in her neck. On his first attempt, the doctor punctured her carotid artery so had to apply pressure for 15 minutes to stop the bleeding. The second attempt was successful, but the whole experience was distressing for Kari.

She was very uncomfortable for the rest of the day. Rachel and Bruce came and prayed with her.

That evening several friends arrived to visit and play card games. Somehow Kari rallied enough to play a game and was able to think clearly enough to even win some rounds. I took this to be a good sign, but later realised it was just an example of Kari-Lee's incredible bravery and determination. As we discovered the next day, she was actually very, very unwell.

Wednesday: Temperature really high this morning. Feeling very scared. Kari distressed and crying. Read Psalms in my Bible. A lady we don't know, but who has mutual friends, felt God told her to come and pray for Kari's healing. Once Kari would have been embarrassed and preferred people not to make a fuss or pray over her publicly, but right now she's welcoming anyone who wants to pray.

Kari's cousin, Michael flew all the way up from Sydney to visit her.

I received an email from the bacteriophage researcher in Canada. He said it was definitely possible to develop a phage which could destroy the bacteria in Kari's lungs. His team had the expertise, but unfortunately their funding had been cut so they were unable to provide any help. This was devastating news – to know that there was something out there that could give Kari a good chance at life, but she couldn't access it because of funding.

I decided to keep searching for someone else who could offer phage therapy. Kari's doctors were uncertain about the whole idea.

> Transplant doctors came and said Kari's right lung is fully collapsed but they don't want to treat it with anything traumatic like a chest drain or bronchoscopy until they see if the antibiotics are going to work in the left lung. Basically, I interpret that to mean they don't have much hope that she'll recover.
>
> Things are not looking good. Infection progressing – fluid build-up, sleeping lots, shortness of breath, temperatures. The doctors see these as signs her body is shutting down as the infection takes over. We're all very upset, but not ready to give up yet.

On Thursday, I caught up with Kari's CF doctor to discuss her situation. I asked him to be honest with me and tell me when there was no hope. A transplant doctor joined us and bluntly said, "No hope." I so badly wanted God to prove this doctor wrong.

The doctors decided to do a CT scan. During the CT, Nic uncharacteristically reached out and held my hand. We prayed for a miracle and sang a chorus, but the CT showed things were worse. The infection had spread further. The afternoon doctors said they might try a few things to reinflate Kari's right lung but felt it probably wouldn't work.

> The doctors told Kari she had only 2–3% chance of survival. After they left Kari was distraught, crying with Nic and me. She talked about how she had so many more things she wanted to do with Nic – take him travelling, set up home together, have a baby. Things which most people take for granted in Australia. Just normal things. It's so not fair. Why Kari? Lots of prayer this afternoon.

A friend came and did Thai massage for two hours. Kari thanked her profusely. She was such a precious girl, so grateful for the little things in life, so appreciative of anyone who did anything for her. She even thanked her nurses when they gave her painful injections or ripped off painful sticking tapes. She almost never complained, even when she was obviously in lots of pain or had so much nausea that all her food just hit her stomach and then launched back out again.

> She never gives up. It's so hard to see her distressed and hopeless, but doctors have left little room for hope. Still, we're not willing to give up yet. It would take a miracle, but our God is a miracle-working God. I really hope so, because right now a miracle is all that will save Kari.

CHAPTER TWENTY-SEVEN

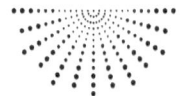

Friday 26th September: This week's transplant doctor arrived on the ward. Shocked to hear Kari's right side sounded better. Sent Kari for urgent X-ray, which showed the right lung re-inflated! Thank you, Jesus. That's the miracle we needed. Doctors were amazed and impressed. No raised temperatures today. So many answers to prayer. We're full of hope again.

Kari had lots of visitors. A guy we didn't know came and prayed with Kari for healing. He assured us she'd soon be sharing her testimony in his church and everywhere.

Nic's parents brought dinner for everyone. Eleven of us crammed into Kari's room and ate together. Took a photo. We're all overjoyed. Kari ate lots but then hit a wall, absolutely exhausted. We left her to sleep.

Discovered a teacher from Kari's school started a fundraising page yesterday for Nic and Kari. It's already passed $10,000! Unbelievable.

Over the weekend, Kari slept a lot. In between, my emotions

continued to churn, constantly in motion, like clothes in a washing machine, my brain stuck on the spin cycle.

There were shocking moments: washing Kari's hair and having great clumps come out in our hands; joyful moments: watching *My Big Fat Greek Wedding* and seeing Kari have a great laugh; sweet moments: seeing Kari's friend give her a gentle foot spa and paint her nails beautifully; fearful moments: as Kari's temperature continued its wild fluctuations.

On Tuesday, the doctor brought catastrophic news.

> The bacteria has spread to Kari's bloodstream. Things can rarely be turned around once that point is reached. He said, "Dr Hopkins will be back from America tomorrow. He'll fix you."
>
> I'm so frustrated. It feels like we're all just marking time, with no decisive changes being made, even though the current regime doesn't seem to be working. I'm trying hard to stay in faith and not let fear overtake me.
>
> Our pastor phoned from USA with encouragement. I decided to stay strong and trust God. Felt better. Slept well.

On Wednesday, Dr Hopkins was back on the evening ward round. He wanted Kari to have a blood transfusion and was thinking of changing all her antibiotics to eradicate the bacteria.

> It feels so good to have someone making decisions and doing something. He's positive and proactive. It's very refreshing and encouraging. We put the word out to get EVERYONE to pray for wisdom for him and the bacteria specialist in England regarding Kari's antibiotics.

The next day, I arrived to find the blood transfusion just finishing.

> Lots of drama overnight. Kari had very rough night. Nurses doing observations all night, repeated toilet trips caused by medications, then a bad reaction to second bag of blood with high temperatures

and racing heart. No sleep at all. We let Nic and Kari sleep all morning.

When Dr Hopkins came, he decided to change all the antibiotics, starting immediately. Kari felt very restless and agitated, missing the grogginess of the strong painkillers which weren't given the previous night in all the drama.

I don't know how Kari's stayed so positive for so long, but even she's starting to feel hopeless and over it all.

Over the next few days, Kari continued to struggle with restlessness and agitation. Sleep eluded her and her appetite diminished even more. She was distressed and crying, so unlike our strong, upbeat girl.

On Sunday, the doctors were questioning whether drugs could be causing her restlessness, so they added Valium and an antidepressant.

My work friend came and gave Kari a massage. She had a lot of visitors. We took her to Rose Cottage for lunch where she sat on the back deck in a camping recliner. She was now very uncomfortable with pressure areas on her tail bone and elbows.

On Monday, Kari seemed to be generally feeling better, although she continued to vomit most food.

A wheezy noise in her lungs bothers her a lot and she's very weak but otherwise feels almost normal. Perhaps the new antibiotics are working and things are improving?

CT to check progress. Unbelievably, rather than improvement, the CT showed the infection has spread even more. Kari's very, very upset.

We were all terribly upset. Things seemed to be on a downward spiral. We feared what the future might hold.

Yet, surprisingly, Kari felt better. The next five days were an absolute gift, as we were able to take Kari out of hospital for an outing each day.

Wednesday: Went to Redcliffe beach with Maloo for fish and chips. Kari relished being out in the fresh sea air. Inflammatory marker down to 63. So good.

Thursday: Kari continues to feel well, so we drove to Mt Coot-tha with Rachel for café lunch. It's wonderful to see her out of that hospital room. Hoping the change of antibiotics is working. Later, changing the PICC dressing was a nightmare and took hours because the dressing had glued on like grilled cheese. Three of Kari's favourite nurses worked together removing it.

Friday: Tiana's twentieth birthday. Kari's inflammatory marker down to 40. Such great news! I ran back to Rose Cottage and cooked potato pancakes for breakfast, because Kari asked for it.

That evening, the large table on the deck at Rose Cottage groaned with a delicious feast of spring rolls, barramundi with sweet potato mash, green beans with macadamia-citrus dressing, all lovingly prepared by Tiana.

Playful banter and quiet laughter permeated the air around the tiny, frail figure at the head of the table. As she enjoyed her dessert of berry jelly with pannacotta, strawberries and chocolate swirl, I raised a prayer of thanks that she was still with us and enjoying food once again.

As Nic's mum presented Tiana with a magnificent Minion birthday cake, I gave God heartfelt thanks that Kari had survived through Tiana's birthday, something which seemed doubtful just days ago. Despite looking just a shadow of herself, she rallied and gave us her very best that night, a precious gift for Tiana.

The weekend brought two more wonderful outings. Saturday was a picnic lunch on the riverbank at Teneriffe where Tiana worked as an apprentice chef, followed by an outing to West End. On Sunday we went to the beach at Wellington Point for fish and chips. Kari tried, but struggled to eat anything. Kari and Nic went to West End for dinner, where Kari ate well and kept it down.

> **Monday 13th October**: Kari feeling tired and "terrible" all day, with debilitating nausea. She weighs only 45 kg. Yet inflammatory marker was way down to 21 and her X-ray was noticeably better.

WE'D STARTED to dare to hope that she'd turned a corner and it was just a matter of getting her strength back and heading home in the near future. One of the things standing in the way of this was Kari's continued battle to keep food down and gain some weight. So, the doctors planned to insert a nasogastric-jejunum tube.

On Tuesday, Kari had lost another kilogram and was still feeling terrible.

> Surgery to insert a feeding tube was supposed to be today, but now cancelled as two gastroenterologists away. I pushed hard and fought for it today, because Kari really needs to get some nutrition. A long and frustrating day. Just have to trust that God knows something I don't and there's good reasons for this delay.

On Wednesday, I walked Kari down at 2.00 pm for what was supposed to be a half-hour surgery.

> Rang at 4.30 pm, there'd been delays. Rang at 5.30 pm, still no word. Later, doctor rang and said things hadn't gone well. They'd found lots of solid food in her stomach so the procedure took longer. She developed a rapid heart rate (160) and they had to intubate her. She might need ICU. We prayed and waited. They managed to extubate her and she was back on the ward, awake and talking.
> Kari said she felt great. No nausea or hunger. Then Gastro registrar came and said feeds couldn't be started because X-ray couldn't locate the tip of the tube and thought it might have doubled back on itself. Had to wait until morning and do a CT scan.
> So incredibly frustrating. Kari needs nutrition. Now. How can she fight the powerful bacteria without any nutrition? I just can't believe these repeated hold-ups. Tried to contact transplant team, but they'd gone home. Managed to get essential drugs down.

On Thursday, the transplant team were surprised to discover feeds hadn't started. I was incredibly frustrated that she'd missed out on over 18 hours of food because the previous day's X-ray hadn't gone low enough. Finally, another X-ray showed correct placement of the tip, so the wait had been unnecessary.

> Kari said she felt "tortured" and almost like giving up. It's like she's "in hell and there's no end in sight". Tube feeds finally started around 1.00 pm. Kari sleeping a lot. While feeds stopped for Taurolidine, I made Kari go for a short walk. She's not feeling great but pushed herself to do it.

On Friday, Kari's weight had dropped again to 43 kilograms. Her feeds were now running continuously, except for two, two-hour breaks for Taurolidine. She was feeling good but very sleepy.

> Nic's sick with sore throat and cough. Tested for influenza. Decided not to sleep in Kari's room anymore because of risk of her catching it. I'll take his place.
> Bronchoscopy today to check for bacteria levels in lungs. Inflammatory marker 127. Way too high.

I went to watch TV in the lounge so I could have a good cry without Kari seeing me. The nurses had indicated that high inflammatory markers were a disastrous sign. Why was it that every time things seemed to be improving and we started to get our hopes up that Kari might recover, another setback slapped us in the face? My emotions had been stretched and twisted and tumbled around like seaweed in the surf. I could only imagine how Kari must be feeling through all of this.

On Saturday, Kari's bronchoscopy results came back. The highest possible levels of cepacia were found in her lungs. She was now vomiting "coffee-grounds" blood and undigested food. Our shared distress choked us, making conversation difficult. Friends came to pray with us and set up a 40-hour prayer roster. Spaces filled quickly.

We managed to take Kari down to Rose Cottage for a couple of hours, in a wheelchair. My dazzling, funny, effervescent Kari lay in a camping recliner with pillows under her back, bottom and legs. She was now so thin and bony that even the camping recliner hurt. A tube up her nose delivered nutrition, prongs in her nose delivered oxygen, a PICC line in each arm delivered super-strong intravenous antibiotics. Her arm dangled over the side of the chair and she weakly ruffled Maloo's hair with her fingers, or held her paw. Mostly, she just lay quietly while conversation went on around her, but occasionally she'd join in briefly. I took photos of her with visiting friends and later wrote in my diary:

> I can't help feeling that I have to drink in every vision I have of her now. I really don't know how much longer she can survive this. My Kari is still there inside that shrinking, pain-wracked body, which is letting her down so badly. I can tell she's suffering and in terrible pain, yet she rarely complains. I wonder what she's thinking. She's so brave through all of this, but she must be contemplating what's ahead. We're still hoping and believing for a miracle, but if I'm honest, only a genuine out-of-this-world miracle could save her now. I'm begging God to spare her. I've asked Him to take me instead. Take anything: my legs, my arms. Take my life, if only Kari can live.

THE NEXT DAY, Kari was feeling a bit stronger, but the doctor came and had a serious talk about whether she wanted to go home because they didn't want her to miss the chance and be too sick to make the journey. They clearly didn't believe she was going to get better.

> After they left, Kari said to me, "What do they think I'm going to do? Just give up? I want to keep on fighting."
> I do too, but it's really not looking good. I'm continuing to stay as positive as I can, standing in faith because I know God can heal her, even now. He can turn this around and I just have to believe that He will. The alternative is simply unthinkable.

I took Kari to Rose Cottage for a few hours, but she needed to go back to the hospital when the effects of her new nausea medication wore off. She had another blood transfusion and magnesium infusion, which made her feel "buzzy" and "weird".

On Monday's ward round, the doctors didn't have much to say.

We went to Rose Cottage and Gaye, Rachel, Winston and Nic's parents were there. Kari was not feeling good at all: headache, bloated swollen stomach, harder to breathe, back pain. She had another toilet accident. They were becoming more common and I felt so bad for her.

Fear melted my heart as I looked at Kari-Lee. She slept most of the time there and lay inside for quite a while.

Monday 20th October: She said she's glad it's me sleeping in her room now, as she's embarrassed by the way her body's letting her down and wouldn't want Nic to see her like that. I reminded her that I'm her Mum and I'm there for her, no matter what. She doesn't need to feel embarrassed with me. I'll do absolutely anything I can for her.

Back at the hospital, a physio did a short treatment on her back and then her friend came and massaged Kari's back for a couple of hours. When asked how she felt afterwards, she said, "My body is singing."

∽

Evening meeting with Popkins. He said inflammatory marker down to 44! Astonishingly, he's talking again about getting her home in a couple of weeks.

THE DOCTOR THOUGHT Kari's symptoms might be from a toxic dose of medication, and he might stop another medication that caused nausea and was usually only given short-term. He planned to get a CT scan done the next day and perhaps put in a chest drain.

I love his decisiveness and positivity. I'd been feeling hopeless, but now I have hope again. Maybe the miracle really is coming. Maybe there'll be a jubilant ending after all. It's not too late.

CHAPTER TWENTY-EIGHT

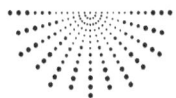

Morning broke, yet darkness descended. Throughout Monday night, Kari's temperature had risen yet again. Infection was taking hold. Hope hung from a fragile, quivering and quickly unravelling string.

We accompanied Kari to the CT scan. As I waited, dread crouched like a ravenous lion deep in my spirit – I was outwardly hopeful, but inwardly terribly, mind-shatteringly afraid.

When the results came, they confirmed our deepest fears. The fight was over. The bacteria had spread throughout Kari's glorious new lungs and had consumed so much that it had spilled out into the surrounding chest cavity.

There was absolutely no possibility of survival from a medical perspective. Only a completely miraculous work of God could save Kari now.

THE RESULTS CAME in the afternoon, around the same time as my work friend left after giving Kari a soothing gentle massage. We all reeled in shock, our minds refusing to grasp the finality of the findings. We increased the intensity and fervour of our prayers for healing, knowing that even at this eleventh hour God could heal our girl completely. In some ways it would show His power even more spectacularly, because there was nothing left that medicine could offer Kari now.

A representative from Kari and Nic's church arrived to pray with her. My mind struggled with unkind thoughts about the irony of them arriving on this day. Kari-Lee had been in hospital, in the fight of her life, battling courageously for her life for the past eight weeks, and only now, when basically all hope was gone, did someone from her church come to pray with her. Maybe God knew better, and this was the time that prayer was going to lead to a breakthrough of healing? I pushed my negative thoughts down.

When he left, another group arrived to pray. We were still in a state of shock, but one person stayed on after praying, performing various kind tasks, unaware of the shattering news we were still trying to come to terms with. We all realised just how precious every single moment with Kari was now and we each wanted to be with her as much as we possibly could. Although I knew this person was acting out of kindness, I'll always regret not clearly asking them to leave so that those who loved Kari best could have that precious, rapidly disappearing time with her.

After they left, each of us had the opportunity to spend a little individual time with Kari, but the most special time for me came in the evening when only the four Vennings were left. The next hour or two formed a sacred time that will live on in my memory forever. We reminisced about family holidays and adventures we'd shared, funny anecdotes that were meaningful only to us. Kari was fully alert and engaged and we shared lots of laughter. It was a precious treasure that I was able to capture and imprint in my memory, a gift of immense magnitude for each one of us. We were the ones who loved her first, knew her best, enjoyed her the longest. Her surname might now be something else, but she would always be a Venning.

After Tiana left to get a few hours' sleep, Peter became demonstrably upset as it started to sink in just how horribly unwell Kari-Lee was. I encouraged him to lie up on the bed beside her so he had some precious father-daughter time with his "little Parbi". He was able to hold her and share some of his deepest feelings about how much she meant to him. He remembers looking into her eyes, feeling that her time was short and goodbye was coming very soon. We didn't know it at the time, but these were the last moments he would have with his "little treasure" here on this earth.

WHEN PETER HAD TO LEAVE, it was just Kari and me. In my spirit I sensed that this was the time to read the letter I'd written to Kari some weeks ago, when things looked very grim. I wanted to make sure she had the opportunity to hear how much she meant to me, while she was still able to comprehend what I was saying. I'd written it all out weeks before, but when her health had improved a little I'd tucked it away in the corner of her cupboard and continued believing for the miracle which would make the words redundant.

Now, appallingly, it seemed the time was here.

It felt a little embarrassing to say it to Kari face to face, but it was very important to me that she heard from my lips all the things buried deep in my heart. Normally I'd have written these thoughts in a letter and given her space to read it in private, but the opportunity for such things was past and it was time to bare my soul.

With tears streaming down my face and frequent sobs interrupting, I read these words to her:

> My darling Kari
>
> I'm so proud of you and how you're so brave and strong in circumstances that would have most people crumbling. Please know that if it gets too much you can lean on Nic and me and on Jesus who loves you so much. You've fought harder and longer and with more dignity than most people could have shown in the face of such overwhelming setbacks. We're still praying and believing for a mighty miracle of God's healing in your life. God is greater than these evil bacteria.
>
> I hope you know how precious you are to me. I longed for a child for so many years. I know that you know how that feels. Being pregnant with you remains one of the happiest times of my life even after all these years. When you were born you were more

than I could ever have hoped or dreamed of. Such a beautiful baby who brought so much joy to Dad and me. You've been the daughter that every woman hopes for. You were such a cute and adorable little girl. So caring, bright, easy to train and funny as well. With your beautiful curls and sweet face, you just melted my heart.

At school you always made us proud. You were so very well-behaved and always excelled at everything you did (except maybe running). Teachers couldn't praise you highly enough. Winning the "Spirit of the College" award demonstrated that. That's not to say you were perfect, as trails of Pancrease used to tell us, but you were seriously one of those kids who other parents wish they had.

As a teenager you were a breeze and although as you got older you made some choices which we didn't agree with, you were rarely openly rebellious and never disrespectful. I'm sure lots of parents would love a teenager like you. I'm so proud of how you've achieved so much. Finishing uni and TAFE so well and then all the amazing places you've travelled so far. You've been fearless and adventurous and so full of life and I've admired you so much.

As you've gotten older, I've relished the fact that you've become my friend as well as my daughter. There's honestly nobody I'd rather spend time with. Whether its trawling around the shops, going to the beach with Maloo, watching a soppy movie, or enjoying a cup of tea from your beautiful teapot, you're such good company and I treasure every minute I can spend with you. Remember that exercise I did recently where I had to tick positive traits about family members and ended up ticking nearly every box for you? There are very few people in the world who could get that many ticks and yet it was all true about you. You're very, very special Kari.

You've always had heaps of friends and I'm not sure there was ever anybody who actually disliked you. I know they recognise just how special you are. The fact that you have more friends than you can keep up with should tell you that's true. And the fact that you've kept friends for so many years is a testament to you. You truly are a blessing to so many people. I'm so glad you've found a beautiful Christian man like Nic who loves you and loves God.

That's what I've always wanted for you. I love to see you snuggled up on your couch together and know that you're being loved in the way you deserve.

Thanks for being there for me through the hard times of the last few years. I honestly don't know if I could have done it without you. You've been a great listener and someone to lean on and have shown maturity beyond your years. Don't take all this praise lightly because I say it with great sincerity and admiration for the woman you've become. I love that you've chosen to follow Jesus and honour Him with your life. You are truly beautiful inside and out.

But most of all I just love YOU. I love the way you light up any gathering. I love the way you bring peace and harmony. I love your quirky sense of humour and dry wit. I love your passion for dance and music. I love driving back from Brisbane with Brazilian music blaring out of the car speakers. I love your compassionate heart that wants to help people and care for the poor. I love all the amazing photos you've taken in all the awesome places you've visited. I love listening to you speaking Italian. I love your bright and intelligent mind. I love watching you playing with Maloo. I love hearing you zip into our driveway in your cute little yellow sunshine car that reflects your personality so well. You truly do bring sunshine with you wherever you go. I love your amazing, beautiful curly hair. I love your eyes.

I love the incredible strength you've shown over the past two years and continue to show right now. I love how you've never let CF define you or played on it to get others to treat you better. I love how you've become tidy and have even managed to make that one granny-flat room into a warm and cosy home for you and Nic and Maloo. I love that you're a better person than me, less judgemental and with a kinder heart.

I love that despite all you've endured throughout all your life you have the most amazing and beautiful spirit of any person I've ever known. You bring me so much joy Kari-Lee and I love you with all my being.

We settled in for what turned out to be the worst night of my life. Kari struggled to breathe throughout the whole night. Early in the evening, the nurse asked if we wanted her to call Peter Hopkins. It was well after hours and neither Kari nor I liked to bother the doctors unless it was absolutely necessary, so we said, "No, thanks." That was a decision I'll always regret.

As the night progressed, her breathing worsened. By now the night shift had taken over and the nurse responsible for Kari was not one that she knew well. Kari struggled to catch any breath at all, despite the oxygen being turned up as high as it could go. She needed to sit fully upright to get any air in her lungs, but she was too exhausted and horrendously unwell to be able to sit up. I sat on the bed and held her in front of me, supporting her in as much of an upright position as I could manage. We remained like that for the entire night. I didn't sleep at all and Kari only dozed intermittently, when exhaustion overcame her.

Several times through the night, Kari became distressed because of the immense effort it was taking to get any air at all into her lungs. She was almost passing out from the exertion. I pressed the buzzer and asked for the nurse to please get the doctor. This happened more than once, with each plea becoming more desperate and more urgent. I was told that there was only a house doctor on call. I realised that this doctor didn't know Kari and couldn't possibly understand that when Kari said things were desperate, they were completely and utterly desperate. Kari rarely ever pushed her nurse call button, because she "didn't want to bother anyone" and "they probably had people who needed them a lot more than she did". Now, she really, really needed help and it felt like nobody could give her the help she needed.

The house doctor suggested a nebuliser of Ventolin – a suggestion which I would have found ridiculously laughable if the situation wasn't so dire and life threatening. Each time I asked, I became more desperate, but felt like someone who was making a fuss about nothing and should just leave them alone and get some sleep. The house doctor came four times. To me they seemed to have no idea what to do to help Kari. Perhaps there actually was nothing more they could do. I'll never know.

Up until this time, I'd almost always been satisfied with Kari's care. I'd always felt people were trying their best even if they weren't succeeding in making her better. Throughout this long, dark and terrifying night, I felt more alone and helpless than I ever have in my entire life.

Anguish and despair twisted inside. Why wouldn't anybody DO something? Was Kari going to die in my arms while I begged someone to help her, to do something, anything, that could help her breathe?

CHAPTER TWENTY-NINE

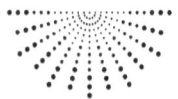

At last, Wednesday morning came. Some of Kari's favourite nurses came to look after her. Kari decided that she wanted to go home. She'd fought as long and as valiantly as she could, but now that there was nothing more to be done she just wanted to be at home.

I informed the medical staff and they told me that it would be impossible to have hospice care arranged so quickly. At this, the mama bear within me rose up and said, "If Kari-Lee wants to go home today, then Kari-Lee will be going home today. Either you make it happen or I'll do it myself." I started phoning friends who were doctors and nurses to enlist their help in caring for Kari at home until hospice care could be arranged officially.

The nurses got Kari out of bed, sitting upright in a chair beside the bed, so that she could breathe more easily. They began training me to use the pump which at home would deliver new IV medications – morphine, midazolam and Valium, along with some of her antibiotics – to ease Kari's pain and anxiety as the end drew near and it became frighteningly difficult to get any breath.

One of the medical staff sat very close to Kari, who always valued her personal space. Afterwards, Kari said to Nic, "Did you see how close they were to my face? I thought they were going to kiss me!" Kari's sense of humour was always close to the surface, no matter how desperately sick she became.

Throughout the morning there were lots of extra visitors. A lady who'd previously prayed for Kari's healing arrived with her team to pray again. They prayed passionately, fervently, even aggressively, believing for a miracle, which we all knew was possible even at this late stage.

Each of the four transplant specialists, as well as the physio and doctors from the CF team, along with some of the nurses, came to say goodbye to Kari and honour her for the courageous way she'd fought, how she'd conducted herself and what she'd taught them. One of the doctors, who'd rarely shown any emotion, said, "Thank you for what you've taught me, not just about CF, but about life."

IN AMONGST THE VISITS, I took the time to talk with Kari about how she wanted things done if the unthinkable happened and the still-hoped-for miracle didn't come. We discussed her funeral and in typical Kari style she asked that everyone wear bright colours, no black. She requested a turquoise coffin and lots of frangipani. She wanted everyone to celebrate and look at photos of the amazing life she'd had. She asked to be cremated, with her ashes scattered at her favourite beach.

She decided it was time to make a will, so she told me all her wishes and I wrote them down, then gave them to the social worker to type into a document that Kari could sign. As she owned very little, this was an easy task. She wanted me to have her little yellow car, Tiana to have all her clothes and jewellery and Nic to have the rest. She told Nic she'd like him to keep Maloo.

Somehow, I don't know how, I was able to operate on another plane on a type of autopilot. I suspended my deepest feelings, boxed them up and put them into a compartment where they couldn't intrude on the unimaginable discussions that I needed to have. Somehow, I don't know how, I was able to discuss her funeral, her cremation and her will. My mind closed itself off to the things that were happening, the implication of things we were discussing, and the fact that my daughter was now officially dying. Somehow, I don't know how, she was able to contemplate those things at the tender age of twenty-five. When she should have been planning her next overseas adventure, or what she was going to wear to a party on the weekend, or which subjects to study next semester at uni, she was facing her own death and helping to plan the details around it. She didn't cry or wallow in self-pity. She bravely faced what was coming and made decisions to make it easier for us when she was gone.

I knew she didn't want to go, but now that it seemed inevitable she accepted it with dignity, grace and immense courage. At one point when we were alone, I asked her if she was scared. She unhesitatingly replied, "No."

She even took the time to put one last post on Facebook, letting people know what was happening.

> I didn't think it would come to this, but I only have a few days left. There's nothing more the doctors can do, so they're sending me home. I just wanted to say:
> Love all people, respect others.
> Be grateful for the little things.
> Peace out.

THE STAFF INFORMED me that they'd managed to arrange everything for Kari to go home. Palliative care would be available in our home and the ambulance was booked for one o'clock to take Kari home. Gaye, Rachel and Winston began packing up some of the things in the room. I phoned my sisters, who agreed to go and unlock our house and move the furniture around to accommodate a hospital bed. Nobody had been living at home for most of the past two months.

Kari managed to doze a little in the chair, but breathing was becoming increasingly difficult so the CF physio was called. He did some airway clearance with Kari, but she was coughing up pink, blood-stained foam and mucous and it didn't seem to help her breathing much.

Each of us took some time alone with Kari that morning. Tiana remembers saying to Kari, "I'll miss you."

Kari responded, "I'll still be around."

∼

BY ONE O'CLOCK when the ambulance was due, everything was ready. Peter had stayed at Rose Cottage all morning, cleaning and packing things up. He and Tiana decided to go ahead of the ambulance and prepare the room. The hospital bed was being delivered and someone needed to be there to let the people in and help them set up. The rest of us were all in the room, waiting to see Kari-Lee off in the ambulance: Nic and his parents; Rachel and Winston; Gaye and her son, who'd come to wait with her until Bruce returned from his uni work.

The sun was shining outside and life in the ward just outside Kari's door proceeded as usual, with lunch trays being delivered and medications being distributed. I heard whispers that the nurses planned to form a guard of honour along the hall when Kari was leaving with the paramedics. We continued to wait, but by two-thirty the ambulance still hadn't arrived. We were used to lots of waiting around for things to happen in hospital, but this was incredibly frustrating as we knew every moment was precious.

As I sat on her bed, Kari said, "I feel like I'm here, but not here."

I suggested that maybe her sedation pump was turned up too high and went to the nurses' desk to find someone to adjust it.

When I returned, she commented, "My eyes are getting blurry."

In came a doctor and adjusted the medication, then sat on the bed next to Kari. When Kari became a little agitated, the doctor started rubbing her arm and soothing her. I cringed inside because I knew how much Kari would have hated this. Kari calmed, but then the doctor started gently caressing her on the cheek. I wanted to push them way, but I wasn't brave enough.

Then Kari started speaking in a very soft and breathless voice. "I want to thank you all for everything you've done."

At first, we didn't realise the significance of what was happening. I thought she might have been thanking the doctors but suddenly I realised that this was something else. Kari had something very important to say, so we gathered closer around her bed.

When she turned to the doctor and said, "I love you," I realised that because she could no longer see properly and the doctor had been caressing her cheek, she thought she was speaking to Nic.

I quickly encouraged him to take his place right next to Kari. The doctor then came around behind me and started very gently rubbing my back. I hate soft touch, particularly from someone I don't know well. I shook it off and sat right up near Kari's head and cradled her in my arms, encouraging Nic to do the same on her other side.

Kari continued speaking to Nic, only managing a couple of words between each hard-fought breath. "Thank you for sticking by me. A lot of people wouldn't have stayed, but you did. Thanks for staying when you could have left at any time."

Next, she turned to me, "Mum, thank you for all you've done for me. I couldn't have done this without you. You're the best mum anyone could ever have."

After a pause to catch her breath, which was becoming more and more difficult, she started speaking to Peter, not realising he wasn't there. I tearfully asked her to hold on while I desperately punched Peter's number into my phone and put it on loudspeaker. While she was waiting, Kari cracked a joke: "Well that escalated quickly," a quote from a movie.

Tiana answered Peter's phone and I said, "She's going!" Having just arrived at our house in Nambour, Tiana thought I meant that Kari was going in the ambulance and would be there soon. "No. She's dying."

Peter couldn't grasp what was happening, but Tiana handed him the phone as Kari spoke to him: "Sometimes you get forgotten, but so many of my best memories were made with you. Look after my baby Maloo for me."

Tiana came back on the phone, and Kari told her, "Thank you. You've brought so much life and energy into our family. I love you."

I brought the phone back to my ear and heard Tiana distressed and crying, but said, "I can't talk," and hurriedly handed the phone to Gaye. My full focus was on Kari-Lee.

Tiana tells me that back in Nambour, she and Peter were standing in the lounge, with Tiana yelling at Peter trying to make him understand what was happening. She desperately tried to call me back. Gaye answered and told her what was happening.

Peter had completely broken down so Tiana put him in the car and drove as fast as she could, with tears streaming down her face, back to Brisbane.

Back at the hospital, Kari struggled to breathe, with the effort to speak taking every ounce of her determination. Another joke: "Those paramedics aren't very punctual, are they?" referencing the fact that she was training to be a paramedic herself.

She then thanked Bruce (who wasn't there) and Gaye for their support. "Thanks for fighting for me. You always believed for my miracle and I almost have it." She told Rachel and Winston, "You've been like a rock for me. Thank you for being my best friend for all these years. Winston, thanks for being a good friend to Nic."

Then she went silent, apart from the rasping of her breaths, gradually becoming slower and further apart. I whispered in her ear how much I loved her, how amazing she was and that she was safe now, Jesus had her.

I encouraged Nic to speak to her too; he was so overwhelmed with emotion he was missing that last opportunity. "She can hear you, just tell her what you want to."

Rachel was standing at the foot of the bed and she recalls something that wasn't visible from where I was sitting. "Kari-Lee leaned forward, possibly trying to breathe, and looked up to her left with her eyes really wide open. I remember thinking how beautiful her eyes were, they were big and clear and fixed on the corner of the room, not moving or anything. She just looked like she was focused on something, regardless of all the people standing around her in the room. I'll never forget it."

Gradually Kari's breaths slowed even further and the time between them stretched and stretched and stretched until…

there were no more.

KARI IS GONE

AFTER: CHAPTER ONE

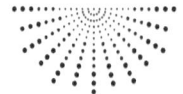

I don't think I cried.

Life as I knew it had ceased to exist, but I don't think I cried. A deep fog descended and I felt like I was living outside myself. One part was taking care of practicalities and seemingly "in control", while inside was a deafening, shrieking noise that screamed of my unfathomable loss. Somehow, I became surrounded by a "bubble" where my senses were distorted and life came at me in a series of images.

I remember Nic's face. It's imprinted on my brain. A look of utter disbelief and despair. I remember him letting out a long moan and sinking to the floor, sobbing loudly, being supported by his parents. I remember him saying that he wanted to die, to be with Kari.

I don't think I cried.

I remember Kari's precious nurses, with tears running down their faces, saying that they'd look after her now, asking what I'd like them to dress her in. What I really wanted was what she was already wearing, her favourite "bird pants" a comfy pair of harem pants with a black background covered in colourful tropical birds. However, I knew they would now be soiled, so I chose a brand-new dress Kari had bought online but never had the chance to wear. It had striking blocks of black and white and seemed suitable for the occasion.

I remember all of us going out to the little lounge and sitting, staring. I remember they gave me the "comfy" chair, as if somehow that could make a difference to the excruciating pain. I felt a deep ache in the middle of my chest, surely my heart breaking. My stomach contracted as if someone had kicked me. Hard. I wanted to vomit. My whole body WAS pain.

I don't think I cried.

I remember Peter and Tiana arriving back from Nambour, the trauma and anguish refashioning their faces. Tiana falling into my arms. Peter standing by, helpless, horrified. My heart broke for them.

I don't think I cried.

I remember the Charge Nurse coming to speak to me, to tell us how she admired Kari's grace, courage and humour, even in the darkest of times. She shared with me that she also was a Christian and had been praying for Kari, but knew now that she was at peace.

I remember the nurses coming to tell us that we could go back in to Kari now and to take all the time we wanted. I remember looking at her with that dress on, black up near her face, and knowing it was wrong. Those two nurses, loving Kari too, took those soiled bird pants, put them through a speed wash-and-dry cycle and brought them back to us fresh and warm, then tenderly dressed Kari in them with a blue tank top. There now, that was our girl.

I don't think I cried.

I remember the nurses telling us to take as long as we wanted saying goodbye to Kari. We took seven hours, most of it a blur. I remember we each took time to sit with her, to drink in that beautiful face one last time, before it was taken away from our sight for the rest of our lives. I held those precious hands. I ran my fingers through that amazing hair. I remember I snipped three locks of Kari's beautiful curls: one for Tiana, and the others to keep with me always. I remember Tiana and I took photos of Kari's tattoos. I wasn't a fan of tattoos, but Kari's were very special to her and I never wanted to forget them.

I don't think I cried.

I remember ringing just a couple of people in our family and asking them to tell others. I remember posting on Facebook that Kari was now "Safe in Jesus' arms" when all I really wanted was for her to be safe in mine. I remember my Mum and sister coming down from Nambour to say a last farewell. My Mum saying over and over how Kari looked like she was just sleeping. And how I wished with all my being that it was true. I remember Peter's sister and her husband, bringing her cousin, her "twin" Rebekah, all of them weeping over Kari.

I remember my faithful friends Gaye and Bruce, and Rachel, Kari's devastated best friend, along with her husband Winston, packing up the room, eight weeks' worth of Kari's life, all the hope and prayers and gifts and everything we had tried to keep Kari alive.

I don't think I cried.

I remember when it was time to go. The impossibility of dragging myself away from this shell that was once my vibrant, funny, beautiful, full-of-life daughter. Just one more hug. Just one more gaze at that precious face, the answer to so many hopes and dreams and prayers. Just one more touch of that body which had taken her on so many amazing adventures, but which ultimately had let her down so badly. It might only be a shell, and an empty one now, but this was the physical form of my beautiful girl that I'd loved and held through all of the ups and downs of her life, since she grew inside me, right under my heart. Oh, how I would miss her physical presence. How could I tear myself away, knowing I wouldn't see or hold her again until the end of my own physical life?

I don't think I cried.

I remember walking out that door, the door of "Kari's room", the best room on the wing, Room 9, which the nurses always gave to Kari if they possibly could. I remember walking down that hospital corridor, which had become a second home over the past two years, a place of hopes raised and held and dashed, of struggle and laughter and fear, of love and faith and tears. A corridor where, just that morning, the nurses had planned a guard of honour for Kari when the paramedics carried her out for the last time, on her way home to Nambour. Instead, after we'd gone, it would be her body which they escorted out to the cold, dark mortuary – a thought I simply could not bear.

I don't think I cried.

I remember walking to the car and driving back to Rose Cottage, unable to speak, unable to think, unable to breathe.

I remember all the young people: Nic, Tiana, Gaye's son and Nic's brother sleeping on mattresses on the floor in the lounge room of Rose Cottage, because none of them could face being alone. I remember Peter and I going into the bedroom, changing and getting into bed like robots, not being able to speak or think, existing in a bubble, turning off the light.

And then I cried. And cried. And cried. And cried. And cried. And cried. And cried. And cried…

AFTER: CHAPTER TWO

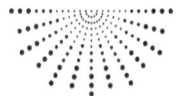

*I*s it possible to imagine a worse day than the day your child dies? For me, yes. The next day, when I wake up to a world with no Kari-Lee in it. A world that will never again have Kari-Lee in it, for the rest of my life. Every single day of my life on earth will have to be lived without her. It's simply unimaginable.

As I slowly come to consciousness, I resist fully waking up, not wanting to open my eyes to this world that I no longer want to be part of. How can the world continue without her? How can my life continue without her? I really have no answers, nor any capacity to even think about the way forward. I feel like I've crawled into a dark tunnel and it's collapsed on top of me, crushing the life out of me. I just want to die, right here in this bed, but Peter and Tiana need me.

Somehow, amidst copious tears, I drag myself out of bed. Seemingly insurmountable tasks stretch before me, beginning with packing up two months of living at Rose Cottage. It's been such a blessing to be close to Kari during these past months, but I never expected it to end this way. No matter how sick she had become, I always expected her to be coming home with us. It sounds strange even to my own ears considering all that's gone before, but I'm in a complete state of shock. Nothing could ever have prepared me for this day.

Practicalities of dealing with food, toiletries, clothes: it's all beyond my current ability and yet, somehow, it's done. Everything I touch is a painful reminder of a moment I've spent with Kari, or getting ready to see her. I'm so blessed by our friends who last night bravely packed up Kari's hospital room so I don't need to deal with that heartbreaking task.

Now, as we face a devastating homecoming without our precious girl, I feel the need to spend time with those who've been in the "bubble". Those who've stood by the bedside in these last dreadful days, who've witnessed Kari's courageous spirit in the face of horrendous suffering and imminent death. Those who've seen that beautiful, yet empty, shell which remained when her spirit flew off with the angels.

These are the people who "get it". That's who I need to be with. And so, the time of the "bubble" begins.

~

MUCH OF THE next ten days is a blur to me. I'm in a complete fog, often unaware of people around me, as my mind and heart struggle to come to terms with a reality that's impossible to process.

Kari died.

Everything swirls together in a cloud of coexisting pain and yet numbness. Gaye and Bruce's house becomes a safe gathering place for us, and we go there on that first afternoon. Nic is there. His parents are there. We talk about Kari. We cry. We drink cups of tea.

We tentatively approach the unthinkable topic of a funeral. Such things will have to be discussed. Time won't wait for us to be ready. Nic's dad suggests a funeral director he knows, but internally my mind rebels at the thought of a funeral director having anything to do with my vivacious daughter. We make an appointment for Monday and I realise that this is now my purpose. The next ten days are my opportunity to plan a service that will somehow do justice to the sparkling presence of Kari-Lee and honour her inspiring life and courageous death. This becomes my focus, my mission, my last gift.

We meet again the following day at Gaye and Bruce's, struggling to process what's happened and what now needs to happen. Then, on the Saturday, Peter and I have much-needed haircuts. The mundane things of life continue, even when your world has exploded catastrophically and nothing seems to make sense anymore. I ask my hairdresser to shave my head. The inner anguish needs an outward sign. Wisely, she refuses. What she does do is colour a small section of my hair in the colour of Kari's hair. This patch of colour will be renewed in my hair for years to come. People will sometimes comment on it and I will love the opportunity it gives to talk about my girl.

Later that day, we all get together for a barbeque at Nic's parents' house. While I only want to be with members of the "bubble", they've invited some of Nic and Kari's friends who've been very supportive to Nic. He's moved back home with his parents. He mostly ignores us, focusing instead on playing video games with his friends. I'm told by his parents that this is what he does all day and much of the night until he collapses from exhaustion on the couch. Some of his faithful friends stay with him. He can't bear to sleep alone in the small bedroom he's been given, but feels the need to be close to his parents so the couch is the best option. It's his way of coping.

The conversation of funeral planning flows around me: flowers, decorations, food. Suddenly, it all becomes too much for me. I'm struggling with Nic's apparent lack of interest. I know he's young and devastated by Kari's death, but I'm frustrated that he can't seem to take part in the discussions at all. I go for a long walk around the nearby streets to clear my head and prevent myself from saying something that I might later regret. It's the first clear indication of how differently we will all grieve and how that might sometimes rub up against each other's raw wounds.

THE NEXT DAY, Sunday, is the most horrendous so far. I literally want to die. Right now. The emotional pain inside me is bursting to get out. It's too monstrous to contain. I need a physical outlet. I need pain. I rake my fingernails down my arms, over and over and over again, until they bleed. I can't believe how physical my grief is.

My entire body aches all over. I feel nauseated constantly. I feel like someone kicked me in the stomach, hard. My chest aches. It feels like I'm having a heart attack.

I want to scream at the top of my lungs. I want to hit things, throw things, break things. A tidal wave of grief and pain and anguish explodes through my being. Nothing I can do is enough. Only death would free me from this unbearable pain. I long for it, yet I can't cause any more pain to those who love me and have also lost Kari.

Somehow, I have to get through this. I really don't know how.

I SPEND hours each day browsing through photos, choosing the right ones to convey the amazing life that Kari lived, just as she asked me to. I choose songs with meaningful words, some of which have prowled through my consciousness for years as I secretly contemplated the incomprehensible possibility of her early death. I aim to be uplifting, to share the highs, because I know that's what Kari wants, but it's so hard, because that's not how I feel.

I know that people come and go from our home, but I only have a foggy awareness of their presence. A few friends bring meals and I somehow speak to them, appreciative of their kindness, yet unable to leave my cloud of numb grief to connect with them. My sisters come to lend a practical hand by cleaning my bathrooms, but I pay them little attention as I focus solely on Kari's farewell. Beautiful flower arrangements arrive, sent with loving care from all sorts of people. I notice them, appreciate them, but somehow it doesn't help. The smell of lilies permeates our home, a sickly smell which makes me feel like vomiting and which I will forever associate with this time.

On Monday, we make the unavoidable visit to the funeral parlour. We sit in an office and discuss the mind-bending event of a funeral for my daughter. I look out the window and the world seems normal: blue sky, leaves rustling in the breeze, birds flying past. Yet inside, absolutely nothing about this situation is normal or believable. We talk about Kari's wishes for lots of photos showing all the amazing adventures she experienced. The funeral director says, "It's best not to show more than sixty photos. People get bored." I nod, but take no notice, because this farewell will be what Kari wanted in every single way I can make that happen.

We discuss practicalities, like what Kari will wear, as if it matters. Yet somehow, it does. We want her to look her best, even though probably no-one will see her. They mention a hearse and my mind jolts with the thought of vibrant, colourful Kari in a drab, black hearse. It's wrong. We decide that she would like to make the journey in a Kombi van, a very "beachy" vehicle, which she admired. We tell the directors that we'll find one, although we have absolutely no idea how or where. As it turns out, it will take a great deal of effort and searching before we find one. Peter will even resort to speaking to random strangers on the side of the road, asking whether they happen to have a Kombi van in a beach colour.

Then comes one of the most horrifically surreal moments, when they take us into a room filled with coffins and ask us to choose one for Kari. They show us polished wood versions with shiny handles and my stomach turns over at the thought. I'm relieved that this is something that Kari gave her clear decision on – she wanted a turquoise coffin, the colours of the ocean. There are two options and I'm wishing we could ask Kari's opinion on which one she'd prefer. Finally, we manage to choose and escape from the claustrophobic atmosphere of the funeral home.

A huge challenge presents itself in trying to find a "black African choir" to sing *Amazing Grace* as Kari requested. None of the leads I follow go anywhere. Eventually, after weeks of searching, Peter's sister will discover that her pastor, who comes from Africa, is willing to sing with his family. I know it's not what Kari had in mind, but with no other apparent alternative I gratefully accept.

ON TUESDAY, we spend time at Nic's parents' house again. There's talk of climbing Mount Coolum to watch the sunrise. Tiana decides to stay the night with them so she can leave early with everyone in the morning.

I let them know I want to join them, then head home. Next

morning, I discover that they've gone without me. I'm angry at being left out. Seemingly small things like this take on huge dimensions when my emotions are so close to the surface. It hurts. I take Maloo for a long walk on the beach, looking at Mount Coolum for much of the walk, crying most of the way. I'm like a walking case of severe sunburn, so sensitive to every tiny thing. Bumps that would normally be unnoticeable become a huge issue.

Later that day, Peter and I go to the studio of the local Christian radio station, where we've arranged to pre-record our messages for Kari's service. I'm planning to read the letter that I read out to Kari on the night before she died. I've added a little bit since she left us. Peter has written a letter to his "little Parbi". We really appreciate the offer to use their facilities, because we both want to share our thoughts of Kari-Lee, but don't feel we'll be able to hold it together at the service.

I go first and as I sit with the microphone in front of me, I'm transported back again to that hospital room with my dying daughter. Now I share those very private thoughts with others, through my recording. I'm so glad I was brave enough to share them with Kari while she could hear them. Amazingly, I manage to complete my whole recording without a pause and without breaking down.

We're contacted by a local journalist we know. He wants to write another story about Kari for the newspaper. I gladly agree, always willing to share the story of my courageous girl with anyone who'll listen. We meet at our friends' house and take turns sharing about our special girl.

Nic shares a deeply meaningful thought which ends up being quoted in several articles: "We were all praying for a miracle, but actually Kari was the miracle."

We share photos and stories and tears. The journalist listens respectfully and writes a beautiful piece which is published in our local paper, as well as many regional newspapers and online.

Gaye takes me to the church where the funeral will be held, to meet with the videographer who'll bring my photo montages to life. I need it to be just right. He takes my need seriously and does a great job.

On Friday, the day before the service to celebrate Kari-Lee's life, Peter and I choose to do the unimaginable. We go to the funeral parlour to view Kari's body. We have asked Nic whether he wishes to see Kari one more time, but he declines. In Australia, unlike the US, this isn't customary.

While in many ways I would have preferred to remember Kari alive and joyfully laughing, I feel the need to see her just one last time. I go in alone and there she is, lying in the beautiful blue dress that Nic had chosen because it reminded him of their very special moment together. Of course, it's obvious as I look down into the coffin that Kari isn't there. The outward shell which had held the spirit of our sparkling daughter is here, but Kari is gone. And yet, this is the body that we held, the face we cherished, still precious in its own right.

I lift the covering and check that she's wearing her fluoro orange sandals as she'd requested. I daringly wipe off the shiny pink lip gloss that's definitely not what Kari would have worn. I say a few last words to her and kiss her cold face. Then Peter has some time alone with her before I join him to say our final farewell together on this earth to our immensely precious first-born treasure, as our tears drip down onto her still-beautiful face.

How grateful we are to have been blessed to be her parents. What a privilege and honour it's been and always will be.

AFTER: CHAPTER THREE

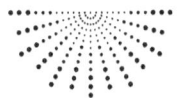

You painted me a picture of tomorrow
A place where you and I walked hand in hand
A world without despair and without shadows
But things just didn't turn out how we planned
Now you're gone
And I believe that there is somewhere
Where the angels fill the sky
And I believe we'll live forever
You and I, you and I
Will never die
I wonder if you knew that you were leaving
I thought that I saw something in your eyes
You painted me a picture of believing
I'll see you there on the other side
And I'll be there…

— *MICHAEL W. SMITH,*
WESLEY KING

*A*s these words blare brave and loud from the speakers, a declaration that Kari's death is not the end and that I'm confident I'll see her again, I sit in the front row of the auditorium, pondering. I do believe it, I have to believe it, and yet.

As stunning engagement photos of Kari and Nic gazing into each other's eyes flash up onto the three large screens in front of me, so cruel in their innocent promise of a life together, my mind closes off to the awful reality of that tiny turquoise coffin in front of me containing all that's left of the earthly presence of my vibrant, sparkling daughter.

The day has already been long and difficult...

UNABLE TO SLEEP, awash in tears, tortured by nightmare images of Kari's last moments on this earth, I rise early and start my preparations, intent on getting everything just right for her farewell. Somehow through what is presented today, I want people to get a sense of Kari, to know her, to love her, to miss her. To capture just a little of the enormous magnitude of our loss.

In my mind is a picture of an auditorium filled with the scent of frangipani spilling over the steps and stage, creating a beautiful tropical garden for Kari's coffin to nestle in, a huge room filled with photos and reminders of Kari to somehow convey all there is to know about how absolutely amazing she was.

It's never going to be enough. There are only a few helpers and they are doing their best. It can't live up to my expectations – probably nothing could.

Instead of a fragrant garden there are a few lonely bunches of sunflowers, some strings of bougainvillea and a few palm branches, beautiful in themselves but lost in this huge building. My sisters are out hunting along roadsides for frangipanis, Kari's favourite flowers, so important to me in this last offering to Kari. In a cruel twist, she's died just a bit too soon for frangipani season.

An artistic display aiming to capture something of Kari's essence has been set up in the foyer by Nic's mum. Kari's teal beach-cruiser bike; her wood panelled sign bearing one of her favourite sayings: "Life is not about waiting for the storms to pass, but learning to dance in the rain"; her surfboard covered in summer photos. It's lovely, but Kari is so much more. There have already been disagreements about whether certain decorations, which other people thought were a great idea, are actually something Kari would have wanted. Feelings run high.

Gorgeous framed photos of Kari and Nic line the back of the building, positioned so that people will see them as they walk to their seats. The pedestal where her coffin will rest has been draped in waves of sheer turquoise fabric, creating an effect of the ocean. It looks good, but it needs to be better.

There's never going to be enough to capture my girl in a building, in a couple of hours. I've done my best, but it's just not enough. I feel I've failed her.

AS THE STARTING time draws nearer, the Kombi van arrives from the funeral home with Kari in her beach-covered coffin. I direct them to the front, where they busy themselves with setting things up. I find it impossible to think about the fact that the now-empty husk that was my effervescent daughter is lying in that pretty box, sitting right at the front of the huge auditorium. I focus on details: beach-themed napkins, thoughtfully bought by my sisters; the order of service booklets with a page for people to share their stories of Kari-Lee; baskets filled with paper cranes from Kari's hospital room, to be given out as guests arrive.

I gaze at the giant photo of Kari on the screen in her magnificent dancing costume from the Carnival in Rio, which will be the still photo everybody sees as they walk in. I listen to the Brazilian music playing softly, a painful reminder of Kari's once active and joy-filled body dancing at every opportunity.

It's all too much. I can't do this. And yet, I must.

I take a last look around, then leave the auditorium before people begin to arrive. As we haven't eaten all day, some drinks and nibbles have been set up in a small room for us and we're able to wait there, out of sight, until the service begins. I have no appetite, but I'm grateful for this small oasis of calm before I face the inconceivable task of farewelling my girl. The "bubble" members are all present: Peter and I, Tiana, Nic, Gaye and Bruce, Rachel and Winston, Nic's parents and brother.

I take some time in the bathroom getting changed. I've chosen to wear the same dress I'd worn just ten short months ago to Kari's wedding. It's one of her favourite colours and she'd asked us all to wear bright colours. It feels so wrong and yet I know it's the right dress for this occasion.

THE MOMENT I've been dreading is upon us. We walk slowly to our seats at the front of the auditorium. I keep my head down as I walk, not wanting to make eye contact with anyone, but I can tell that the auditorium, which seats over one thousand people, is nearly full. I say hello to my family, sitting just behind us, then sit and wait for the faith-filled words I've chosen to start this service. I wanted to set the right tone, hoping it will somehow permeate my being as well.

As the words sung by Michael W. Smith fade to silence, Bruce stands and makes his way to the front. We've asked him to lead the service, because he was *there*. He gets it, but he also gets God. He doesn't disappoint.

As Kari requested, the service is full of photos of her life, her adventures, and all the amazing places she was able to visit in her short time on this earth. First are photos of Kari growing up, shown as the recorded messages of Peter and I ring out through the auditorium. In some ways it's too much, too personal, too intimate, these words I've spoken to Kari in the dead of night, just the two of us on her last night on this earth, now being heard by hundreds of people. And yet I want them to know who she was to me. Each person in this auditorium knows a different aspect of Kari, but she was mine first and I want them to know how incredibly blessed I've been to be her mother.

Next, an act of bravery that has a huge impact on me. Tiana, looking so small, supported by her big, strong cousin, Michael, walks to the podium and shares with this crowd about the unique relationship she had with her big sister, her wingman, her expected companion for life. It's funny, it's heart-wrenching, it's honouring. I'm so proud of Tiana in that moment.

Throughout the service, I don't cry. I wonder if people can see and if they think I'm unfeeling. My eyes are dry because I've heard these songs and looked at these photos for hours and hours over the past week. I've cried oceans of tears as I've worked to get everything exactly right. I've put photos in. I've taken photos out. I've rearranged photos. I know everything that's going to be seen and heard, inside and out.

The painful truth is that I'm in a state of disbelief that this can possibly be happening at all. Kari can't be dead. We can't be farewelling her for the last time. It's simply, absolutely impossible.

Michael W Smith's song *This is Your Time* brings a lump to my throat as photos of Kari's overseas adventures scroll through, beaming her infectious smile, loving life, living in the moment. This song is one I've earmarked since the first time I heard it. I always knew I'd play it at Kari's funeral. I'd just hoped it would be a long time in the future. The words are so appropriate:

> This was her time
> This was her dance
> She lived every moment
> Left nothing to chance
> She swam in the sea
> Drank of the deep
> Embraced the mystery
> Of all she could be
> This was her time

So true of Kari-Lee. Followed by the verse that would continue to bring me hope:

> Though you are mourning,
> and grieving your loss
> Death died a long time ago

> Swallowed in life,
> so her life carries on
> Still, it's so hard to let go

Bruce stands to share a few encouraging words and does a great job in finding the balance between our complete devastation that Kari is gone, and the sure and certain hope that we will see her again. He reminds us that she's no longer suffering. Instead, she's more alive than she's ever been, enjoying a life of joy and health and laughter.

Another song, *I Lived* by OneRepublic, plays while more photos of Kari's adventurous life scroll through for people to enjoy. This song has been a new discovery for me and it includes the words of a young man with cystic fibrosis. Because of this, I have taken the opportunity to share some photos of Kari-Lee's life with CF. Not many, just enough to remind people that her life wasn't one big adventure of travelling overseas and dancing. Right from the beginning of her life, CF poked its nasty head into everything she was doing, intruding in ways that most people here are unaware of, stealing Kari's time, relationships and opportunities, but never her courage, joy and optimism. The song is uplifting and catchy. I'm not sure if Kari ever heard the song, but I think she'd love it.

Winston stands to read Nic's farewell letter to Kari, full of love and gratitude for all that she brought to his life.

> The past two years have been unforgettable and life-changing and this is all because of you. I know that we've been praying for a miracle for the past eight weeks, but I think you were the miracle. I thought our time together would be longer than what we had, but even though it was so short, it was amazing right from the start.

The next song is the deal breaker, the one song that does bring tears to my eyes – today and every time I hear it for years to come: *All of Me* by John Legend. The song that played as Kari walked out of Nana's house and across to marry Nic, on that joyous day just a few months ago. As photos of Kari and Nic during their short life together scroll through I glance to my left where Nic's sitting, in time to see him clutch his mum's hand and wipe a tear. I think again, "Life's not fair."

∿

BRUCE PRAYS the service to a close as the men we've asked to carry Kari out to the waiting Kombi van make their way to the front. Kari will leave the auditorium accompanied by a song written by Bruce just last week as he flew to Tasmania to visit his sick mother. It's sung by Kari's childhood friend, one of her "brothers". The words to this song, titled *Sunlight on the Ocean*, are printed for everyone to see – so poignant, so moving.

> Did I ever get to tell you what you meant to my life?
> How you taught me what it is to overcome
> In your quiet unpretentious way
> You moved your mountains every day
> And never bowed before a single one.
>
> Though your journey saw its share of pain
> Of cloudy skies and driving rain
> You opened up your heart at every chance.
> And if life is Heaven's Broadway show
> You took the stage and oh how you danced
> Oh how you danced
>
> When I think of you
> I can see the sunlight on the ocean
> When I think of you
> I can see right out to the horizon
> When I think of you
> I see forever
> And forever's how long I will love you
>
> You always told me not to mind the storms
> But to dance in the rain

And Heaven knows your dance was short, but it was sweet
And though my arms ache to hold you now
Someday I'll see you again
But until then...

When I think of you
I will see the sunlight on the ocean
When I think of you
I will see right out to the horizon
When I think of you
I'll see forever
And forever's how long I will love you
Yes, forever's how long I will love you.

As Nic and Peter lead the way, carrying the small coffin up the long aisle, it brings to mind that other long aisle that Peter so recently walked Kari along as she made her way to marry Nic. Then, both Peter and Nic's faces were filled with joy and anticipation. Now, they're deformed by unspeakable grief and suffering. My brother Charlie and Kari's cousin Michael are lined up behind Peter, with Nic's dad and brother on the other side. As they slowly make their way to the front of the church, we file in behind and drag ourselves forward to the moment when we will have the last sight of the coffin holding the earthly form of our darling girl.

As directed by Bruce, the hundreds of people present begin to form a guard of honour on either side of the long driveway. As the Kombi begins its slow exit, the sound of Celine Dion singing *Fly* floats out on the breeze. This is a song that Celine sang for her niece, Karine, who died from cystic fibrosis, aged just sixteen. It's another song that I've had tucked away for years, just for this occasion. Kari has already flown to Jesus, but it's a fitting farewell, the tender and touching words releasing Kari's spirit.

Then, the hardest part of the day. Hugs. So many hugs. Hugs from people I know. Hugs from people I've never met. People mingle and chat, laugh and cry, eat and drink. At some point, some of Kari's Latin dance friends do a short dance in her honour.

It's all a blur. I know I speak to people, I somehow interact, but I'm not really present in my body. When everyone finally leaves, Peter, Tiana and I go out for dinner with our friends, Janine and Cam, who've travelled down from Cairns.

It seems a strange thing to do, but I can't face going home, because then it will all be real. Kari will really be gone. There'll be nothing I can ever do for her again. I just need to postpone that moment for as long as I can. I need to not think about what awaits me tomorrow. And the next day. And the next.

I can feel the darkness creeping up on me and I fight to keep it away for just a couple more hours. Once I go down the rabbit hole, will I ever be able to return?

AFTER: CHAPTER FOUR

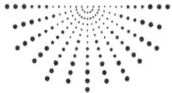

Kari is gone…

I've done the best I could to give Kari the farewell she wanted and deserved. There's nothing more I can do for her. Nothing. A huge black void opens up before me, sucking me in, pulling me down, down, and away into the darkness. I don't want to live. I don't think I can go on living. I don't think I want to.

Kari is gone…

I need to be alone. I just can't be with anyone right now. I can barely stand being with myself, but I can't escape from me. I'd like to just disappear, cease to exist, but that doesn't seem possible. I need to get away by myself and try to process some of this overwhelming pain that threatens to devour me.

Kari is gone…

I remember that Kari had booked a mini holiday for her and Nic at a farm stay, to enjoy after her transplant. It was sponsored by the local Apex club for families living with CF. I remember she never got to use it. She died before they had a chance. I phone to see if there's any way they'd let me use it instead. I explain the circumstances and they're kind and compassionate enough to agree to cover the cost of the three nights there, starting Tuesday.

Somehow, I need to get through the next two days. I don't know how to deal with all that's going on inside me. I feel like I'm losing my mind. I can't deal with the completely incomprehensible fact that Kari is gone. My head is exploding. I constantly review everything that happened, to see if there's something that could be changed, something that could be done differently that would somehow mean the outcome would be changed. As if, somehow, I can bring Kari back by going back in time and changing some detail. My rational mind knows that this is nonsense, but hours are spent lost in this swirling, tumbling confusion of ideas. What could I do differently so that we don't end up here?

Sleep eludes me. Whenever I close my eyes, my inner vision is filled with pictures of Kari, struggling to breathe; Kari, exerting all of her energy to thank us; Kari, pale and lifeless.

THE DAY AFTER THE FUNERAL, the bubble group gathers at Gaye and Bruce's for lunch. We sit outside and the talk swirls around me.

I can't do it. I can't bear it. I can't be here. I leave.

I don't tell anyone where I'm going, just mention to Gaye that I need to leave. I start walking, keep walking, trying to outrun my feelings. I need a physical outlet for the emotions that are too huge to contain in my body. I walk for miles, up and down hills, through mud and rocks and long grass, uncaring and unseeing. I realise that I'm heading for my parents' house, a place I can feel safe. At some point, I hear a loud muffler coming closer and Nic pulls up beside me in his ute. He asks if I'm okay and if I want a lift. I tell him I'm fine and he drives off in a haze of dust.

The next day is Tiana's last before she has to return to Brisbane and sort out her life there. It'll be hard to let her go. I feel so bad because I know she needs me, but I'm really no use to her or to anyone else. I'm in a deep, dark fog of pain and I have nothing to offer to anyone. She tells me that she's okay and she'll be back in a week to see us. Work needs her back. It's the busy season for chefs – leading up to Christmas, with lots of functions and weddings booked. I know she doesn't really want to go, but feels she has to if she wants to keep her apprenticeship.

Later that afternoon, I go for a walk to clear my head, desperately seeking something, anything, to calm the storm raging within. At the halfway mark I stand staring up into the sky, as if somehow an answer will appear in the heavens.

A plane, far off in the distance, enters my line of vision. It slowly traverses the wide canopy of the evening sky which begins to glow with the approaching sunset. The plane transforms into a golden arrow, reflecting the dazzling colours of the sky. I'm mesmerised, as I remember the joy Kari always found in flying. Deep within I feel a warm glow of peace. This exquisite shining plane feels like a sign from above that my Kari is flying now with the angels. She's flying off to Heaven and she will be okay.

As I watch the plane slowly progressing across the wide arc of magnificent colours, my heart feels a tiny hug of comfort. In days to come, I will see many planes flying high up in the sky, "winks" from God to let me know He cares and He knows how much I miss my girl. It seems that on the hardest of days I see more planes.

ON THE TUESDAY after Kari's farewell service, I drive myself up into the nearby hills. I don't tell Peter where I'm going, just that I need to get away totally by myself. He doesn't really understand, but I don't give him a choice. It's non-negotiable.

I leave when he's not home. The views are spectacular, right across the farmlands, the towns and out to the ocean. I think of Kari and wonder where she is. I cry. I drive on, winding through the green countryside, past horses, cows, picturesque farm sheds and fences, but my mind is elsewhere. Tears stream down my face as the inner turmoil of my soul spills over and out of my red, weeping eyes. I repeat to myself, "Kari is dead... Kari is dead... Kari is dead."

How can that vibrant, joyful, fun-loving, bright bubble of life just be gone? I know it's true, but my mind just can't grasp it, refuses to accept this impossible fact. It simply can't be true. And yet it is.

An hour later I turn in at the farm-stay and collect my key from a kind woman who explains that the cabins are a little further up the hill. There are daily feeding sessions of calves and chickens which I'm welcome to join. There are eggs collected daily which I'm welcome to eat. There's a bush walk which I'm welcome to take. I nod and thank her and try to arrange my face into the appropriate shape, but I just want to escape from her and from everyone and everything and disappear into nothingness.

I drive further up the gravel road where I find my cabin, one of only three, and let myself in. As I step onto the deck of my tiny, cosy cabin, the view takes my breath away. Far down below me is a stunning lake which takes up most of the vista, with trees and flowers and birds in abundance. Even in my decimated state, I can appreciate the awesome beauty before me and I silently thank the God I'm not sure I want to talk to anymore.

I've brought no food because I'm simply not eating these days, so there's little to unpack. Just a few tea bags, a couple of books, and all the scrapbooks I've made of Kari-Lee's life. I've also brought a set of DVDs of *Downton Abbey*, lent to me by my precious friend Gaye.

I spend my days and nights crying, reading a little about other people whose children have died, crying at what they share, drinking tea, looking at photos of Kari, crying some more and watching endless episodes of *Downton Abbey*, while crying. Years later, just hearing the opening bars of the introductory music to *Downton Abbey* will be enough to bring me to tears.

The book I'm reading, *Choosing to See*, is written by another mother who had to say goodbye far too early to her precious daughter. Mary Beth Chapman is open, honest and real and I see myself reflected back from her pages of unspeakable pain, lostness and deep darkness. I had read her book before Kari died and it's the first one I turn to now.

One afternoon I make my way up to the animal area and collect two eggs, which I manage to cook and eat, the only food I consume during these three days. I feel constantly nauseated, like someone punched me hard in the stomach. The mere thought of food is enough to make me gag.

I have a continual pain in my chest that aches non-stop. Later I read that this is a common symptom among grieving mothers – a sign of a broken heart.

Another day, feeling a need for movement, I set out on the bush-walk. The path isn't very clearly marked and I become completely lost, trapped in undergrowth and not even knowing which direction I should be heading. I sit and have a good cry but decide it really doesn't matter if nobody ever finds me. I'm ready to die and go to find Kari. Eventually though, I find my way out and head back to my cabin for more tea, more *Downton Abbey* and more tears.

I spend a lot of time just lying on the bed, crying. My mind goes round and round, often not able to follow a path of thought, but twisting and turning through grief and questions and doubt and despair and hopelessness.

Why Kari? Why now? What more could I have done? What more could anyone have done? What if she'd never caught glandular fever? What if she'd been able to continue on the new drug? Why didn't God answer our desperate but fully faith-filled prayers for healing? Why can't I just die now? What's the point of living? What's the point of praying? Why couldn't someone save her? Why couldn't she live long enough to have the baby she longed for? Why do other people with CF get to live longer?

Most of the time there's nobody in the other two cabins and I feel safer in the isolation, far away from "normal" people. I feel like I'm existing in a parallel universe of sorts. This gives me some freedom to express my feelings and I find myself wailing and groaning from far down in the depths of my being. With only the cows to hear me, I can let out noises that would be embarrassing and unacceptable were anyone else to hear me.

Each morning I receive a text message from Gaye. Initially, she starts them with "Good morning", but I soon tell her that there's nothing good about my mornings anymore and she modifies it to simply, "Morning". The texts are usually short, mostly that she's thinking of me and maybe praying for me. I do appreciate this, although I'm no longer convinced about the purpose of prayer. She often mentions Kari's name and something about her, which is the best gift of all. These morning texts become something I look forward to and they will continue faithfully for over a year.

ON THE FIRST NIGHT, I have a phone call from Peter who's concerned for my safety. I assure him that I'm not intending to harm myself, although, if I'm honest, it's very, very tempting at times.

On the second night I tell him where I am and agree that he can come and spend the final night with me, to see that I'm okay (well, not really, but sort of). He does come, but I draw no comfort from his presence. I'm an island. My grief feels too personal, even with the one other person who shared Kari fully with me for her whole life.

As time goes on, I'll discover that grief is a very isolating experience. Each of us had a different relationship with Kari while she was alive, so each of us has a different experience of grieving her now that she's gone. It drives a wedge between us, while at the same time keeping us together, bound by invisible cords of understanding who she was, how special she was and what a gaping, raw, heart-rending hole has been left by her leaving us.

He stays the night and we leave together the following morning. I'm still devastated, still wanting to disappear into nothingness, but the time alone has made it possible to be with Peter, to take the next tentative step towards the future that I wish I didn't have to live in. We've booked ourselves on a flight to Cairns, leaving in just a couple of days. It's something that I knew I would need if my worst nightmare ever came true.

THE NEXT DAY we take Maloo to the beach. It's a welcome respite and we love to see her joy as she runs in and out of the waves and rolls in the sand. At the same time, it's another reminder of the immense hole in our lives. It should be Kari at the beach with Maloo, not us. None of this is right.

We meet with Nic for a coffee and talk. I have no idea what we talk about, except that he says he doesn't want Maloo back, but wants us to keep her. Although we love Maloo dearly we're upset at the thought, because we heard Kari say she wanted Nic to keep her.

During our time together at the hospital, especially as things became more dire, I felt Nic and I had developed a deep bond as we prayed for, cried over and tried to cheer Kari. That seems to have vanished into a vapour and we're back to discussing inconsequential things. He seems unable to share his feelings or even his deeper thoughts, certainly with me. Yet another loss.

I sleep that night, and many future nights, in Kari and Nic's bed in our granny flat, anything to feel close to her. There's very little of her scent left because she's spent so much time in the hospital, but still, I feel her presence. It brings me a modicum of comfort when little else does.

AFTER: CHAPTER FIVE

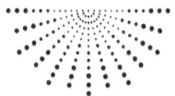

*I*t's been ten long days since Kari's service. I'm taking Maloo for one last walk before we go away, before dropping her to Nic.

I let her run free off the leash on a quiet road. She revels in the freedom, disappearing into the long grass, finding thrilling treasures. She returns with a dirty toy tiger in her mouth, a valued find in her eyes.

As we head up the long hill towards home, I hear her breathing become laboured as she tries to breathe around the tiger. She insists on carrying it in her mouth rather than letting me carry it for her. I try to convince her, repeatedly saying, "Let go," a command she usually obeys, but not today. She's not letting go of that tiger. She doesn't trust me to keep it safe and return it to her. Instead, she struggles all the way home.

I feel God is showing me a parable. Rather than letting go of Kari and trusting God to carry her safely for me until we're both "home", I'm clinging tightly to her and struggling to breathe in the process.

I need to let go. I'm not sure I can.

We board the plane for Cairns and I spend the entire flight crying softly. Kari-Lee revelled in flying and I feel her near me during take off, her favourite part. I hear her joyful "Wooohooo!" as the force pushes us back in our seats and I weep for all the journeys she's never going to take, all the times I'll never get to see the joy on her face as she anticipates the next exciting adventure.

I pray the pain will end. I pray the plane will crash. I tell Peter and he's appalled. "What about all the other people?" he asks.

"I don't care," I reply. "I just want to die."

The tug towards oblivion is so strong that if I could do something to bring the plane down, I probably would. But instead, I hunch in my seat, tears streaming down my face, and stare unseeingly out the window.

We arrive in Cairns and our lovely friends, Janine and Cam, are waiting to pick us up. Cam's mother is away and has offered us her cosy unit at Trinity Beach, a relaxed seaside village just north of Cairns. It's perfect. We need the solitude, the privacy, the peace. Even in my despair I appreciate her wonderful generosity.

We settle into a routine of sorts. There are two bedrooms and two TVs (one upstairs and one downstairs). We gravitate to different levels and tend to stay there for the duration. I sleep in brief snatches, waking at about 3.00 am most mornings, crying as I face another day without Kari in it.

Reality strikes again and again as I wake hoping it was all a nightmare. Waiting for it to become light, I drink a coffee in bed. I read books written by parents whose children have died, trying to understand how they survived. I head down to the beach, striding up and down for an hour, tears streaming, until I can feel the exhaustion kicking in. I look out to sea and think of Kari. The beach was her special place and I feel close to her here. I pray and beg for her to not be gone.

I head back to the unit. I swim laps of the pool, any exercise I can find to try to make myself tired enough that sleep will come at some point through the night. I lie on the bed, sweating under the fan. I cry. I watch *Downton Abbey*. I cry. I read more books. I cry. At some point, I usually eat a small salad, my one concession to the physical needs of my body. I have no desire for food; the feeling of having been kicked in the stomach continues, along with nausea, which takes away all desire to eat. I doze a little. I cry. I head back out to the pool and do another twenty laps. I cry. I walk back down to the beach and continue my relentless striding up and down, up and down.

PETER USUALLY COMES to join me at the beach in the late afternoon. He sits on a picnic rug with a glass of wine, a sudoku and his radio. He smiles as I join him. I cry. I can't understand how he can smile. "Doesn't the water look beautiful?" he says. I snap at him, disgusted that he can find anything beautiful in a world without Kari.

We go to the shops to get simple supplies for Peter to eat, because he's not having any trouble with that. I can't bear it inside the grocery shop. *There's* Kari's favourite snack, *there's* the tea she liked to drink, *there's* her go-to breakfast. It's all too much. Everywhere I look there are reminders of what we've lost. I have to leave. Peter has no such difficulty and continues shopping without me. It will be months before I can face grocery shopping. It will become a job that belongs to Peter for years to come.

OCCASIONALLY, we spend some time with Janine and Cam. It's bearable, because Janine is compassionate enough to let me talk. I probably repeat myself over and over as I ruminate on why things have happened the way they have. We talk about Kari. We talk about unanswered prayer. We talk about healing. She's generous with her kindness and does lots of listening as I try to make sense of what's happened.

I'm not much fun to be around. I'm not eating. I'm not laughing. My conversation is fairly one-track. I'm aware enough, though, to be grateful for friends like these who loved Kari-Lee and who don't run away from the shambolic mess that's currently me.

Janine lends me a book, *A Grace Disguised*, which makes a lasting impression. Its title has me convinced it will be full of Christian platitudes, but that's not the case. It's written by Jerry Sittser, who lost his daughter, wife and mother all in one car accident, in which he and his remaining children were injured. I feel he's earned the right to speak, as he obviously understands great loss.

There are some passages in this book which have a profound effect on me. One section, about facing your grief not running from it, helps to shape the way I grieve. It speaks of not turning away from the darkness, but rather plunging into it, to eventually come out into the light.

I choose to plunge.

On a day close to the end of our two weeks away, I decide I need to drive to Palm Cove where Kari spent some of her happiest days on her honeymoon with Nic. Peter has no wish to accompany me, so I set off alone.

I don't know why I feel this compulsion to visit. I know it'll cause me great pain, imagining Kari so full of happiness and love. Still, off I go and find the resort. I wander about and look at things she would have looked at. I take photos and I cry for all that could have been, for the dreams that were never fulfilled, for the unfairness of only ten months of marriage, for the pain and trauma which accompanied so much of their lives together. I pick up some frangipani flowers and take them with me to press and keep as a reminder of this special time in Kari's life.

OUR TIME in Cairns is over. Instead of flying home, we've chosen to do something different and catch the train. We thought it would be good to relive that special time on the *Sunlander* with our girls back in 1997. The *Sunlander* has been retired, replaced by the *Spirit of Queensland*, a modern train with sleeping pods something like business class on a plane.

I lie awake and read to distract myself. Another book written by a bereaved parent, this time *Only Spring* by Gordon Livingston. His young son becomes ill and spends weeks in hospital, improving and declining, while prayers bombard the heavenlies. The similarities are somehow cause for comfort, even though the outcome is dire. Somebody else who hoped and prayed but whose child died anyway. The need to feel understood and not alone in my experiences is powerful.

∼

WE PLAN to be home for only a few days, just time to repack our bags and do a few tasks. Foolishly, I've chosen to have a job interview – because the thought of returning to my usual place of work seems ridiculous. I'm not the same person who left there four months ago. Of course, in my present state I make a hash of the interview and realise there's no chance I'll be offered the position.

We drive to Bellingen, a small town in the mid north-east of NSW, to the home of friends who've graciously allowed us to stay with them for a few days on our way to Canberra. Maloo has accompanied us and has a great time playing with their golden Labrador, Honey. Their home is in the country – peaceful, restful, quiet. They're gentle with us, allowing us to speak of Kari-Lee when we wish but not forcing the issue. We appreciate their sensitivity.

After a couple of days in this oasis we continue to my brother's home in Canberra. His girls are away, so the house is quiet. We're given the bedroom downstairs which offers us privacy and separation, both very much needed at present.

My brother and his wife experienced the loss of their precious baby girl, Ruby, on the day she was born, so grief is no stranger to them. Kari had a special connection with my brother because of shared travel experiences and her time looking after their twins, so it feels right to be here.

We spend a week, visiting a few scenic spots, but mostly reading at home and being entertained by the interactions between Maloo and their dog, Pearl. I'm still struggling most of the time to be with people, but I feel safe here. Soon it's time to leave and we head for Bellingen again.

WHILE OUTWARDLY I might appear to be functioning somewhat normally, in reality I'm an exposed raw nerve, sensitive to the slightest wrong touch.

My first meltdown comes just before we arrive at our friends' place. Someone shares the news that Nic's brother has announced his engagement on, or very close to, Kari and Nic's first wedding anniversary. For some reason this sets off a bomb in my brain. In my mind, that day should remain sacred to Kari and Nic's wedding. I think, "How could someone so close to the family be so utterly insensitive to the sacredness of that day?"

Peter tries to reason with me that it doesn't mean anything and they're probably not even aware of how hurtful this might be to us. He genuinely can't understand my distress and later, looking back, I won't really be able to understand it either, but at the time it's very real.

I declare that I'm too upset to stay with anyone. I just want to go home. We compromise by finding a motel in the nearest town and by morning I've calmed down enough to go and spend a couple of days with our friends. They're very understanding and don't talk about my complete loss of control.

WE ARRIVE HOME in time to help Tiana move house. She's been struggling with young flatmates who don't seem to have any comprehension of the devastation Kari's death has wrought in her life. She's moving into the granny flat underneath the home of family friends. The three children are adopted from the same nursery in Taiwan as Tiana and our families have been friends for years. Just two years ago, their mum died from cancer, so Tiana knows that they will understand her deep grief. There are two bedrooms in the granny flat, so we stay with her for a week to help her settle in.

CHRISTMAS. Somehow, it's Christmas. A time of peace and joy and hope.

I feel none of those things. I'm struggling with deciding what I believe about the One who Christmas is all about. I don't want to join in laughter-filled family celebrations. I just want Christmas to go away and leave me alone. How can it possibly be "Happy Christmas" without Kari-Lee?

I discover that Peter and Tiana are feeling much the same so we decide to skip Christmas this year. It sounds easy, but there are expectations. We always have a big family get-together on Boxing Day, my mum's birthday. We feel we can't do that this year, but nor can we face Christmas at home, where Kari should be. Too many memories of cheerful Christmases past.

We somehow discover that some friends will be away for Christmas. They offer us their house. Nobody will know where we are and we'll be left in peace to just pretend Christmas isn't happening. It seems the ideal solution and we move there, with Maloo, for a few days.

It seems so simple. We go about our lives quietly, acting like it's any old ordinary day, reading books and watching TV.

We start off well, but ultimately it all comes crashing down. Tiana and I have a disagreement about food. What I've provided doesn't meet her expectations. She hoped for something a bit special, while I couldn't care less. I'm barely eating anything anyway. Emotions have already been very close to the surface, like a pressure cooker primed to explode. And explode it does. We end up shouting at each other. It's all so stupid, but the pain inside can't be contained and bubbles up, spilling out in meaningless arguments that drive us apart when what we really need is to draw together. Finally, Tiana packs her bags and takes off, back to Brisbane.

And that's our first Christmas without Kari-Lee.

AFTER: CHAPTER SIX

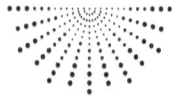

*T*ick...tock...tick...tock...tick...tock...

The clock slowly but incessantly moves towards midnight. I sit, trying to look at anything but that cruel clock, yet always drawn back to watching it, dread and resignation twisting together inside me. I focus my mind in a vain attempt to will those hands to stop their forward motion, stop what's about to happen, stop the inevitable.

"At the stroke, the time will be midnight." Fireworks explode up and down my street, echoed by the exploding emotions rippling through my body.

2015.

A new year.

A year that Kari-Lee has never inhabited.

The first of many she won't ever inhabit here on this earth.

The thought is unbearable. "Please God, make it stop." If I go forward, I'll be leaving her behind. The gap between us will stretch wider and wider. I can't do it. But I'm powerless to change things. The clock keeps ticking and the calendar turns over to another year. "Goodbye, my Kari."

JANUARY

Tiana's all alone in Brisbane, completing her apprenticeship. The family she lives with have gone away on holiday. She's so brave to continue on alone, so we head to Brisbane to keep her company.

We spend our days quietly, swimming, walking Maloo and reading, while Tiana continues working her crazy chef hours. My grief is ever-present, all-consuming, heart-shattering, but I push it aside when I can, to try and be there for Tiana. She needs me.

So often bereaved siblings are the forgotten ones. She's been asked more than once how her parents and Nic are doing. She's been told more than once to be strong for us. She's been unmentioned on some cards and flowers which bear the names of Peter, Nic and me.

Kari was her constant companion for all of her life and under normal circumstances she could have reasonably expected her sister to be there for the rest of her life. Their relationship was deep and wide and long. Her grief is immense.

We all try to support each other as best we can, although often we retreat into our own private misery.

THEN SOMETHING HAPPENS which exponentially changes things for me. I discover a book called *Heaven* by Randy Alcorn. I start to read and I'm captivated. I read about where Kari lives now. There's so much more in the Bible about this topic than I ever realised. I read about the New Heaven and the New Earth, where I'll live forever with Jesus and all those who put their faith and trust in Him, including Kari.

I devour the book. It's over five hundred pages long, but I sit by the pool and read for much of the day. I lie in bed at night reading. I read at every opportunity. I've been a Christian and follower of Jesus for most of my life, yet so much of this is new to me. I've read through the entire Bible several times, so how could I have missed all of this incredibly important information about the future?

Of course, my grief remains huge, robbing me of breath at times, but now, in amongst the black gloom a tiny beam of hope peeps through. Kari is still gone, but somehow knowing more about where she is and where we'll ultimately be together changes something deep within me.

OTHER HELP COMES from a stranger in America. Back in November, a local friend whose son has CF put me in touch with a mother in the US whose daughter with CF died the year before Kari. She's been a wonderful encouragement, genuinely keen to hear all about Kari and fully cognizant of all that end-stage cystic fibrosis entails.

Tragically, towards the end of 2014, her husband had been diagnosed with a terminal glioblastoma brain tumour. I had encouraged her not to worry about me but to focus on him.

What transpires now is something that ends up helping both of us. She starts a closed Facebook group called "After 65 Roses" for bereaved mums whose children have died from cystic fibrosis, so that there are others to support me while she tends to her husband. The name is based on the way a young child said "sixty-five roses" when he couldn't pronounce cystic fibrosis.

Initially there are just a few mums, but the group grows quickly, eventually reaching over one hundred mums. This becomes a great source of comfort to me because these are people who really get it. Their children went through many of the things Kari endured. As mothers we've all been powerless to prevent the decline and ultimately the death of our children.

BUOYED by the benefits of chatting online with other bereaved mothers, once I'm back on the coast I really want to connect face-to-face with other bereaved parents who are believers. I find a local group called Compassionate Friends whose online resources I've used. Gaye kindly offers to come with me to the first meeting and, after checking details on their website, we set off.

We drive for an hour, then sit and wait. And wait. And wait. Nobody shows up.

The nervous anticipation that has been building within me for days segues into frustration with myself. Have I got the wrong place, the wrong time? I phone the contact number, only to be told that the meeting finished several hours ago. The time on the website is out of date and we've missed the whole meeting. I feel completely deflated as we make our way home and, in the end, I don't try again.

~

Long before I'm ready, it's time to go back to work. I'll be returning to the same job I had before Kari died. I'm not sure I can do it, but Peter's still unemployed, struggling with ongoing depression and anxiety. I have to step up.

I've tried to reduce potential minefields by asking my senior therapist to request that client families don't talk to me about what's happened. I don't think I'll be able to handle any outpouring of sympathy.

The weekend before I'm due back at work, I go in when I know there'll be nobody there. I've arranged to move to a new desk in a corner, facing into a wall and as far away from the front reception desk as possible. I take some laminated A4-sized photos of Kari and cover the walls around my desk with them. I need her close to me. I walk around the centre, mentally preparing myself for what lies ahead.

It's very early the next day. I'm all alone. I've already set things up in preparation for the goal-setting interviews I'll be involved with today. I'm as prepared as I'm able to be.

I head to the staff tea room for a bracing cup of coffee, mentally fortifying myself for what's to come. Will people's sympathetic words bring me to tears? Will I be able to cope with their kindness and caring? Will I break down and completely lose my composure?

I hear the front door open. In comes the first staff member with a huge smile on her face. "How was your holiday?" she asks.

What? My brain does a double-take. Holiday? I'm speechless.

Maybe I misheard. Holiday? Does she seriously think I've been on a holiday? I know that she and the rest of the staff have been on a six-week-long summer holiday, but me? I've been watching my daughter die. They all know what's been happening in my life. I can't believe I've been asked this question. I'm not sure if or how I respond. My mind is blown.

Now another staff member appears, coming to make her coffee. She glances at me. "I like your hair," she says.

I feel like I'm in a parallel universe. What's going on? Gradually the rest of the staff arrive and conversation swirls around me as they discuss their holidays and the fun they've had. A couple of people mention that it's nice to have me back after six months, but nobody, not one single person out of the twelve staff members, mentions Kari's name. These are all highly trained, dedicated, caring professionals, who work with families of children with disabilities. Some of them I've worked with for twenty years. I know they care. I simply can't believe that they're all just ignoring the huge "elephant in the room".

When this continues all morning, I realise that the staff must also have been asked not to mention what's happened in my life, to spare me more pain. That makes some sort of sense, until I ask my senior therapist and she says, "No."

I feel completely unseen. I know that some of these people genuinely care about me. Several of them will step up over the coming days, weeks and even years, mentioning Kari frequently and supporting me in an ongoing and meaningful way.

Later, when I've had time to process what happened, I will come to believe that they felt they were being kind and sparing me more hurt. I will learn that people really have no idea how to approach a bereaved parent.

I'll never forget that first day back at work and the unbelievable nightmare of nobody mentioning Kari-Lee's name for the entire day.

∽

I LIE ON MY STOMACH, my face cocooned in a ring of warm fluffy towels, my lower body encased in more towels, my back exposed to warm air. Restful music drifts from hidden speakers. Scents of coconut and frangipani infuse the atmosphere as I float in a weightless state of relaxation. Strong yet gentle hands firmly knead my muscles, obliterating tension, rigidity and stress. Peace descends, even as tears drip from my eyes and sobs threaten to erupt from within.

I'm being pampered, cared for and comforted by Kari's final birthday gift to me. A voucher for a massage, which I've deliberately saved until I have completed my first traumatic week back at work.

It's the twenty-second today, exactly three months since she left us. My girl may be gone, but she continues to bless me with her thoughtful gift. I cry with gratitude, with longing and with deep grief at the thought that I'll never be the recipient of her tangible love again. I miss her so much.

A FEW DAYS later I try to make an appointment to see the lung-transplant specialist who cared for Kari. I feel a need to talk to him, to try to fully understand why Kari died. I know that he, and all the medical staff involved, did absolutely everything they could to save Kari, yet still she died. He seemed optimistic that Kari would beat the bacteria and recover. I was so sure she'd bounce back like she always did, yet still she died.

Subconsciously, it somehow feels that if I can find out more detail of what exactly happened, I can travel back in time and do something differently, somehow undo Kari's death, and she'll be back with us. Consciously I know that makes absolutely no sense at all, but different scenarios swirl round and round in my brain on a never-ending loop, often when I'm trying to get to sleep at night. Maybe he can help me understand. Maybe that will help me accept the reality that she's gone. Maybe my guilt at not being able to save her will subside.

After multiple failed attempts over several months, I give up. He's an incredibly dedicated and busy doctor whose time is precious, especially to those who are still fighting to live. Probably there really is no point discussing things because it can make no difference now.

Yet the tornado of churning questions about what I could have done differently doesn't abate. Hours each day are spent in mental gymnastics trying to change multiple parameters and ultimately "undo" Kari's death.

ANOTHER SOURCE of unexpected pain is the way Nic seems unable to be around us. During those dark, frightening days in the hospital, it was often just Nic and me alone with Kari, sometimes with Kari asleep. I felt we'd formed a deep bond through these mutual experiences and the deep love and hope we both shared for Kari-Lee. I'm learning that we all grieve differently. I've seen that with Peter and Tiana. We all loved Kari deeply and miss her profoundly, but the way our grief expresses itself differs greatly.

Nic, too, has his own experience of grief, different from ours. While I can understand that in my head, my heart hurts with the way he appears to avoid us. I want to help him, to support him, to be there for him, but I can see he wishes I'd leave him alone. He rarely responds to my "supportive" texts.

I finally stop, realising he doesn't want my help. It hurts, but I can't blame him for needing to grieve in his own way. Avoidance of Kari's family seems to be a primary factor in his way of coping.

A PASTOR VISITING from Western Australia comes to Nic's church. This man has much in common with Nic. His first wife died unexpectedly in her sleep not long after they were married.

The church arranges for Nic to have coffee with him after hearing him speak. Following this, Nic asks to meet with us at Gaye and Bruce's house. He expresses that he finds it very hard to be around us, but the pastor's words made him reconsider. This man shared that his biggest regret was not keeping in touch with his first wife's family, especially at the beginning. He encouraged Nic not to make the same mistake. Nic said that he wants to keep in touch with us, but he wants to be the one to initiate any contact. We are grateful for any interaction, so we agree.

Nic also shares that he's started Bible College and joined Red Frogs, an Australian organisation providing positive peer presence at large events, helping keep young people safe. It seems a good thing for Nic to be doing and he feels it's helping him.

We're glad he's found something that gives meaning to his life, because for a while he appeared to be drifting, lost and purposeless. We look forward to a new, more adult relationship, where he'll organise some get-togethers and we can share memories of the good times, as well as share some of the pain of missing the girl who meant so much to each of us. It means a lot to us to be able to keep in contact with the man Kari chose to give her heart to.

AFTER: CHAPTER SEVEN

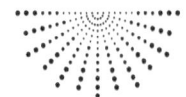

It's late. I'm physically exhausted. I can't believe how utterly exhausting grief is. I lie next to Peter who snores gently, completely oblivious to the depths of turmoil wracking his bedtime companion. I've been here for hours, tossing, turning, then lying quietly, willing my worn-out body to surrender.

Every night it's incredibly difficult to actually fall asleep. As soon as my eyes close, my mind fills with pictures. Kari taking her last breaths. Kari with tubes coming out of everywhere. Kari after her spirit had left her body. They haunt me and taunt me and drive sleep far from me.

Despite increasing my walking and swimming in a vain attempt to tire myself enough for oblivion to overtake me, when I finally lay my body down it often takes multiple attempts before my brain will finally succumb to shutting down.

In between are hours of wakefulness, countless cups of tea or warm milk with a dash of Kahlua, sometimes a walk outside to look up at the stars, tearfully sobbing, often with Maloo as my faithful companion. Frequently I wake during the night and run through the whole sequence again, maybe several times each night. Sometimes I get up and go into Kari's room, touching the things she touched, reading the things she wrote, trying to connect with her.

She's not here. What can I do? How can I survive this? Will it ever get better?

~

IN THE MIDDLE of the night, while rummaging in her room I find an unexpected blessing. Messages that Kari's nurses wrote at her funeral.

> Kari was the best patient I've ever nursed and one of the best women I've known. She burned and sparkled with light. She was joyous and full of grace right up to her last day. Even as she struggled for breath, she smiled and gave love to us.

Although I shed copious tears, reading these messages touches my heart in ways that are healing. I'm so grateful that we included a sheet of paper in the order of service folder, asking people to share a special memory of Kari. They become a lifeline. I read them and reread them repeatedly.

> It was a privilege to be one of Kari's nurses. Kari, you taught me so much about life and you probably never realised it. You were the bravest person I've ever known. I will never forget you, Kari.

Kari-Lee's nurses saw the truth of what she went through in a way few others did.

> Kari was an inspiration to us all. She inspired us by her graciousness, her positivity, her smile, her humour, her loving nature and so many other ways.

Why do these help me so much? I think it's because her nurses recognised that Kari was someone special, even as she lay there wracked with pain and overcome with unending nausea.

> Kari taught me so much. I never heard her complain. She always remained positive and dignified. I feel so privileged to have known

> and nursed Kari. She taught me more about life and about CF than any textbook. I miss her.

It may have turned out to be a losing battle for her life, yet Kari ceaselessly added sunshine to the world. Reading these words helps me know that it wasn't just me who was blessed by her life and example. Others saw it too.

> I loved looking after Kari. I would sometimes spend time in Kari's room because being around her would make the shift better. Her smile, calm nature and wonderful sense of humour were to be admired. Having met and nursed Kari has made me a better person and nurse. I'm very grateful for that.

It seems counter-intuitive, but reading about how valuable the treasure of Kari is, even now that I've lost that treasure, somehow still helps me.

> Kari-Lee was such an inspiration – so young, so beautiful, so amazing. A patient that was always so positive, never giving up. Kari, you touched all our hearts.

Of course, people always say nice things at funerals, but the fact that ten of Kari's nurses took the time on their day off to drive two hours to share our celebration of Kari's life speaks volumes to me.

> Kari-Lee was one of the most beautiful people inside & out I have ever met. I remember her smile and soft voice, despite the hard time she was having battling the infection.
>
> She was the most beautiful girl here on earth. She will be forever missed.

These people only knew Kari for a relatively short time but saw through to who she really was. She made a difference in their lives. They appreciated her enough to miss her, now she's gone. That means so much to me. One of the deepest desires of my heart is that Kari-Lee will never, ever be forgotten.

From January onwards, Peter, Tiana and I see our psychologist, sometimes individually, sometimes together. As we've been seeing her on and off for some years throughout Kari's decline, we know she's someone who can help.

Some people think using a counsellor or psychologist is unnecessary, but the value to us is unquestionable. Sometimes her main role is just to listen – maybe to the same conversation over and over. It's something I don't feel I can ask many friends to do, yet it's so needed. It's a huge part of how I process what's happened.

I can say things to her that I wouldn't share with anyone else, knowing I'm not being judged. Sometimes she gently steers me in a direction to help me see that something I'm doing or thinking might not be helpful, but there's no condemnation attached.

Throughout January and the months that follow, Gaye and Bruce's house continues to be a sanctuary for me. Now that I'm back at work there's less free time, but often I'll drop over for a cup of tea and a chat, knowing I can speak freely about Kari. It's so important for me to speak her name.

If only people could realise what a priceless gift that is to me. I've spoken to countless other bereaved parents and they all concur. Speak the name of our child to us. It's a gift beyond measure.

Together, Gaye and I thrash through some of the deep questions of how this could have happened and what it all means in the grand scheme of life and God.

Another faithful friend who welcomes my lamenting and reflection about Kari is Leanne. Occasionally, we sit on her verandah with its glorious views across the cane fields and nearby mountains to the ocean. She listens and shares from her deep knowledge of the Scriptures. Her wisdom and understanding of God and His ways are profound. She also blesses me on a weekly basis with a beautiful hand-made card in the mail, one which always mentions Kari by name and acknowledges how much we must miss her.

These two women are the constant support that I rely on. I'm so thankful to God for their willingness to listen and to hash out the really hard questions with me. Friends who are willing to sit and say nothing, to sit and listen, to contemplate with me the questions that seemingly have no answers are rare gems. I hope they know how deeply I appreciate them.

∼

FEBRUARY

Another seemingly small thing leads to a huge change in the odyssey of my grief. A fellow bereaved mum invites me for a coffee and chat. She gifts me a CD called *Beauty Will Rise* by Steven Curtis Chapman. I'm familiar with a couple of his songs and also with the story of his little daughter Maria, who died in a tragic accident in 2008. I've read the book his wife wrote.

I take the CD without thinking too much of it, not realising the profound impact it will have on my life. I play it over the next few weeks and realise that he's written so much of what I'm feeling into these songs. He's written a lot of what I've learned about Heaven from Randy Alcorn. He's written sad, dark, deeply pain-filled songs and he's written others which shine hope. Initially, I can only listen to the first category. I'm not ready for too much hope.

I play this CD on a permanent loop whenever I'm in my car. I drive and I cry. I cry and I drive. What I don't realise is that the thoughtful and perceptive lyrics which describe so much of what I'm feeling are helping me process aspects of my grief, even as I drive along, crying.

Songs like *Our God is in Control* have me wrestling with the sovereignty of a God who could have healed Kari, yet didn't. The song *Questions* addresses many of the exact questions that I wrestle with. The answers aren't all provided, but that in itself makes me trust these words more. The song *Jesus Will Meet You There* aptly describes situations where your world just falls apart, which is what my life feels like right now. It then assures us of Jesus' presence in the midst of it all, something I'm still exploring.

No longer willing – not that I ever really was – to accept superficial, pat answers that some people try to cast my way, I need to wrestle with this and with so many other aspects of my faith and my life and decide again if what I believe is true. I've been accused of reshaping my theology based on my experiences rather than on what the Bible says. Yet for me, if what's in the Bible can't make sense of what is happening in my life, I'm not sure it's something I want to hang all of my trust on. I need to re-examine everything in the wake of Kari's death.

Soon I purchase the follow-up CD, *The Glorious Unfolding*, and these two CDs are almost the only music I listen to for the next two years. This man has earned the right to speak into my grief. He's stared into the abyss, he's asked the hard questions, he's chosen to still believe.

One song has me crying as soon as I hear the opening bars. It's called *See You in a Little While* and captures so much of my pain, yet hope. I hold onto the promise that I will see my precious girl in just a little while, even as I sob my heart out with longing and yearning to see her right now.

The title song, *Glorious Unfolding*, speaks to my struggles in understanding how life has turned out the way it has, yet offers hope for a wonderful future forever.

It's a sunny day in February when I park in the Coles car park. I've made an appointment for a mammogram with the mobile BreastScreen van. My health's been neglected during the last few years, yet routine aspects of life need to go on even though in some ways I couldn't care less. My recent eye check-up confirmed my fears, when it determined that my eyesight had deteriorated five years' worth in the past year.

Now I sit inside the van, filling out forms, listening to music in the background, undoubtedly designed to help relax patients. Over the speakers comes the beginning of the song *All of Me*, the song which played on Kari's wedding day and at her funeral.

I flee. I don't care what the lady at the desk thinks. I run to my car, where I sit sobbing. I gradually gather myself and make my way back to the van, embarrassed yet unapologetic.

Regardless of how much I try to avoid triggers, grief bombs lurk everywhere. It's not the last time I'll be caught out, ambushed by grief.

Soon after this, Nic visits to remove his bed which he and Kari shared in marriage. He comes with his dad, unable to face being alone in the space where he and Kari-Lee spent so many happy, memorable times together. He dismantles the bed, then wanders aimlessly around the space, staring at everything that was part of their life together. I ask if he wants to take this item or that, but mostly he says no. I offer him a framed photo from their wedding.

"Is it okay if I take that?" he asks hesitantly.

"Of course," I answer, wishing he wanted more to remember our girl. I'm not sure how he's processing his grief and he's made it clear it's none of my business. The contact he asked to initiate with us hasn't materialised.

I care about Nic. To me he seems to be avoiding anything to do with Kari, as if by shutting the door on his grief it will just go away. I fear he's setting himself up for deeper pain in the future, but he's also metaphorically closed the door on me. I have no option but to leave him alone and ask God to take care of it.

This is the only time he ever visits our house after Kari's death, apart from dropping in briefly in October.

On the last day of February, Peter, Maloo and I are enjoying our regular outing to North Shore dog beach, where we're entertained by Maloo's antics chasing sticks and riding waves.

It's become a haven where I walk for miles – currently even more miles than usual because I've booked myself on a walking trek along the Great Ocean Road in Victoria. I'm the fittest I've been for years, due to all the walking and swimming I've been doing in an effort to sleep at night. I find peace and healing in the beauty of God's creation so the planned trek seems an ideal getaway from the sad story my life has become. I'm looking forward to it as much as I'm able to look forward to anything these days.

I stride along the beach, soaking in the sunshine and the fresh sea air. It's my thinking time and also where I feel closest to Kari. I gaze at the sunlight sparkling like jewels, dancing on the ocean, then beyond to the horizon where blue sky melds with blue ocean. It reminds me of the song Bruce wrote, describing Kari so well:

> *When I think of you, I can see the sunlight on the ocean,*
> *When I think of you, I can see right out to the horizon…*

I head back to join Maloo frolicking in the waves and somehow as she races past me in her usual frenzied excitement at chasing a stick, her leg gets caught between my little toe and the rest of my toes. I feel a snap. Instant pain shoots through my whole foot.

I limp up the beach in agony. My toe has already started to swell and change colour. I'm pretty sure it's broken. In an instant my much-anticipated dream of a healing walking trip is gone.

AFTER: CHAPTER EIGHT

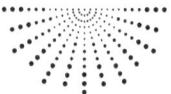

MARCH

I stand, my eyes glazed with unshed tears, my heart broken by unfulfilled dreams. Apart from the removal of Nic's bed, the granny flat is set up just the way Kari had it. Her cosy little nest. Her temporary home with her beloved husband, symbolic of the hope she had for the future.

All of her treasured wedding presents are gone with Nic. Kari-Lee was ecstatically looking forward to setting up home with him. Now that's never going to happen. This one big room is all they'll ever share together.

I walk around, touching, reading, trying to absorb the essence of Kari. Sticky notes with cute messages of love from Nic still adhere to the wardrobe door. Her calendar, still open at August, taunts me with its bright colours and a quote that reads: "I've decided to be happy." Her box of post-transplant medications, which were going to save her life, sits mocking me.

Tiana will soon be moving into this space. I need to make it hers now, not Kari's. I'm thrilled she's chosen to come home now that she's completed her apprenticeship, yet it breaks my heart to dismantle the solid evidence of Kari's hopes and dreams. I know I'm more fortunate than many bereaved parents because Kari's childhood bedroom stands ready to receive her belongings. I don't have to rush to sort or dispose of them.

After photographing her little "love nest", I move almost everything into her bedroom, where it can wait until I'm ready to face thinking about what to do with it long term. There are some things I'm happy to distribute to her friends. Her current handbag goes to her friend Rachel, her shoes all go to her "twinnie" friend who has the same size feet, her Latin dance CDs go to Kristal.

I carefully and lovingly arrange her things, then spend the rest of the day rearranging the granny flat so it bears no resemblance to how Kari had it, now a fresh canvas for Tiana.

AT THE END OF MARCH, I attend a work conference in Brisbane. I take my seat in the huge auditorium and when I look up, there, seated directly in front of me, is Kari.

Wait. No, it's not Kari. It's someone with hair exactly like hers. My hand itches with wanting to stroke that beautiful curly hair. I have to physically sit on my hands to stop myself reaching out.

I barely hear anything the speaker says. My mind tosses and turns with memories, with missing, with yearning.

It's something that happens again as time goes on. I "see" her, at all different ages, in all different places. There she is, running on the sand with her little ringlets bobbing up and down. There she is, crossing the road in front of me in her school uniform, laughing with all her friends surrounding her. There she is at the shops, with her baby tucked in a pram, as she window-shops with her mum.

The air vibrates with the presence of Kari, popping up when I least expect her.

APRIL

After getting so much out of *Heaven*, the book by Randy Alcorn, I'm excited to start watching a DVD series showing him teaching this subject to seminary students. Gaye, Bruce, Peter and I spend twelve weeks meeting weekly. Deep discussions are bathed in frequent tears, as the subject matter is all too readily applied to our Kari, so recently departed for this previously vague destination.

Learning even more about Heaven – both the present Heaven, where Kari now lives, and the New Heaven and Earth where we'll all live together forever – answers so many questions and brings a sense of some peace. The phrase "she's in a better place" while often offered as a perfunctory response, is actually a profound and life-changing statement.

Of course, questions remain. If Kari is safely in Heaven and if I'll see her again and if everything will be made right at that time, then what am I going to do with my time remaining on earth? I don't want to waste it wallowing in the depths of despair. Naturally I'll grieve. Definitely I'll miss her, yearn for her, long to see her. Of course, everything is not hunky-dory just because I know she's in Heaven and I'll be with her again when my time comes.

But it's a complete mind-shift.

I must ponder deep-seated beliefs and weighty questions. Randy Alcorn has a saying "Live for the line, not the dot." This refers to the concept that our time on earth is just a dot compared to the neverending line of eternity. Rather than focus all our efforts and all our meaning on that little dot, we should spend our time doing things that will count for eternity.

So, I ask myself, "What will count for eternity?" According to the Bible it's people's spirits, it's our family, it's caring for others like widows and orphans. It's making a difference in this world for the better – for others, rather than focusing on making it better for me.

This becomes my goal. I would still rather go straight off to Heaven and join Kari. Life is still incredibly challenging and difficult to participate in while carrying the enormous burden of living without her. But here I am. I start to try to think of creative ways that I can be part of the change.

I start giving blood and plasma again, something I did before Kari became dreadfully unwell. It seems such an easy way to help other people and make a difference in the world.

I reconsider starting a foundation or charity in Kari-Lee's name, but I still don't have the emotional energy to tackle this, even though I'd love for Kari to be remembered in this way.

May is approaching. May is Cystic Fibrosis month, also known as 65 Roses month. CF Queensland encourages fundraising events involving the number sixty-five. I've helped in the past with the annual Run65km4CF, started by some of my friends here on the Sunshine Coast. I'm not a runner, but I'm a swimmer, so I decide to get a team together and swim sixty-five kilometres.

I request that any money raised by my swim-a-thon will go towards upkeep of Rose Cottage. Having free accommodation close to the hospital was such a blessing to us while Kari was recovering from her transplant, but even more so in those last, horrific two months. To know I could be with her in a matter of minutes if she needed me was so reassuring. Rose Cottage, like most CF Queensland work, is funded predominantly by donations and fundraising.

I enlist swimmers and encourage them to find sponsorship of sixty-five dollars each. I start training with an adult swimming squad three times a week, so I can fully participate. People willingly sign up. Kari's death is still fresh in their minds and they're keen to contribute.

MAY

Mothers' Day. The first without Kari's cheeky grin, cheery text and meaningful words she always wrote in my card. It hurts. It hurts so bad.

I hate the helpless feeling of not being able to do a single thing to change the circumstances. I just have to live through the pain burning up inside me, while presenting a relatively normal outward façade. I'm not sure how well I'm doing that.

On Mothers' Day, Tiana goes out of her way to spoil me, aware of how much I'm missing Kari. After breakfast in bed and morning tea at Nana's, she takes me for lunch to a fancy Japanese restaurant in a beautiful setting on the Noosa River. She makes me feel very special. I appreciate her thoughtfulness.

Soon, it's my birthday. Another day of immense pain and intense awareness of the absence of Kari. I'm mindlessly scrolling through Facebook when something catches my eye. Steven Curtis Chapman is going to be performing on a cruise to Alaska. Max Lucado is the guest speaker. I decide it's providential that I've seen this on my birthday and I'm meant to go. It's happening next July, when hopefully I'll be in better shape to enjoy travel.

I inform Peter that I really want to go and, knowing he no longer loves to travel, I'd like him to come. It gives me something to look forward to, making me think there might be some moments of joy in my future.

A fun opportunity comes up just after my birthday, when my sisters and I take Mum and Dad to Tin Can Bay for a long weekend. They're aging fast now, at eighty-seven and eighty-five, so we realise this might be the last opportunity for a holiday together. Helping to care for them in their own home is taking increasing amounts of time from us.

In the past, I was the one living closest, so much of the responsibility of driving them to appointments fell on me. I've been unable to be much help over the past few years while caring for Kari. My sister has moved closer and stepped into that role, but over the next couple of years, as their needs rise, I'll play an increasing role again.

I've struggled with visiting my parents since Kari died, because Mum has insisted on asking me whether Nic has found a new lady yet. Every time I visit, that's her question. It's not something I'm ready to consider. Despite Mum's explanation that, "Men who've been happy in their marriage often look for a partner to make them happy again very quickly," it hurts my heart to think of Nic with someone else. He's Kari's.

I know that inevitably in the future he will find someone else. He's young, attractive and kind. I want him to be happy. I just can't face that thought yet. It's only been six months.

I stop visiting my parents for a time because I just can't face that question again. Mum has always been a huge support to me and I feel robbed of her presence in my season of deep grief. Eventually, I confront Mum and explain how hurtful the thought of Nic with someone else is for me. Thankfully, she takes notice and stops.

Now, in Tin Can Bay, we're able to enjoy special times together, reading, chatting, visiting coffee shops, playing board games and reminiscing about our lives together. I'm grateful to be part of it.

Losing Kari has reminded me to take these opportunities whenever I can. None of us is promised tomorrow.

AT WORK, I'm enjoying a special week with Rachel as my work experience student. She's studying Occupational Therapy, so she's come to stay at our house and work with me for a week. It's great to have her close and we share lots of wonderful Kari memories.

One day, a staff member catches me at the photocopier to deliver a criticism that she feels I need to hear. She's shocked when I suddenly burst into tears, drop what I'm doing and rush into another room to hide and sob my heart out.

When she finally comes to find me and discuss the incident, she's surprised that I'm so fragile because she saw me at Kari's funeral and I "seemed fine". It's my first indication of the huge chasm between what I'm experiencing and other people's understanding of it.

It's been six months since Kari died and some people think it's time to move on now. So many people seem to think that child loss is not much different from losing your elderly grandparent, something I was well and truly "over" after six months. That wasn't to say I didn't miss them, but it wasn't central in my life.

What people looking on obviously don't realise is that Kari is constantly front and centre in my brain and my emotions. No matter what I'm doing I'm thinking about Kari-Lee. My concentration may momentarily be focused on what I'm doing, particularly at work when I'm treating a child, but there's only a thin veil between that and Kari. She's always there. Her loss is always there. Everything I'm missing is always there.

Thoughts about Kari take up so much room in my brain that there's very little space for anything else. That's why work is so exhausting. There are grief triggers lying in wait everywhere.

A sight. A sound. A smell.

Anything. Anywhere. Anytime.

~

Splash!

"Go!"

"Hooray!"

Sounds of excitement and activity surround me as a silent tear hovers at the corner of my eye. The swim-a-thon in memory of Kari-Lee is in full swing. And she's not here to enjoy it.

I leave my quiet moment and step back into the chaos. People are arriving to swim their laps. Lanes are being assigned. The smell of coffee mingles with the strong vapour of chlorine emanating from the heated pool. We're at Goodlife Community Centre, my church home, which has a swim school that meets here regularly. We've moved in with our Brazilian music, sausage sizzle and photo boards showing Kari's life along with information about CF.

Gaye and I have spent hours organising times for people to arrive, trying to assign lanes so that all six are being used consecutively and continuously, without too many double ups.

There's a carnival atmosphere as everyone steps up to do their bit for Kari, for Rose Cottage and for CF Queensland. Most people swim a few laps, several swim a kilometre or two, but one man, whose wife lives with CF, swims 6.5 km himself.

Children who've never swum a whole lap in their lives before thrash along with their heads out of the water like turtles. Older people cautiously yet doggedly make their way down the pool. Others zip up and down the lanes like it's no big deal.

At the end of each lane, helpers tally the laps being swum, then the total is posted on a huge whiteboard for everyone to see.

Slowly at first, then faster and faster the numbers approach our goal of sixty-five kilometres. Before the afternoon is out, the goal has been surpassed and I haven't even had a chance to swim my laps.

Sausages are consumed. Huge cupcakes – baked by one of Kari's friends – are sold to add to our contribution. Other donations of food disappear fast.

We're visited by the local newspaper, by staff from CF Queensland headquarters in Brisbane and by curious onlookers coming for their session at Goodlife's gym, cafe or squash courts but distracted by the noise and excitement.

As darkness falls, I jump into the pool to swim my kilometre. My heart is full. Over eighty kilometres have been swum. Over eight thousand dollars has been raised to support Rose Cottage. Kari has been remembered, honoured and celebrated.

I won't allow my girl to be forgotten while I still have breath in my body.

AFTER: CHAPTER NINE

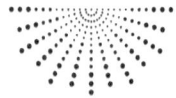

JUNE

The sun rises and so do we. Tiana, Peter and I load Maloo into the car and head for Kari's beach.

It's her birthday, but she's not here.

In the absence of a grave, this beach is where we go to remember her. Somehow it seems more fitting than a cold, lonely cemetery. It's where she asked for her ashes to be scattered, something we haven't been able to face yet.

The sun glistens on the turquoise water, the crashing surf breaks over the rocks. I imagine her here, head thrown back in pure joy, frolicking in the waves, basking in the sunshine, lying with upturned face and closed eyes on the icing-sugar sand.

My Kari. How we miss you.

On the way home we stop at North Shore dog beach, where Maloo can run free and frolic in the surf. Kari loved to bring her baby here, so we do the same today.

After dropping Maloo home, Tiana and I dress ourselves up before driving to Silva Spoon at Cotton Tree, Kari's favourite teahouse. It's hard, but we try to enjoy the things Kari loved, chat about special times with her, remember all the amazing things that made her unique.

The day passes painfully slowly. I spend time in her room, reading messages people wrote last year, Facebook posts this year, looking through photos of her adventures, sobs wracking my body as I contemplate, yet again, the gut-wrenching reality of her absence. I can't bring myself to be happy. Not yet.

I've deliberately kept her actual birthday private. We're still in mourning and I couldn't pretend otherwise. I need this day to sit in the pain and sorrow, so that tomorrow I can put on my "victorious Christian" face and celebrate Kari in the way I want to, with others who knew and loved her.

At dinner time we eat her favourite meal of macaroni cheese. We watch videos of her birthdays through the years, tears and laughter mingling as we hear her voice and see her alive again.

Thankfully, eventually, after what seems forever, the day is done and we head for bed. As usual, sleep eludes me as I contemplate the thought of many years ahead facing June nineteenth without the one who made it a special day.

Morning comes. The door is open. The food is ready. A magnificent cake takes pride of place in the centre of the dining table. Piles of scrapbooks wait hopefully to see who will come through the door and whether they'll take the time to open them. But something is missing.

Is it Kari's infectious giggle pealing through the air? Is it her dancing feet prancing down the hall? Is it the sparkle and glow that accompanies her entry to a room? It's all of these and so much more. There's a giant Kari-shaped hole in our home and never has it been more pronounced than today, as we attempt to celebrate her birthday without her here.

I want to make her birthday a positive time, a celebration of the amazing gift we received on that day, twenty-six years ago. We've issued an open invitation to anyone who wants to come and share stories, memories, tears or laughter as we remember.

Flowers arrive from thoughtful friends. An unexpected bunch comes from a school friend of Kari's. She's accompanied it with a note.

> I remember when Kari-Lee called me from hospital on my birthday, which is two days after hers. She'd just had her transplant two days before so I wasn't expecting a message, let alone a phone call. I couldn't believe she'd call me during such early stages of recovery. I cried hearing her voice. It was a demonstration of how caring and selfless she was. In so much pain after major surgery, yet she put that aside to call me. Kari never showed any fear or sadness. She was always the light in the room, making everyone laugh and smile. I don't feel words are enough to explain just how amazing she truly is.

Now it's time to celebrate our amazing girl. People start to arrive in dribs and drabs. Not necessarily the people I expected to show up, although the ever-faithful ones are here. I'm grateful for everyone who takes the time and is brave enough to come close to the shattered mess that is now me.

The tantalising smell of sausages fills the air in honour of Kari's love of sausage sizzles. I've asked people to bring a plate of "Kari food" to share, so we have coconut chocolates, jelly slice, an antipasto platter, pineapple dip, Tim Tams, watermelon and chocolate jelly babies. My sister Claire has brought a gorgeous coconut-flavoured cake, iced in Kari's favourite shades of bright blue. We sit around the dining table, sharing stories, wiping away tears, laughing at the funny girl who filled our lives with magic.

A spectacular birthday cake's been made, to my specifications, by another wonderfully creative and generous friend. It's a representation of Kari in Heaven. Her favourite ocean colours predominate, but there's also a waterfall and tumbling colourful flowers. Kari herself is dancing, her arms uplifted, her long curly hair flowing behind her, an expression of joy and peace on her face. It's an incredible gift. This is the way I imagine Kari now. This is what brings moments of peace, in brief glimpses which make life bearable enough to get up each morning and face another day without her here.

I call the day a success. People came. People shared. People remembered. It makes my mother-heart glow.

~

A FEW DAYS LATER, school holidays begin and we head for Canberra to visit my brother on the way to Melbourne for a family wedding. Last time we visited him was only weeks after Kari's funeral.

It's freezing in Canberra, but we manage to enjoy lots of winter activities with Charlie's family. Bike rides around the lakes, picnics by icy rivers, walks in nature and times with the family fill our days. We're much easier to be around, this time – much more sociable, much more "normal".

JULY

After a week, we drive off to Melbourne to stay with Peter's brother and sister-in-law while we attend their daughter's wedding. It's the first time we've seen this family since Kari's funeral. Last time we were at their house, Kari was with us. It was a great family time where Kari introduced Nic to her many Venning cousins. He obviously made an impression because they've invited him to the wedding. He arrives a day after us.

We haven't seen him to talk to since he told us in January that he wanted to be the one to initiate contact with us. That hasn't happened yet. I've seen him briefly when I've called in at his parents' café where he works, but usually he acknowledges me and that's the extent of interaction.

It's awkward and strange to now be thrown together with him in front of the family who have no idea what's been going on. He jokes and laughs and pulls funny faces with the cousins and seems to really enjoy being with them. I try to find opportunities to chat with him, to ask how he's doing, but he manages to avoid any situation which forces him to talk to me. I long to be able to help him, to talk with him about Kari-Lee, to somehow be a part of his healing journey, but it's very obvious he doesn't want that. It's not my role and I need to let him grieve the way he wants to, even when it tears at my heart.

~

A DAY OR SO LATER, Peter and I leave to have some quiet time at a seaside town nearby. It's restful and just what we need. I'll be flying home at the end of the week, but Peter is staying on for another niece's wedding.

Unfortunately, after a few days, the weather forecast turns bad. A strong cold front is heading our way bringing gale force winds, storms and sleet. I hate thunderstorms, particularly windy ones and especially flying in them. I fly out earlier to avoid the coming storm.

My dislike of storms stems from when I was ten years old and the town where I lived was struck by a freak tornado. The building I was in disappeared entirely, with only the stumps left. A girl my age who I'd known all my life was sitting near me. She died. I could easily have died myself if not for the intervention of one of the leaders, who caught me by the hair as I flew past her. I was extremely traumatised, particularly as we watched that poor young girl dying, moaning in pain in the corner of the room where we sought shelter, while an ambulance tried to get through to us.

That experience had a huge impact on my life and faith. When I'd show fear during storms, people would comfort me saying, "God will keep you safe. You can trust Him." I knew that wasn't true in the way they meant it. The girl who died loved God and was a sweet, kind girl, yet she died.

What does "God will keep you safe" actually mean? Obviously, people who love Jesus still die "before their time". Sometimes they die horrific deaths. Christians might pray for protection, but what does that protection look like?

My mum loved to share the story of her mother who would kneel down and pray for God to keep them safe every time they boarded the train to go into the city of Brisbane. When they arrived home safely, she would kneel down and thank God. A sweet story of a faithful mother.

Is that it? We just need to ask to be kept safe and we will be? I know there are Bible passages that seem to indicate that, but I now know too many Christians who are bereaved parents just like me, who prayed for God to keep their children safe, fully believing and trusting that He would. And their children died.

That's part of the reality I'm still wrestling with. I'm no longer willing to accept pat answers or Christianese cliches. I need to dig deep and decide if God is someone who I can really trust with my life and the lives of those I love.

∼

IN MY CONTINUING quest to find meaning in this life I've decided to become a Make-A-Wish (MAW) volunteer. Kari's MAW trip to Tahiti had such a positive and lasting impact on her life that I'd like to be involved in bringing joy to other children facing life-threatening conditions.

I'm nervous as I make my way to a local coffee shop to meet the President and the Volunteer Care Coordinator of our local branch, but they soon put me at ease and confirm that this is something I really want to do.

Towards the end of August, I'm excited to be starting another small group watching the *Heaven* DVDs by Randy Alcorn. The content is so deep and full that I'm sure I didn't grasp it all when we watched it earlier. This time my friend Leanne and another friend will watch it with me along with Kari's godparents, "Mr and Mrs Moon".

I'm keen to share it with others, but also interested to hear what Leanne thinks of the content. She has a deep understanding of the Bible and I'm looking forward to her input and opinion about how this lines up with her knowledge of the Word of God.

I long for it to be true and solid. I need it to be true and solid. My life depends on it.

∼

SEPTEMBER

It's only September, but Christmas is on my mind. It's time to pack my boxes for Operation Christmas Child, a project of the charity Samaritan's Purse.

Kari-Lee loved buying items for Christmas boxes. All through her childhood we packed four boxes, one from each member of our family, to send clothes, toiletries, school supplies and toys to a child living in poverty.

This year I decide to ramp up my contribution and pack twenty-five boxes in memory of Kari-Lee's twenty-five years on earth. I can no longer buy her Christmas gifts, but I can bless other children with the overflow of my love for my absent Kari.

When some friends contribute items for the boxes or money for postage, I feel a great warmth enveloping me and spreading out to the children who will be blessed by these boxes. Buying, sorting and packing occupies my mind for a time, giving me a focus while honouring my girl.

LATER IN SEPTEMBER I'm at Brisbane International Airport. Tiana is leaving me for adventures in far-flung places.

I've been here before. Many times. This time is different.

My emotions twist and turn. My stomach heaves. My eyes leak. Just four years ago, in this very place, I farewelled Kari-Lee as she jetted off to explore Central and South America. Now she's left us on what I believe is her greatest adventure yet, one she's not returning from. This airport overflows with grief triggers.

I'm struggling, but I'm here to support Tiana, who's made the brave choice to travel alone to Japan. She's chosen this trip to mark her twenty-first birthday next month. A traditional party is not something she wants to contemplate, but an escapade to Japan ticks all the boxes.

She's taking with her an origami paper crane, similar to the ones that used to hang in Kari's hospital room. We've decided to start a tradition of leaving a crane in countries which Kari never got to visit.

We're planning to give them to friends and family who visit other destinations Kari-Lee would have loved. Tiana is the very first.

I'm happy for her, have actively encouraged her to seek this adventure, yet fear lurks at the edge of my consciousness. I'm only too aware how fragile our lives are. My head knows that, statistically, she'll return to us safe and sound, but my heart isn't picking up that message. One daughter has left me. Would God be so cruel as to allow another one to go?

These are the times when all my questions about trusting God rise up and shake me to the core. I know there are no simple answers. The sovereignty of God is still a concept I grapple with when it intersects with my own life. It's all very well in theory to agree that God is in control over absolutely everything, but when that involves the death of your child it becomes a lot more complicated.

Trust is the key. Absolute trust. Trust that says that even though I don't understand, I believe that everything God allows in my life is for my eventual good.

I'm not there yet.

AFTER: CHAPTER TEN

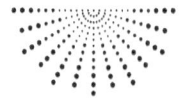

OCTOBER

Before I'm ready, October is here. The month I've been dreading. Soon it will be one whole year without Kari.

In the beginning, I doubted my ability to survive one minute, one hour, one day, one week. Yet somehow, here I am, almost one whole year later and still mostly upright.

One question has been haunting me for the past few months. Is Kari really in Heaven? Now that I've learned so much about Heaven and how wonderful it is, now that thinking of Kari there brings me peace, now that I'm looking forward to the day I see her there and have endless time together, this question plagues me.

I'm well aware that Kari didn't live a perfect Christian life. There were several years in her young adult life where God definitely took a back seat and she made choices that were outside what she knew He would have wanted. Some of those choices she tried to defend to me. Some I'm unaware of, just like most mothers of young adults. Tiana occasionally hints at aspects of sin in Kari's life, which she doesn't always see as sinful. I understand that Tiana doesn't want me to put Kari on a pedestal, so pointing out areas of her life that would disappoint me is her way of preventing that. I realise she doesn't mean any harm by it, but the solid ground of trusting Kari is in Heaven and that I'll see her again starts to show cracks, and begins to crumble beneath me.

I think one of the reasons it bothers me so much is that I had planned to discuss deep spiritual topics with Kari when she went home for what was supposed to be her last few days. I had thought we'd have quiet, private time together in those days at home and I could ask whether there was anything she needed to confess and make sure she was right with God before she got to meet Him. She never made it home and I've always regretted not having the conversation with her sooner. What if my negligence stops her entering Heaven? How can I feel secure that she's safely home?

In the first few weeks after Kari left us, several friends shared "pictures" or visions they had of Kari when they were praying. Most involved Kari dancing with freedom and joyful abandon, wearing a flowing dress with flowers in her hair, entering a stadium full of cheering people. As she proceeded towards where Jesus was waiting, someone announced, "May I present Kari-Lee," causing the crowd to cheer even louder. While these visions are very precious to me, they don't have a lot of details specific to Kari, except perhaps her hair and her dancing.

What happens next is astounding to me.

My After65roses friend in the US contacts me to share a dream she's just had. She tells me:

> I saw Kari-Lee alone, not paying any attention to me. She was wearing green shorts and a soft-looking shirt. She didn't look like she had CF. She had far bigger boobs than Jordan (her daughter with CF) ever had, pardon my description. Her weight looked normal. Her hair was pulled back in a ponytail with curls escaping. She was wearing a backpack. She was exploring, totally engrossed in what she was doing. She was alone, but didn't mind at all. She was in a place that reminds me of Kualoa Ranch in Hawaii. It was more beautiful than anything I've ever seen before, lush and green. It looked like a mountainous area, with a waterfall behind her. She

looked excited, as if she was exploring another country and excited to see everything.

She saw me and seemed to know who I was. She said she wished she could send you postcards and photos like she did before (is that what she did?). She referenced her time in Egypt and said it was like that time. I don't know what that means. (Did she really go to Egypt? I don't know anyone else with CF who's ever been to Egypt.) She said she was saving the pictures until you get there. She seemed very happy and content. She was planning on you coming, in the way any daughter does when her parents stop by for a visit. CF seemed but a distant memory, part of what got her there, but not thought about anymore.

I saw her again. This time she wasn't alone, but had travelled to wherever she was. I can't explain that better. She was with people who were dark-skinned, a different race from her or me. They were showing her a dance and she was studiously trying to learn it. I left then and she waved goodbye, happy and content in the knowledge that her mum would be there one day.

This dream is different. This dream has facts this friend couldn't have known. What Kari had said on Facebook about her time in Egypt was "I LOOOOOVE EGYPT !!!!!!" It sounds like she loves Heaven, unsurprisingly.

I feel a bit sad when I read the part about postcards, because I don't think I ever received one from Kari while she was in Egypt. Other places, yes, but I have no memory of a postcard from Egypt. A few days later, I'm tidying some papers when something drops out. Unbelievably, it's a postcard from Kari in Egypt.

Of course, none of this is definitive proof that Kari is actually in Heaven, but once again I believe God has seen my need and orchestrated a sign for me, to bring me comfort and help allay my doubts and fears.

SOON IT WILL BE the twenty-second, but before I have to face that traumatic anniversary there are things to enjoy about the month of

October. I choose to put aside the building tsunami of overwhelming feelings and focus mindfully on the positive and exciting dates ahead.

Tiana's twenty-first birthday is in early October. She's already celebrated in her own way with her memory-making trip to Japan, but now that she's home I want to make the actual day of her birth special.

Charlie is visiting from Canberra, so I arrange for Mum and all my siblings to join Tiana and I for high tea. Tiana loves tea in teapots, delicate teacups and saucers, dainty nibbles and the atmosphere of a high tea. We dress up and act very posh. Tiana is in her element. We're all aware of the missing smile at the table, but do our best to focus on Tiana, celebrate her and help fill the gaping chasm in her life.

Next day we invite Nic to join us for a birthday lunch for Tiana at a nearby winery, with great views and delicious food. We've not seen him since the wedding in Melbourne, but with the approaching first anniversary of Kari leaving us we want to build bridges so he can mark the day with us.

We chat and laugh together as we enjoy the scrumptious food, but there's an air of awkwardness hovering. Nic tells us all about the overseas trips he's been taking, made possible by Kari's life insurance payout. Kari desperately wanted to take Nic travelling, so I know she'd approve. He takes us to see his massive, brand new four-wheel-drive utility truck with personalised number plates that he's recently bought.

Tiana and I both notice that Nic isn't wearing his wedding ring. We wonder whether he's just forgotten to put it on or whether that's a deliberate signal to us that he's thinking about dating again. We understand that this is something he'll do in the future, but it stabs like a knife in our hearts.

We talk with Nic about our plans for the anniversary of Kari's death, which we're choosing to call her "Heaven Day". We feel it's time to scatter her ashes as she requested, at her favourite beach where Nic proposed to Kari. We assume he'll want to join us, but he says he'll think about it. We're a bit shocked, but understand it might be difficult to contemplate such a thing. Although I haven't been involved at all in his grief journey, I do care about Nic in spite of the distance he's chosen to keep between us. We really hope he'll come. It's a significant milestone and a symbolic farewell.

Several days later he asks us to join him for coffee at a nearby café and informs us he doesn't want to come with us to scatter Kari's ashes. I'm devastated, but acknowledge that it's his choice to make.

∼

BRRRRIIIINNG! My alarm jolts me from a restless, interrupted sleep. It's still dark. Why am I awake?

Reality hits. I need to get up. Today is October twenty-second. Kari-Lee has been gone a whole year.

We gather the special tubes I've covered in turquoise and frangipani paper, to scatter Kari's ashes. We bring the frangipani bowl Tiana's prepared with all Kari's favourite tropical fruits. We collect our bunches of frangipani and hibiscus. We're going to do this in style. Kari style.

We load Maloo into the car and head for Kari's favourite beach. As we navigate the steps in the dark, a lightening on the horizon signals the approaching dawn. We gather our scattering tubes and step tentatively into the foam, a little distance from each other, yet synchronised in our movements.

As the first golden rays poke above the distant edge of the ocean, we glance at each other, then start shaking our tubes. Out flies the powdery mix, all that remains of our beautiful, precious girl, all that's left of the dynamic, lively body that took her on adventures to exotic locations, creating priceless memories that live on long past the end of her physical life.

Tears fall, hearts break, longing sucks at our souls. There's a sacred hush in the beauty surrounding us as we fulfil one of Kari's final requests.

We write Kari-Lee's name in a big heart on the sand, our flowers arranged round it. We run up and down the sand with Maloo, throw a few sticks in the waves for her to chase, laugh at her antics. We sit on the sand, enjoying our plate of "Kari" food, reminiscing about all the wonderful times we shared, wondering what Kari is doing right now. Can she see us? Does she know it's been a year? Does she care?

We know it's time to leave as people start to arrive for a fun day at the beach. We glance back, watching our flowers now floating out to sea, Kari's name washed away by the incoming waves, her virtual presence erased just as her actual presence was erased on this day one year ago.

Back home, we find a bunch of flowers and card from Nic, reading: "Thanks for letting me be a part of your family. I will never forget Kari-Lee." It sounds like a farewell. I'm not sure what to make of it.

Other flowers arrive from kind-hearted friends, touching our hearts and blessing us in the knowledge that we're not alone in remembering and missing our girl. Later, Gaye and Bruce, Rachel and Winston arrive. I've bought beautiful helium balloons in ocean colours and we hold them tight as we stand, sharing a few words out by the pool. At my signal, the balloons are released, flying high in the blue, blue sky, climbing on towards the place where Kari now lives.

Tears drip as we watch them grow smaller and smaller, further from our sight, just as our girl flew from our presence, further and further away as this year progressed.

THE NEXT DAY, at Tiana's request, we take a drive in the beautiful countryside around Mount Glorious near Samford.

This is where she found solace while living in Brisbane alone, mourning her sister. This was her place of escape and she wants to share it with us. We eat lunch at a quaint restaurant set on the edge of rainforest and soak in the tranquillity of the mountain bush setting.

A WEEK LATER, we're shocked to receive a phone call from Nic, asking if he can come to our home and meet with us. A sense of foreboding descends. What could he possibly want to talk to us about? Tiny pinpricks of hope peek through. Perhaps he regrets not coming with us to scatter Kari's ashes, but now that emotional task is finished he wants to have more contact with us.

Somehow, despite my hope, I sense that's not the case. We've heard vague rumours of him having a special girl who sits near him in church. Clawed talons of resentment grip my stomach at the thought of Nic with someone other than Kari. It's been less than a year since we waved off that tiny turquoise coffin carrying the shell of our beloved girl. My heart is still in a million pieces. I'm not even sure where those pieces are, let alone whether they can ever be put back together in any meaningful way. The wound is open, fresh, gaping, still so tender. Surely Nic, her husband, feels the same?

A large photo of Kari and Nic waits on the table, a special gift for Nic. We hear a knock at the door. He enters, awkwardness emanating from him. It's obvious he's nervous. Not a good sign. He refuses tea or coffee. Not a good sign. He looks down and mumbles as he starts to speak. Not a good sign. Words come from his mouth, but after the first sentence a fog of disbelief, horror and anger envelopes me. My worst fears are realised. He's found someone else and he wants to be the one to tell us.

Even in my numbed state, I can appreciate his bravery in coming to tell us face to face. Despite that, my emotions flare up into a blaze of indignation, incredulity and stupefaction. The sound of his voice warps and distorts as blood pounds through my brain. My hands shake, my knees quiver. I feel like I'm going to vomit. How can this be happening? How can he be ready to move on? How can he be able to gaze into someone else's eyes, hold their hand, laugh with them in shared private jokes? It feels like the ultimate betrayal.

I lose control. The deep pain of the grievous wound inside me erupts out of my mouth. Crying. Sobbing. Stumbling over words. I say unkind things. Most of it is a blur, but I remember I say that he wasn't much of a son-in-law. I regret saying it immediately but I can't take it back. Passion is flooding my veins. I take the photo and rip it down the middle. If he wants to be with someone else, then he won't want photos of Kari looking at him with love.

He looks shocked. He leaves. I never see him again.

AFTER: CHAPTER ELEVEN

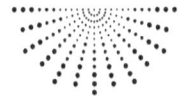

NOVEMBER

It takes me days to recover from our meeting with Nic. I'm still dazed and shocked by his words. I'm also ashamed of my reaction. It was like an out-of-body experience where my rational self was completely overtaken by my emotional self. All the hurt from his continued chosen absence in our lives bubbled up and spilled out. I'm not proud of it.

Rationally, I know he's done nothing wrong by finding love again. Even Kari loved movies like *P.S. I Love You*, where a widow finds love again just a year after her husband died. Yet, for some reason, it hurts my heart so badly. For some reason it feels like he's betraying Kari-Lee. For some reason it feels like she couldn't have meant much to him if he can move on so quickly to love someone else.

I know it's not true. He loved her until her death, which is what he promised to do. I know it's not true in my head, but my heart is struggling.

The first day of November marks one year since we farewelled

Kari at the celebration of her life. I ponder whether I've made any progress since then. I can see that I have, yet so many things remain the same. I still cry every single day, multiple times a day. Sometimes it's silent tears sliding down my cheeks. Sometimes it's sobbing while building mountains of soggy tissues. Sometimes it's gut-wrenching, body-wracking, all-consuming groans that drive me to my knees. I'm still sleeping very little. Visions continue to haunt me as soon as I close my eyes at night. I'm getting better at finding strategies to cope. Sometimes I give in to it and have a good cry. Sometimes I go into Kari's room and look through her things, searching for a sense of her, trying to stem the missing, the longing, the yearning. Other times I find a task to distract myself and to accomplish something useful in the long, lonely stretches of the night.

I wear some of Kari's jewellery, especially her silver bangle with the inscription of Psalm 139:16 (NIV): "Your eyes saw my unformed body. All the days ordained for me were written in your book before one of them came to be." It's a constant reminder to me that God knew her days; her death was no surprise to Him. She wasn't robbed or short-changed. On my other arm, I wear the silver and blue bangle she brought back for me from the Greek Islands. I wear some of her silver rings that she loved so much. I've been wearing some of her silver charms around my neck, but now I buy a beautiful silver frangipani necklace and have her name and dates engraved on the back. When it arrives, I love it and wear it on a black thread, never really taking it off again. I order a bracelet from a website which can inscribe jewellery with your loved one's handwriting. I choose to have Kari's unique trademark signature stamped onto the front. When it arrives, I wear it always, glimpses of her name catching my eye at random times and making her feel close. Wearing Kari's jewellery, especially her bangle and ring which she wore, which touched her skin, which may even have particles of Kari still embedded somewhere, brings a measure of comfort to my broken heart. I wear no other jewellery.

TIANA ARRANGES a special surprise for me. She's booked a long weekend just for the two of us at a unit in Coolum. It's such a thoughtful gesture and something we need. We spend our days eating, walking, resting, talking. It's a great mother-daughter bonding time, where we can talk openly about how much we miss Kari-Lee, but also forge an adult-to-adult relationship between the two of us. I love having her living at home again, something we haven't enjoyed since she left home soon after finishing high school.

One evening we wander down to the local shops for dinner. We bump into a couple we know who have a daughter the same age as Kari. They share about each member of their family, update us about what's been happening in their lives, enquire about each member of our family. Except Kari-Lee. She doesn't get a mention. It's as if she never existed.

I realise they're probably trying to be kind, trying not to upset me. Maybe they feel awkward because a year has passed, so they don't think they should bring up her name. What they don't understand is that mentioning Kari's name, even if it's just to say they're sorry about what happened to her, is the greatest gift they could give me. What they can't understand is that even though Kari may not physically be here, she's just as much part of my life, my thoughts, my love as she ever has been. What they can't understand is that not mentioning her hurts me deeper than any prying question about her death ever could.

The sound of her name is so precious to me that I've started a new habit. Whenever I order coffee and they ask, "What name?" I say, "Kari." That way I hear her name called out loud and clear, music to my ears, a blessing to my heart.

SO MANY QUESTIONS still gnaw at my brain, day and night. Why weren't my faith-filled, heartfelt, desperate prayers for Kari's healing answered, along with the thousands of other prayers offered over the years by countless believers? Why did God let Kari go through all of the trauma and pain and suffering if He knew she was going to die anyway? Why did God allow Kari to catch glandular fever which would lead to her death? And still, the biggest question of all, can I really trust that she's in Heaven and I'll get to see her again? My friend's dream helped, but still doubts persist.

When the questions become unbearable, keeping me from sleep, robbing me of peace, I organise a meeting with my pastor. He met with Peter and me in March offering comfort and reassurance, but this time I need answers to my specific question, "Is Kari in Heaven?"

Of course, he has no definitive answer to this, but as he guides me through the truths in the Bible, he reminds me that we aren't guaranteed entry to Heaven based on whether we lived a perfect Christian life or not. If that was the case, none of us would make it.

I'm already aware of this, but it helps when he spells it out for me. Yes, Kari sinned, sometimes knowingly. We all do. I do. Is that our basis for entering Heaven? Do we need to be good enough? Does every unconfessed sin create a roadblock to that final destination? NO. It's trust in Jesus and His finished work on the cross that opens the gate into Heaven for us. Only Jesus lived a perfect life without sin and He paid for us to reap the benefits of that, if only we will accept our inability and trust in His ability.

Kari did that. Kari loved Jesus. Kari trusted Jesus. Kari is in Heaven.

DECEMBER

As Kari's second wedding anniversary approaches, it's no easier than the first. In fact, it's a whole lot harder, because now I can't even share memories with Nic. He's moved on. He's found a new love. We've recently discovered that he actually started dating just seven months after Kari's funeral. When I saw him at our niece's wedding, he was already besotted by someone else. On their wedding anniversary, I find myself questioning the validity of the vows they made.

When I discuss it with my counsellor, I'm reminded again that his promise was to love Kari-Lee "until death separates us". And he did that. He's done nothing wrong. Logically, I can accept that, but my heart still struggles with it all. The thought of Nic with someone else pierces my heart with daggers of fire. I try not to think about Nic anymore. At all.

I ATTEMPT to go back to church, but despite God and I being on speaking terms now, it's still incredibly hard. Peter's been going occasionally without me. Now we decide to go to the evening service where hardly anyone knows us. I can't face seeing familiar faces and having to deal with sympathy or, possibly even worse, no sympathy.

We begin by deliberately arriving late and leaving early. That way, we don't need to interact with anyone. It also cuts out the singing and "worship" time. There's absolutely no way I can sing any of those songs. Worship time was already an emotional time for me before Kari died. Now, every song brings tears and sobs and embarrassment, so it's easier to just avoid it.

It seems to work, at least to the point that I can attend church sometimes.

I CONTINUE to search for unique ways to honour Kari-Lee. I decide to have some business size cards printed, requesting acts of kindness in memory of Kari. I come up with the acronym I.R.A.K. KARI, standing for Intentional Random Acts of Kindness, using Kari's name backwards. I have my favourite photo of Kari-Lee on the front and a small explanation on the back. "This random act of kindness has been offered in memory of Kari-Lee."

When I order them at a local printer, he seems interested in the story behind them. When I go to pick up the finished cards, he refuses any payment. It's such a kind and generous act from a complete stranger that it brings me to tears.

I share them with any friends and family who answer my callout on Facebook. I ask for people to let me know if they do any kindness acts for Kari. I hear from a couple of people, but mostly nothing happens. It's disappointing, but I have enough cards that I'll be able to try again in the future.

∼

I FIND some online groups for bereaved parents that offer support. "Still Standing" seems mostly aimed at those who've lost babies, but some posts are helpful. "Silent Grief", facilitated by Clara Hinton who's lost both a baby and an adult son, seems to be the most relevant and helpful. "An Inch of Gray" is more of a blog, written by the author of *Rare Bird*, a book I found very honest and helpful. Another blog which really speaks to me is written by Lexi Behrndt, whose young son Charlie died around the same time as Kari. Although he was so much younger, many of her hospital experiences and questions about healing mirror mine.

In the absence of a face-to-face support group to attend, these Facebook groups go some way to filling that gap. It's immensely helpful to find that most of what I'm experiencing isn't unique to me. It's part of the so-called "new normal" world of child loss. I'm not sure I'm happy to accept that this will be my normal going forward, but I'm glad to know that I'm not losing my mind or grieving inappropriately, as some would have me believe.

Something else that brings great comfort is connecting with Kari's friends and occasionally being invited to catch up with them. I'm sure they never fully understand just how much it means to me. Similarly, when I'm invited to two weddings, knowing I'm there in place of my girl, it brings both great joy and deep sorrow.

In early December I receive a wonderful surprise. I've been looking at a jewellery website in the US called Shine. It was started by a Christian mum who experienced loss. The pieces she makes are meaningful as well as beautiful. While I'm contemplating what I'd like to buy, I enter a competition they're running to win a piece of jewellery inscribed with your loved one's handwriting (similar to my bracelet). I choose a disc with the words "I love you so much, Kari" on one side and "Mumsalicious" on the other side, followed by "see you soon…" I've copied each of these phrases from cards Kari-Lee gave me in her last few months. "Mumsalicious" was written on the envelope of the last birthday card she gave me. Soon after, I'm surprised and ecstatic to discover that I'm the winner. I add the silver disc to my silver frangipani.

CHRISTMAS ROLLS AROUND AGAIN, as it will every year. I share on Facebook about my tradition of buying a special ornament for my girls each year: an angel for Kari and a star for Tiana. This built a collection that they each took when they left home. Some of my friends and family generously send me angel ornaments in memory of Kari-Lee. This carries on for several years. Such a blessing at a difficult time of year.

This Christmas I need to be brave and join with the rest of the extended family. I need Kari to be there too. I need her to be thought about, honoured, remembered. I know that she is, but I need it to be tangible.

I bring a snow globe with a picture of Kari frolicking in the snow in Urbino. I place it in the centre of the table where it can't be ignored.

I place a canvas of my favourite photo of Kari in the window behind the couch. Unmissable. Inescapable. Unforgettable.

When it's time for the traditional family photo with us all wearing silly hats, I bravely join in, but hold the canvas of Kari to my chest. She may not be here physically, but she's part of this family and she always will be.

AND SO, we come to the end of 2015. We've now experienced all of the "firsts" and even a few of the "seconds" like Christmas and Kari's wedding anniversary. Somehow, I've survived. I'm not sure how.

I've tried to follow the advice penned in one of Steven Curtis Chapman's songs, *Take Another Step*. The title really says it all. He paints a picture of a normal life abruptly interrupted by disaster and the helpless confusion that makes moving in any direction seem impossible.

As another friend puts it, just do the next right thing. It doesn't help to look ahead at years and years without Kari-Lee. When it seems I can't survive another day without Kari, I need to focus on the next step, the next hour. If I can make it through that, gradually the hours will add up and I will have survived another day. I'm still not entirely convinced that I want to go on, but really there's no viable alternative at present.

AFTER: CHAPTER TWELVE

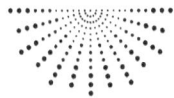

*T*all eucalypts form a guard of honour as I push myself upwards, leaning heavily on my walking poles. Dust motes pirouette in rays of sunshine that intermittently penetrate the leafy canopy. The air, fresh and crisp, sucks into my lungs as I test the limits of my endurance, hiking up the steep grassy hill.

Then, the reward. Spread beneath me is a picture postcard of wild whitecapped ocean meeting tall rocky cliffs. Seabirds wheeling, squealing, soaring. Intense blue sky dotted with whipped cream clouds.

I've made it to the summit on my hike of the Great Ocean Walk. A year later than I originally planned, but well worth the wait. It's been such an adventure, hiking each day, sleeping in the lighthouse keeper's cottage each night, making new friends, sharing hearty meals and life stories. For the first time in a long time, I feel a sense of freedom, of exhilaration, of revitalisation. The shadow of Kari's death is ever-present, yet momentarily subdued while I pour all my energy into the physical challenges of the walk. Even on the third and final day, walking alone the entire time in pouring rain can't ruin the benefit to my spirits.

I return home invigorated.

MARCH BRINGS bittersweet moments when Tiana moves back to Brisbane. She has enrolled in a patisserie course with hopes of adding to her cheffing repertoire. She's also reconnected with a young man who's caught her eye in a different way from their previous encounters. Matt was an apprentice chef with Tiana in 2013, when they were both dating other people. Now she's keen to spend more time with him and see where it leads.

We're happy that Tiana's looking to the future with hopes and plans, but we'll miss having her presence at home. Further sad farewells for me when Gaye and Bruce leave to live in Tasmania, over two thousand kilometres away. Bruce has family and a new job waiting for him, but selfishly I wish they could stay close. They've been such a great support to me over the past two years. Still, there are always phone calls and a visit to Tasmania now has added attraction.

Back at work there are more challenges. Drastic changes are being brought in with new leadership. Most of the therapists who've worked at the centre for ten years or more don't feel it's for the better. The atmosphere is changing. Financial viability becomes a focus. Team camaraderie is wavering, fault lines are appearing. It's no longer a welcoming, supportive place to work. I begin to dread going to work each morning, grateful it's only three days a week.

THANKFULLY, I have an amazing upcoming adventure to focus my attention. As June approaches, final preparations are made for our month-long holiday to Canada and Alaska, culminating in the cruise with Steven Curtis Chapman.

We board the plane, filled with hope for a refreshing time together. After a twenty-four-hour marathon journey to Vancouver, we arrive bleary-eyed and fuzzy-brained. It's early morning when we land and we struggle to stay awake until bedtime in an attempt to reduce jetlag. Finally, we allow ourselves to drop into bed, totally exhausted but ready for our escapade the following day.

Rudely awakened by our shrilling alarm clocks fracturing the silence in unison, we make our way to Vancouver train station for a two-day journey on the *Rocky Mountaineer*. We revel in the luxury offered to us, above and beyond what we expected. Even more awe-inspiring is the spectacular scenery rolling past our huge windows. Majestic soaring peaks covered in glistening white snow. Wild, fast-running rivers. Lakes of immense dimensions and jaw-dropping beauty.

It's a mind-blowing start to our holiday and we relish every moment. At the back of our carriage is an open caboose where I spend most of my time, hair whipped by the wind, fingers red and stiff from the cold. I've brought Kari's digital SLR camera, her pride and joy. It's way too fancy and professional for me to really know what I'm doing, but I've taken a few lessons so I can attempt to take amazing photos with it. The opportunities are endless and I swivel about snapping glorious scenery left and right, in front and behind, trying to emulate the photographic talent of my girl.

The trip has so many highlights that I could fill several books with the stories. In amongst eye-popping vistas and breathtaking scenery, certain moments stand out. After exploring the picturesque town of Banff, with so many hidden wonders, we make our way to Calgary where I worked as a nanny in 1982–3. I've kept in touch with the family I worked for all those years ago, although the little boy who I primarily cared for has sadly passed away. He had very severe quadriplegic cerebral palsy and died aged eleven. We spend several nights with the parents, who understand the trauma and heartache of saying goodbye to their child. As believers, they also share the hope of seeing their little boy again in Heaven, healed and whole. Even with the passing of thirty-four years, that instant bond which occurs between believers whose children have run on to Heaven before them means that we're able to share deep and meaningful conversations.

Our next stop is Lake Louise, an area of world-renowned beauty. It's Kari-Lee's birthday and we've booked a special experience at the famous Fairmont Chateau Lake Louise. We're going to celebrate her with a fancy high tea, overlooking the lake with its stunning backdrop of grandiose mountains.

The high tea is everything I imagined and more. The staff are aware it's someone's birthday, but when we explain whose birthday they're extra caring and kind. Mixed emotions ripple through me. Awe and wonder at the sight in front of us. Gratitude and appreciation as I remember the incredible gift of Kari in our lives. Longing and yearning for her to be present with us on this, her twenty-seventh birthday. Sadness and regret as I think of how much Kari would have loved to be here, experiencing yet another country on her long list of places she wanted to visit.

We marvel at the breathtaking beauty of the area, with awe-inspiring lakes in every shade of Kari's favourite ocean colours, each one seemingly more beautiful than the last. They literally have to be seen to be believed. As I stand mesmerised by Moraine Lake, nestled in the Valley of the Ten Peaks, it feels like a glimpse of Heaven. It's hard to think how anything could be more beautiful, yet I know it will be. I'm thankful to God for this reminder of what awaits me and what Kari is experiencing even now.

We make our way north to Jasper along the Icefields Parkway, visiting the Columbia Icefields and walking on the Athabasca Glacier. Arriving in Jasper, we take the Skytram to the top of Whistlers Mountain, then hike a little further until we're on our own, gazing out over the panoramic view stretching for miles around us. It's the perfect place to leave one of the origami paper cranes we've brought. We tuck it behind a rock, before taking a photo with the town of Jasper far below. Little rituals like this help us with tangible memorials to Kari. She didn't make it to all of the countries on her list, but we can leave a symbol of her there – our girl who loved to travel.

For the next segment of our holiday, we catch a Greyhound bus back to Vancouver, travelling via Clearwater so we can experience some of the country we haven't yet passed through. The long hours on the road give me opportunity to reflect. Thoughts of Kari dominate. Missing her surges to new heights and tears frequently wash my face. I realise that not a day has passed yet, since she died, when I haven't cried. I'm not sure that day will ever come, although others who are further "ahead" say it does eventually happen.

Having wonderful adventures helps, as does being away from the routine of our normal lives. Lots of brainpower is used in planning the next days' activities, taking photos, keeping a diary, yet always, there at the edge of my consciousness, a curly-haired laughing girl peeps through. Hopefully, it's happy, healthy Kari who makes an appearance, but sometimes it's dreadfully unwell Kari who surfaces, struggling to breathe. In one form or another she's ever-present, and I wouldn't want it any other way.

Soon it's time for the catalyst that started this whole dream trip, a cruise through Alaska with Steven Curtis Chapman. My excitement levels skyrocket as we board the gigantic cruise ship. Our room has a balcony, a luxury which will prove to be worth every hard-earned dollar as we cruise along the Inside Passage and later spend a day in Glacier Bay. The scenery almost defies description: towering glaciers, floating icebergs, quaint seaside villages. During each of the seven days, we either enjoy the passing spectacle of panoramic scenery or make our way into one of the three stopover towns, alive with fascinating culture, breathtaking vistas and exciting adventures. We manage to leave another origami crane high in the wilds of Alaska.

Evenings onboard are a wonderful time of blessing, singing worship songs led by Steven Curtis Chapman, along with his band and the thousand other Christian travellers enjoying the cruise with us. Tears often accompany my singing, as the words which have become a lifeline for me are echoed by myriad voices raised in song around me. Teaching by Max Lucado, always preceded by at least six jokes, tops off each evening. A highlight of the cruise is meeting Steven and Mary Beth Chapman, along with Max and Denalyn Lucado. I even enjoy the special privilege of sharing a coffee with Mary Beth, something I'm brave enough to request. We talk about our girls in Heaven and I share with her how much her book meant to me.

Back in Canada we enjoy a last few fun-filled days in Whistler. An unexpected highlight occurs one afternoon when I make my way to the outdoor hot spa pool. As I'm relaxing in the bubbling water, my thoughts drifting aimlessly, three young men attempt to enter the enclosure. Their door key won't work, so I let them through and we start chatting. They're world-champion downhill skateboarders, competing on nearby mountains. Two of them are Brazilian, very good-looking, friendly and chatty.

Momentarily I think, "I must tell Kari about this," then realise that's impossible. I imagine how much she would have revelled in my situation. She could probably have spoken a little in Brazilian Portuguese with them.

I hope that, somehow, she knows. I'm not sure how it all works. Some of Randy Alcorn's fiction books include the idea of portals in Heaven where the inhabitants can occasionally glance at significant events on earth. I'm not sure this qualifies, but I hear Kari's melodious giggle at the thought.

After a day of bike riding and exploring back in Vancouver, we board our plane home to Australia, back to reality, grateful for the cache of memories we've tucked away to help carry us through the hard days.

RETURNING to work is unexpectedly life-changing. While I've been gone, things have deteriorated dramatically. Our senior therapist has resigned under difficult circumstances and gradually, as the term progresses, each of the therapists and most of the family support staff hand in their resignations, including me.

It's a traumatic end to twenty years in what's been a wonderful workplace with meaningful relationships, both with client families and with staff.

As I'm working out my four weeks' notice, I decide to try a change of career. It's something I've been contemplating since returning last year. My OT job is emotionally and mentally demanding and after losing Kari I've been considering looking for work with children that isn't quite so challenging.

A nanny job I see advertised in the newspaper sounds like a description of me. I'm thrilled when my application is successful and even before I finish at the therapy centre, I begin my new career as a nanny on my days off.

The family has an adorable eleven-month-old baby girl and two seven-year-olds. I work three ten-hour days each week, which is physically exhausting, but fills my days with joy and laughter as the baby and I form a strong bond.

In online grief groups there's much talk of the secondary losses that accompany child loss and for me the loss of Kari's future children is devastating. She loved babies as much as I do and longed to have her own. It's an aching void that can never be filled. There will never be a child of Kari's. Hopefully Tiana will one day have children and they'll be immensely precious to me, but in the meantime, I can enjoy my days with this enchanting child.

⁓

ONE OF STEVEN CURTIS CHAPMAN's songs, *A Little More Time to Love*, reminds me that we only have limited time here on earth to make a difference. In the blink of an eye our life here will be over and we will live forever in the unimaginably wonderful world that awaits us.

In the spirit of doing my best to make a positive impact in the world, I've accepted a committee position with Make-A-Wish. It involves welcoming families from other parts of Australia who come to fulfil their child's wish on the Sunshine Coast.

In August, I volunteer for the first time at the Royal Queensland Show, known locally as the Ekka, on a stall operated by the hospital where Kari spent so much of her last two years. For over twenty years this hospital foundation has operated the strawberry sundae stands at the show as a fundraiser, now a much-loved Ekka tradition. I spend my shift chopping countless boxes of fresh strawberries. I think of Kari-Lee, who loved watching the Ekka from her hospital room, who loved strawberries and especially strawberry lip balm.

⁓

CHRISTMAS RETURNS, as it always does, but this year we have a new family member in the silly hats photo. Matt has become firmly ensconced in the family and seems to take our raucous gathering and silly shenanigans in his stride.

One day in December I have a startling realisation. I get to the end of the day and realise I haven't cried. At all. All day.

It's a first for me and marks a very subtle turning point. Grief remains my constant companion and missing Kari my ever-present consciousness, but perhaps there's a tiny glimmer of hope that I might survive losing her and somehow find a way back to meaning and joy again. It definitely won't happen overnight, but perhaps it might actually happen.

AFTER: CHAPTER THIRTEEN

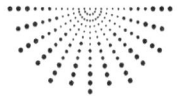

*L*oudspeakers crackle with indecipherable announcements. Harassed travellers check tickets and passports while others saunter along enjoying the thought of restful days to come.

I'm at the international airport again. Seeing my daughter off again. Sparking grief triggers again.

This time, Tiana is travelling with Matt to Thailand and Vietnam. Impatient anticipation is fizzing in the air around them as they give us one last hug before descending to the lower floor for customs and security checks. They reappear in the secure area below us as we watch from the balcony. The mixed feelings, which are becoming a standard part of my life, churn in my gut. We wave them off, with their bright cheery grins. I pray they'll be safe and come home to me again, knowing there's no guarantee.

Valentine's Day arrives, and with it some exciting news. Matt has proposed to Tiana on the Phi Phi Islands in Thailand and she's said yes! We're so happy for them. They've left a "Kari crane" there to mark the spot, a place she'd have loved to visit.

Soon after, we're thrilled to hear that some of Kari's Latin dance friends are planning to hold a gala ball in her memory, as part of a whole weekend called the Sunshine Coast Latin Dance Festival. For the next few months we'll be involved with helping to sell tickets, decorating tables, finding sponsors, sourcing raffle prizes and lending a hand in any other way we can. Any profits will go to Cystic Fibrosis Queensland in honour of our Kari-Lee, who was a treasured member of the Latin dance community on the Sunshine Coast.

Another new activity I've started, in my attempt to process and work through my grief, is writing.

I've joined a writers' group and recently I've written two poems to be included in an anthology of work being published as a fundraiser for school chaplaincy on the coast.

Writing is often suggested as being helpful and cathartic when dealing with grief. One of the leaders of our writers' group, Suzanne Strong, has written a book called *Freedom Writing* for this purpose. Some other books I find that have prompts aimed at working though grief include *Writing to Heal the Soul* by Susan Zimmermann and *On Coming Alive* by Lexi Behrndt.

I've started small with my own writing, but in the recesses of my mind is the thought that one day I'd love to write a book about Kari's life so that she'll never be forgotten. One of the poems I've written expresses thoughts that I'm still wrestling with.

> What if...? What if...?
>
> What if my precious, beautiful, fun-loving, vivacious daughter hadn't died?
> What if the fervent and faith-filled prayers of literally thousands of people asking for her healing had been answered in the way we wanted?
> What if her life hadn't been cut short when she caught glandular fever which, along with cystic fibrosis and an antibiotic-resistant bacteria,

formed a lethal cocktail for her usually strong body?

What if she could have lived a long life, helping people in her career as a paramedic and making a positive difference in the world?

What if as a mother I could somehow have protected her from a horrendous death at the terribly young age of twenty-five?

What if she hadn't been born with cystic fibrosis in the first place?

What if there is a completely different perspective, an alternative way to view all the "facts"? One which turns everything on its head, which seems so totally counterintuitive that it's hard to even consider?

What if being born with cystic fibrosis was what made her the incredible, amazing person she was, touching thousands of lives throughout the world in her quiet, unassuming way?

What if, somehow, in spite of everything within me rebelling against the notion, dying at just twenty-five years of age was really always the plan?

What if Psalm 139 really means it when it states that "all the days of her life were written before even one of them came to be"?

What if "dying before her time" means she is spared future pain on this earth and lives in perfect peace and health and favour, bathed and immersed in love we can only dream of?

What if the difference she makes in the world comes through her courage in suffering and how she never let it break her spirit or steal her smile or diminish her heart for others?

What if the true purpose of her life was to show others how to be brave and live fully in the face of insurmountable pain and challenges?

What if someone whose life she touched goes on to

- change the world because of what they saw in her?
- What if her grace and dignity through suffering spoke volumes to all the doctors and nurses and others who watched her day by day?
- What if it affected them so much that the ripples spill out to benefit all their future patients and families?
- What if, rather than being the one whose life was "cut short" she has a better life than any of us?
- What if, rather than feeling sorry for that poor girl who died at twenty-five, we should all be so envious that she got to catch an early flight to eternity?
- What if this life is just a foretaste of what LIFE is really meant to be?
- What if, even now, as I miss her with every breath, she is living a life of so much beauty and joy and happiness that I can't even imagine it?
- What if the fervent and faith-filled prayers of literally thousands of people asking for her healing really were answered in a way far better than the one we wanted?
- What if my precious, beautiful, fun-loving, vivacious daughter is not really dead, but truly and fully alive for the first time and forevermore?

What if…? What if…?

~

IN APRIL, we're invited to stay at Trinity Beach in Far North Queensland again. It's an opportunity we gladly seize. This time we're emotionally able to spend more time with our friends Janine and Cam and to visit local nature spots.

The relaxation and processing I'm able to achieve while walking on the beach and resting at the unit continues, but unanswered questions, regrets and "what ifs" continue to challenge me.

All of Kari's life involved a huge effort to keep her well enough for long enough that a cure could be found, or at least until medication could be developed that would significantly extend her life expectancy. The Vertex study she signed up for in June 2012 had that potential and now the resulting new medications are looking like they might lead to unbelievable improvements, adding potentially twenty or more years to those living with CF.

I wrestle with the apparent unfairness of it. Why couldn't she have stayed alive long enough to benefit? Would she still be here if she'd had access to those drugs? Why did all our efforts appear not to make a difference to her lifespan? Of course, I'm so happy for those who are benefitting, but it's bittersweet.

I still don't understand why God would bring a beautiful Christian husband along, seemingly in answer to my prayers, and then allow Kari to catch glandular fever. I still regret letting Kari-Lee go to New Zealand with Tiana. The glandular fever hadn't yet been diagnosed, but she was probably sicker than any of us realised. Because I was so caught up with all the terrible things happening with Peter, perhaps my attention wasn't as fully on Kari as usual and I didn't see how sick she was. I didn't notice that she wasn't eating or exercising. I feel deep guilt over that. She wasn't living at home and would never have admitted those things, because she hated me making any fuss – but still I should have paid more attention.

Maybe I missed an important opportunity at the clinic in January, when she was obviously unwell but wasn't seen. Maybe if I'd pushed harder, tracked down the nurses, if someone had admitted her to hospital then, she would never have become so gravely ill. Maybe if I'd realised just how dire the situation was, we would have returned to the clinic before March. Unseen by any of us, her health was deteriorating drastically that whole time. She was far sicker than any of us comprehended.

I know these ruminations aren't helpful, yet they bubble up uninvited during quiet moments.

In my search for help and answers to questions that threaten to destroy any peace I might find, I spend time online, accessing various support groups for bereaved Christian parents, which mostly seem to be in America. Late last year I found a helpful Facebook group called *Heartache and Hope: Life After Losing a Child*. There's a blog attached by Melanie DeSimone and I soon discover that she seems able to read my thoughts and put them into words better than I can. Her son died in a motorcycle accident six months before Kari-Lee, at a similar age. I appreciate her honesty and authenticity and find myself agreeing out loud with many of her writings.

Most bereaved parents I speak to, either in person or online, particularly those who are followers of Jesus, seem to have much in common in the way of questions, challenges and experiences after their child died. It's incredibly validating to find that what I'm thinking, feeling and experiencing is "normal" for the abysmally abnormal situation we all find ourselves in.

Through Melanie, I discover and join another group called *While We're Waiting* (WWW). This group was started in Arkansas USA by two bereaved couples, Brad and Jill Sullivan and Larry and Janice Brown. They began with retreats for bereaved parents, adding support groups and building a refuge where retreats are now held on most weekends. I'm not initially aware just how life-changing this group will be for me, but I benefit from reading and interacting with posts from other believers whose children have gone ahead of them to heaven.

IT'S MAY. My birthday month. We're in a huge hall. The air hums with expectancy as we take our seats. The lights dim. Conversation ceases. Anticipation rises.

Suddenly, a spotlight flashes on the back of the room as a stream of dancers in exotic and colourful costumes burst into the room accompanied by an energetic samba band. As they thread their way through tables filled with people, they dance to the front and up onto the stage. We're transported to Brazil, swept up in the glamour and wild celebratory atmosphere of Carnival.

It's an awesome opening to the Gala Latin Ball honouring Kari. Tears fill my eyes, even as a smile illuminates my face. Kari would absolutely love this.

The night is a great success. Entertaining acts fill the stage for hours, interspersed with dinner courses, then followed by Latin dancing for everyone to join until midnight. A video of Kari-Lee is played, the highlight of the night for me. The photos flash through, mostly Kari enjoying life, to the background music of *I Hope You Dance* sung by Ronan Keating. I've included a few pictures showing her courageous battle in hospital, something many of these people are unaware of. I see people dabbing their eyes with tissues and know that her story is touching people's hearts. I'll never let her be forgotten.

∼

JUNE 19TH. Kari's birthday. I've had my early morning walk on Kari's beach with Maloo, my mind filled with memories, my heart squeezed with longing.

Now Tiana, Nana and I are off on a momentous outing, heading to the shop to make a final decision on Tiana's wedding dress. When she steps out from behind the dressing-room curtain, spontaneous gasps of admiration slip from our lips. It's perfect. It's an auspicious moment, one that Kari should have been sharing, one of many where her absence is deeply felt. My momentary sadness turns to laughter when Tiana spins around and we see that the dress is being held together at the back by giant pegs because it's way too big for her.

We take advantage of being together to snatch a moment out for tea and cake at Silva Spoon, Kari-Lee's favourite teahouse. Happy birthday, Kari.

∼

IN JUNE, July and August I attend the *While We're Waiting* support group in Arkansas. Of course, I don't go to Arkansas, but with the wonders of modern technology I can be part of the group via FaceTime while remaining in Australia. While I mostly just listen, it's refreshing to be with others who need no explanation of the manifold emotions which shape my every day.

I start to realise that a support group like this could be a great help in achieving the best outcome for my life after farewelling Kari.

∼

AUGUST BRINGS a joyful celebration of Tiana's engagement, where family members from each side get to meet each other for the first time. Memories of Kari and Nic's engagement party, which became their secret wedding, threaten to creep in and tarnish my enjoyment of the night. I banish these thoughts, so that I can fully focus on Tiana and Matt on their special night. I never want to let the pain of missing the one who's left me cause me to miss the one I still have here with me.

The party is on the same day as Pa's eighty-ninth birthday. He and Mum are still muddling along at home. Their mobility is diminishing, their Meals on Wheels are often left on the bench decaying, their medications somehow muddled up despite being in pharmacy blister packs. They're needing more and more help from all of us, which we're happy to provide, but we wonder if their safety will one day soon be compromised. Mum's already spent a few nights in hospital after overdosing on her blood-thinning medication. They're not willing to consider any alternative care yet.

I'm continuing to thrive in my position as nanny, although I work very hard. The entertaining toddler, along with Maloo at home, are the ones who bring me the most laughter and fun these days. It's important for me to be able to laugh at their antics, because so much of life still seems sad and grey.

A Global Leadership Summit is being held in November and I've been gifted a ticket. I tentatively make my way to a seat, only to notice that sitting quite close to me is a friend I haven't seen for years. It's my best friend of twenty-five years, who started fading from my life when Peter had his breakdown and who disappeared completely soon after Kari died.

It's an awkward situation, but I invite her to sit next to me. We spend the day chatting as acquaintances, the many years of deep, close friendship seemingly wiped out.

I know my experience isn't unique in the world of child loss. So many other bereaved parents have shared how friends they thought would be there for life slowly drifted away after the death of their child. It happened with several of my friends. Initially, I was hurt and upset by their actions, feeling abandoned and betrayed at a time when I needed them most. I've come to understand that there are all sorts of reasons why this happens. Sometimes friendships are for a season, long or short, and when that season ends we just have to accept the situation.

The flip side is the new friends who we meet, and the friends who weren't so close but choose to come alongside us in the depths of our grief and are now treasured companions.

∼

As a result of feeling quite alone at times in my grief, combined with the benefit I've gained from being a part of WWW groups through online access, I decide to apply to be a local support group facilitator. It's quite a bold move as there are no other groups outside the US. I must pass their screening process, but once I'm successful I start planning my group, aiming to commence in January 2018.

I've facilitated many support groups over the years – CF support group, adoption support group and home groups – but this one feels extra important and I want to get it just right. My capacity for organisation, along with many other skills, is diminished since Kari left.

Of course, the best preparation is for me to saturate the whole enterprise in prayer. If I'm honest, my natural inclination is to be a "doer" rather than a "pray-er", but without God's help and presence this group will be worthless.

∼

2018 looms as a big year, especially the first half of the year.

I want to be very involved in Tiana's wedding preparations – as much as she's willing to accept. She's booked a beautiful venue at a historic homestead in the country, an authentic vintage setting, which aligns perfectly with Tiana's vision. We'll be making as many of the accessories as we can – invitations, table decorations, wedding favours, signage – to make it unique and personalised.

As well as the wedding, Peter and I are both turning sixty and we've planned a month-long camping and hiking trip through the Kimberley region in north-west Western Australia.

I decide that now's the right time for me to have some time off work. After tentatively trying work in security for a season, Peter has recently begun steady employment driving school buses, so mine is not the only income. I feel I need the longer break I didn't really get to have after Kari-Lee died. I'm a little wary of telling my employer, but as I start to explain she chuckles and informs me that she was planning to speak to me that day as well. She's wanting to reduce her work hours and so won't need my nanny services anymore.

It's perfect. A God-arranged timing. I finish the year looking forward to new chapters ahead.

AFTER: CHAPTER FOURTEEN

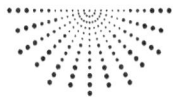

"*I*'m exhausted, Rhyl. I don't think I can do this anymore. I think it's time."

These words from my sweet Mum are the catalyst for huge changes. She and Dad are moving into a nursing home, something Dad swore he'd never do. His gradual deterioration, both physical and mental, has reached the stage where Mum can no longer cope at home, even with all the family support and input from government agencies.

Packing-up over forty years of family life begins in earnest. Their new room, while comfortable and spacious, is small compared to a full home, so difficult decisions need to be made.

Initially, we visit daily to help the settling-in process. Dad, believing he's just there for a short respite, copes better than we expected. It's still difficult though, seeing our strong, intelligent, immensely capable and supportive parents reduced to living in one room, without the ability to even make themselves a cup of tea due to safety rules.

It will be a significant adjustment for all of us. Just because I've lost a child doesn't mean I'm spared the other griefs of life.

MEANWHILE, amongst these changes, on a quiet Tuesday evening in January, eight people gather in a meeting room at Goodlife Community Centre. It's the beginning of the While We're Waiting support group, Australian style.

It's a little strange at first, but we soon warm to the topics brought up by the WWW devotional. We speak freely of our children who no longer live on earth with us, sharing stories, laughter and tears, with a depth of understanding that brings great comfort. This core group will continue to meet monthly for the rest of the year, with occasional visits from parents living in Brisbane.

IN MARCH, I start a new hobby, one which helps me feel closer to Kari-Lee but will also hopefully help my brain function a bit better. I begin Italian lessons with a group of other women, casual lessons where we have lots of fun and challenge our minds and memories.

The end of March brings Easter, during which we're able to enjoy a much-needed break at a friend's home at the beach. Matt and Tiana join us for several days and it's a great opportunity to spend time with Matt and get to know our future son-in-law a little better. A week later, it's time for Tiana's bridal shower at our house. Friends and family crowd into our lounge room. Laughter rings out as we play silly games, eat delicious food and make Tiana feel like a princess.

Around this time, Nic marries again. While the thought of this is traumatic for me, I cope much better with this than I did when he first told us he was dating. Over three years have passed since Kari left us for Heaven, and that's about the time I expected him to be seeking a new partner. Tiana, however, finds the thought of this incredibly traumatising and triggering, with many unresolved issues. I try to help her work through her feelings, but she's prickly and hurt and the anger remains.

May arrives and ushers in the second Latin Gala Ball in memory of our darling Kari-Lee. It's a wonderful night and I delight in the fact that it's honouring my Kari. Next day I'm brought crashing back to earth with yet another Mother's Day without my firstborn baby here to celebrate with me. As the years pass, in some ways it gets easier, because I've survived these days before so I know I can do it. Yet in some ways it gets harder because more time has passed since she was here for Mother's Day, my birthday and all the other special days throughout the years. So many special days without the effervescent presence of my happy-hearted girl.

A week later, amidst animated chatter and peals of laughter, I take a quiet moment to look around me and be thankful. Seated around the table are twelve of my closest friends, women who've been there for me during the last painful four years. Voices rise and fall like waves on the sea, swirling around me as women from different arenas of my life get to know each other, sharing stories and soup and laughter.

It's my sixtieth birthday and I'm celebrating quietly but meaningfully. My sister Ann is hosting at her home and has decorated beautifully with ocean-themed items, along with a masterpiece birthday cake with artistically created frangipani and seashells. My other sister Claire oversees activities, leading my friends in making mini canvases depicting aspects of our friendships and answering silly quiz questions to see who knows me best. Tiana has joined us and is home for the next whole week, leading up to her wedding. I feel loved, valued and appreciated. What more could anyone want?

Except, perhaps, that ever-smiling girl of mine, who contributed so much to my fiftieth birthday party, when none of us suspected that she might not be here for this one.

JUST A WEEK LATER, I'm driving our red Mazda 3 around tight corners of a country road behind the Sunshine Coast. Tiana sits beside me in a state of heightened anxiety, her attention fully focused on the rear seat, where her two friends delicately balance a stunning three tier wedding cake as I hurtle along trying to make up lost time. It's Tiana's wedding day and we're heading to the bridal villa at Glengariff to prepare for the big event.

We arrive safely to find the hairdresser waiting and the makeup artist on her way. Champagne and laughter, breakfast platters and fizzing excitement, are tempered briefly as Tiana takes a moment alone on the verandah. It hits her afresh that one person who should be here by her side is missing, never to be a part of any milestone events in her life again.

Because Kari had a surprise wedding with no attendants, Tiana wasn't able to be a part of the build-up and anticipation, nor to have a major role in that event. And now, she's unable to share all of the emotions of this current watershed moment. One of her friends sees Tiana struggling and comforts her. We're all aware of the gaping hole where a different matron of honour would have stood, had life turned out differently.

Time flies along and before I know it I'm seated in the tranquil outdoor setting, surrounded by peaceful countryside, craning my neck to see Tiana arrive. On the seat next to me is "Kari's" bouquet and bridesmaid's dress in a different colour from the others, providing a poignant backdrop to a small photo of smiling Kari-Lee on her wedding day. Just as I start to drift towards sadness, my attention is captured by the beaming bride walking down the steps on the arm of her proud Dad, making her way down the rose-petal-covered grassy aisle. The moving words of *Turning Page* sung by Sleeping At Last waft through the beautiful outdoor setting, as Tiana passes me, heading for her destiny and her future.

Matt's tears fall as he gazes at his beautiful bride. After a reading of 1 Corinthians 13 (Kari's favourite) and some wise words from Bruce, they vow to love each other for better or worse.

Maloo, the ring-bearer, creates a happy stir as she makes her way down the aisle in her flower-bedecked collar and lead with the ring box firmly attached.

Touching reminders of Kari are everywhere: a decorative tree covered in white origami cranes, a piece of her wedding dress sewn into Tiana's bouquet, the photo and dress beside me.

Time out for photos around the picturesque farm setting, followed by a plentiful banquet, entertaining speeches, cake cutting and sweet dances lead to the culmination of the evening with a sparkler guard of honour.

Next morning I'm in that recurring international airport setting again, waving off two bleary-eyed lovebirds as they jet to Fiji for their honeymoon.

~

WE BARELY GET our feet back on the ground when, a week later, we return to the airport to collect the happy couple. After settling them into their cute inner-city apartment, we head back to Rosemount to prepare for our own departure from the airport, scheduled in one week's time. It's our turn to board a plane and jet off for an adventure.

As always when we take off, I close my eyes and see Kari-Lee, her eyes sparkling with excitement, her smile wide, face glowing as she whispers, "Wooohooo," revelling in the sensation of the plane taking off, flying her to another exhilarating adventure.

We settle in for two long flights, over 5,000 km total. Australia sure is a big country.

White sandy beaches stretching as far as the eye can see are edged with rugged, red, rocky cliffs, plunging into unbelievably intense aquamarine waters, framed by a canopy of dazzling azure sky. We've finally arrived in Broome, on the north-west coast of Western Australia. Our accommodation is perfect: a pool to swim laps, the famous Cable Beach just a few kilometres walk away, a local bus stop at our doorstep and a generous buffet breakfast every morning. After a week exploring the area, we meet our future travelling companions at a hostel in the centre of Broome.

We set off in a specially adapted 4WD bus. On the third day, it's Kari's birthday, a day we can't let slip by without recognition. Even though we've only just met these people, we decide to share a makeshift birthday cake. People are kind as we sit around the campfire, sharing cake along with stories of our cherished girl.

The next two weeks enclosed in our travelling home soon iron out any awkwardness and we spend hours chatting, laughing, dozing. Along the way there are hikes to spectacular locations. Highlights include the Bungle Bungles, Mitchell Falls, Bell Gorge, Lake Argyle.

Late afternoons are spent collecting firewood and stacking it on the roof of the bus, ready for the evening cooking session. As we pull into our campsite each evening, we gather at the back of the bus where our tents, swags and bags are tossed from the baggage compartment. Soon everyone is busy racing to get their tent up, their swag rolled out and maybe squeeze in a quick shower (if there are facilities) before dinner. We all pitch in to help prepare, serve and clean up after dinner.

Although the days are mostly warm, the nights are cold and trips to the outdoor toilets located some distance from the tents are only undertaken when absolutely necessary. The reward for such bravery is a magnificent view of a star-studded sky, brilliant with countless more stars than are visible in civilisation. I gaze up into the heavens, imagining where Kari might be right now, enjoying wonderful experiences beyond my wildest imagining. After a bit of star-gazing, it's time to hurry back and snuggle into a nice warm sleeping bag nestled in a swag, designed to keep the cold at bay.

Just when we're getting used to sleeping on hard ground, using drop toilets and skipping showers when necessary, we reach our destination of Darwin. This is where Peter and I met, courted and spent the first year of our marriage. We crane our necks looking out the windows, trying to recognise familiar landmarks. We sleep gratefully in a comfortable motel bed, before heading to our Airbnb on the marina in the morning. We meet our jovial hosts, who are bursting with local knowledge and suggestions for our stay. Our week is filled with discoveries of many things which have changed greatly in thirty-three years, alongside finding some treasured gems from the past.

August brings the inauguration of a new home group at our place, another stint as a volunteer at the Ekka, and Dad's ninetieth birthday.

In September, we're again invited to holiday in Trinity Beach and we gratefully accept. This time I arrive a week before Peter and travel four hours north on the bus to Cooktown, to stay with a friend from the old days, who's been caring and supportive since Kari died. I celebrate her sixtieth birthday with her and explore this tiny town way in the north of Australia.

On my return to Trinity Beach to meet Peter, I realise that the difference from our very first stay here is enormous. Now we're able to enjoy the beach, the pool and the natural attractions all around the Cairns district.

Unfortunately, Peter becomes very unwell with shingles, so I'm left on my own a lot. While I manage alone, I still see glimpses of that shattered pair of hollowed-out individuals who first brought their broken hearts and pain-riddled bodies to this beautiful setting. Four years has made a big difference, but we're forever changed and remoulded by the tragedy of Kari's departure.

∼

WE RETURN HOME in time to pack up Christmas boxes for children living in poverty – twenty-nine this year, the age Kari would have been.

Around this time, I start to feel odd sensations, like something is wrong but I'm not sure what it is. My sleep is affected. I'm agitated for no apparent reason. I feel melancholy, gloomy, devitalised. I feel fractious, impatient, peevish. Then I realise.

It's October. Kari's Heaven Day is approaching. Even when I don't consciously think about the date, my body and heart remember.

We make our way to Kari's beach in the morning, take Maloo for a run on the dog beach, watch videos, and the painful arrows of loss and grief pierce my heart again. Will this day ever get any easier? I really don't know the answer to that, but it hasn't happened yet.

Christmas follows all too soon, with a similar feeling. I can now cope with the commotion of the extended-family celebrations, which initially were overwhelming and mind-blowing.

Yet still the missing piece, the missing smile, the missing giggle causes unexpected ambushes, tiny trickles of tears and painful wringing of my heart. Celebrations are no longer occasions of unadulterated joy. There's always something not quite right.

Kari's not here. Kari's missing. Kari's gone.

AFTER: CHAPTER FIFTEEN

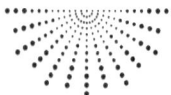

My work life is non-existent. While I planned to have six months off in 2018, that's stretched to a whole year. It's time to get serious about finding another job.

I apply for a position nannying for slightly older children, even though that's not my preference. It starts off well, but the children don't seem to listen and often refuse to do what I ask of them. Emotionally, I'm unable to cope and drive home from work crying most days. I feel trapped. I hate to give up so soon.

I give notice during my trial period. The parents are upset and ask me not to come back. I'm devastated by the whole situation. It's an unwelcome reminder that I'm far from the person I used to be. I don't have the emotional resilience and capacity for stress that I once had. Kari's death has changed me irrevocably and my inner resources will obviously take much longer to return to what they once were. I'm not even sure if that will ever happen.

EARLY IN THE YEAR, I begin to sense that our WWW meetings for bereaved parents aren't working. Most of the dads choose not to attend and those who do seem unwilling to share.

It becomes clear to me after much prayer and working through my feelings of failure that God is leading me in a different way. I make the difficult decision to replace these meetings with a WWW support group just for bereaved mums.

With many of the same participants, we begin meeting in March. Immediately, the spirit of the meetings changes. All who attend are willing participants. Five core members attend every month and another five attend intermittently.

I feel God has his hand on this group and it's making a difference in the lives of these mums, as well as in my own life. It's not always easy, but I feel it's worthwhile.

IN MARCH, my dad becomes unwell and it very quickly morphs into life-threatening pneumonia. My brother flies up from Canberra and we four siblings spend most of the next five days in Mum and Dad's room, as he slowly but steadily deteriorates. I try to speak to him about Heaven, but I'm not sure he's hearing.

After days of laborious breathing, he slips away, leaving Mum a widow after sixty-seven years of marriage.

I'm sad. He was a good Dad. We'll miss him, especially Mum. But, with a sense of guilt, I feel nothing like the devastation I felt when Kari breathed her last. Dad was ninety years old, lived a good life with a long span of years. Everyone must die one day and this was his time. It feels absolutely and completely different from Kari's death.

I'm sure some people won't understand, especially those who've only lost elderly parents. For them, it's the worst loss that's happened so they feel it more deeply, I think. I decide that I don't need to justify my feelings. They are what they are.

We plan a very personal farewell, with each of his four children sharing special memories and some of his favourite music playing. I hope he's gone to join Kari and that I'll see him again one day. His faith was something very personal to him, something he wouldn't talk about with me, so I'll just have to trust my loving and merciful Heavenly Father with Dad's future.

JUNE BRINGS A SPECIAL OCCASION: Kari-Lee's thirtieth birthday. Her life expectancy of thirty at diagnosis makes this a milestone day.

I decide to have a party. One brave friend tells me he thinks it's weird, but I'm past caring about what other people think. I decide to have a picnic, which Kari loved, combined with a sausage sizzle, another of her favourites. I invite some of her friends and mine.

We gather on a sunny, fresh winter's day on a green grassy hill at my sister Ann's place. We sit and share stories of Kari, relax with warm chatter, just as Kari-Lee would have loved. We sing "Happy Birthday" and cut a beautiful cake with shells and frangipani and her treasured name.

Somehow, it feels like a bit of a full stop. I won't have another party in her memory, but her birthday will always be a deeply meaningful day when God blessed me with the inestimable gift of a much-longed-for baby.

IN JULY, a horrific event occurs. My faithful friend Leanne rings, asking me, in a voice almost unrecognisable, to pray. Her son, Michael, has gone spear fishing, but hasn't surfaced from his last dive. People are searching for him, but it's not looking good.

Finally, Mike's body is recovered from the ocean floor. Leanne and her husband John are now facing the devastating loss of their precious middle son. Their Christian faith is deep and strong, but I know from my own experience that they'll need every ounce of faith, strength and courage to survive this loss well.

Leanne has been a trustworthy support to me since Kari left for Heaven, one of only a handful of people who have truly been there for me, not trying to fix me, but listening and sharing in helpful ways. I long to be that support for her. Even having experienced the loss of my own child, it's hard to know exactly how much presence or space they might prefer.

We visit the next day, bringing a meal, but only staying briefly, as family have arrived. I phone and text regularly to offer company, meals, a listening ear, or anything else they might find helpful.

Their large family and multitude of friends gather around them and Leanne expresses her preference for us to wait. Wait until people have returned to their normal lives. Wait until some people might expect them to be getting back to their own lives. I honour her wishes.

∽

After not working since February, I'm employed in August as nanny for a cute eleven-month-old girl. I'm grateful for the time I've had off work, as it's given me time and head space to sort our house, which has been suffering from years of neglect.

When Kari was so sick in hospital, I spent my time either at work or in Brisbane. Then, in the years since Kari died, I haven't had the emotional or mental capacity to care much about housework or tidying.

I'm grateful I've been able to spend time sorting through Kari's belongings in a more thorough and systematic way. It's a deeply emotional task, which takes a toll and which needs to be done slowly and mindfully. I don't think I could have done it before now.

Occasionally I discover hidden treasures, like a card from one of Kari's CF doctors. The words bring tears, yet immense comfort.

"Kari-Lee was such an inspirational, brave and determined young woman. She taught me so much about strength and resilience. Despite being so unwell at times, I never heard her complain. We used to fight over who was going to see Kari in clinic as she was such a delight. I feel privileged to have known Kari and played a small role in her life."

∽

September. In the airport. On the plane. My ears are assaulted by an ever-building roar, as the enormous steel bird carries me up into the sky and away for three weeks' adventure on the other side of the world. I close my eyes and picture Kari, eyes glowing with excitement, mouth wide in a huge smile.

I'm off for an awesome experience learning more about the life-changing ministry of While We're Waiting.

Nineteen long hours later, my stomach churns as we float to the ground in Dallas, Texas. I weave my way through crowds of people speaking in broad Southern accents, out of the doors into steamy sunshine.

A generous couple I've never met before wave me over and bundle me into their car. I'm whisked away for a five-hour drive to Hot Springs Arkansas. As darkness approaches, we wind up a long driveway between majestic trees to the While We're Waiting Refuge, set in beautiful rolling hills outside the city. I'm handed over to Jill and Brad Sullivan, who greet me warmly and show me to a cosy double room with an ensuite. It's one of ten lining the accommodation corridor, providing visiting parents with a private oasis. So begins my three weeks attending retreats at the WWW refuge.

After a good night's sleep in a comfortable bed, I'm raring to go. Just as well, because there's lots to do in preparation for the upcoming retreat. There are beds to be made, food to be cooked, resources to be collated, tables to be decorated. I help in any way I can. Great attention to detail ensures that participating couples feel safe, cared for, pampered.

Friday night comes and couples begin to arrive for the weekend, some shy and hesitant, some more outgoing, some obviously still in the depths of fresh grief. One of the participants is a mum who I've become friends with through our online group After65roses. It's great to meet her in person as well as another couple who also lost their daughter to CF. There's a common bond of understanding.

Attendees span many demographics: different ages, different states, different lengths of time since their child died, different ages of their children now in Heaven. We're all united in our common grief of farewelling a beloved child, while trying to find meaning and purpose in continuing life on earth without our precious child's presence.

Much of the weekend is spent in the Liferoom, sharing our stories, discussing relevant topics, praying and ministering to each other amid tears and laughter. Mealtimes are equally important, mixing in a less structured setting, yet still sharing our stories. Evenings outdoors around the firepit, Saturday afternoon activities, a quiet walk on the bush track, chatting on the verandah or resting in our rooms, give plenty of opportunities for discussion, reflection or solitude. Dinner on Saturday evening is a formal affair with five courses prepared by a local chef who donates his time to the Refuge.

Sunday morning starts with a worship service after breakfast and before we know it, the weekend is over and it's time to say goodbye. Everybody leaves with their hope bolstered that life can go on, it can be meaningful and even, at some point, joyful again.

Things are quiet at the Refuge after everyone leaves, but there's plenty to do. Mountains of sheets and towels need to be washed. Decorations put away. Food packed down. Next weekend, many of the support group facilitators will be gathering for their annual retreat.

During the week, I help with whatever needs doing and enjoy getting to know Jill better. I join in the local WWW support group. The Facilitator's Retreat will have a slightly different focus from the Parent's Retreat, as we discuss our groups and how we might improve them. All the facilitators are bereaved parents themselves, so we share stories about our children in Heaven. It's an uplifting and faith-building weekend.

Following the Facilitator's Retreat, I take some time exploring around Hot Springs. One evening we go to see the new *Downton Abbey* movie. Because of its association with the early days after Kari died, I'd warned Jill that the opening music would probably make me cry, and I don't disappoint.

On my last Saturday at the Refuge, we have a Mom's Day Retreat. Each retreat has volunteers who help in the kitchen, people who've previously attended a retreat themselves. This time, one of the volunteers is taking me back to her home in Texas for a few days before I fly home.

Her husband drives us to the tiny town of Barclay, Texas. My new friend shows me to my room, and there on the bedside table are some very special touches. Photos of my darling Kari-Lee, a notebook with photos of Kari, a wall-hanging with sunflowers, as well as lots of lovely gifts representative of Texas. Only another bereaved mum could understand how precious these touches would be to the heart of someone missing her child every minute of the day. I'm so grateful.

We have a few fun-filled days together, exploring the local area and enjoying some authentic Texan experiences, before I'm dropped in downtown Dallas for a bus tour of the city. Then it's time for the long journey home.

BACK ON THE SUNSHINE COAST, it's October again, coming up to five years since Kari took her last breaths of Earth's air.

It doesn't get any easier. She's still gone.

After a trip to Kari's beach with Maloo, I spend parts of the day with different friends and family members who are kind enough to be with me on this difficult day.

I take on another difficult task that's been churning through my mind. For several years, I've been working through my feelings about interactions with Nic after Kari died. There's a lot of hurt, disappointment and questions. I'm sorry for the way I spoke to him when he came to tell us he was dating again. I was completely ambushed by shock and grief, but I need to ask forgiveness for my reaction.

I've also had to do some serious reframing related to my understanding of things he and his family said and did to me, to Tiana and to Peter. It's taken time and lots of mental grappling, but I've come to understand that he reacted and grieved in ways that were vastly different from mine, but that is his prerogative. He doesn't owe us anything. He promised to love and cherish Kari-Lee until death separated them and he honoured that promise.

I need to let go of any unmet expectations, hurt and disappointment, and choose to forgive. I write a letter, pray intensely over the wording, run it past my counsellor and wait for the right time to deliver it.

IN NOVEMBER, I see yet another Facebook post saying "God is good" when someone gets the job they'd hoped for. It's a recurring theme when people's prayers are answered in the way they'd hoped.

My question is, "What if that doesn't happen? What if the healing, new job, or financial help doesn't come? What if the worst happens? Is God still good? Or is He only good when He does what we want?" It's something I've really had to wrestle with over the past five years.

I volunteer to speak in the "Magnificent 7" segment at our church, where people can share how God is working in their lives. I want to talk about God's goodness, but also challenge people.

This type of opportunity wouldn't have arisen had Kari been healed. It in no way makes her loss okay, but it does show me that there can still be a purpose for my life. Perhaps God can still use the broken, shattered, questioning pieces of my heart to make a difference in this broken, shattered, questioning world.

AFTER: CHAPTER SIXTEEN

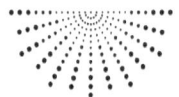

*2*020 ushers in a change in my grief. Something has shifted slightly after five years. It's hard to describe, but I feel like life can possibly be meaningful, perhaps even joyful again.

I still frequently tear up. A sight, a sound, a smell – often for no obvious reason except that Kari's still not here.

I've planned another walking holiday in Tasmania, with Peter joining me afterwards for a few weeks' exploring. Out of the blue, amid ongoing wet weather, I slip, fall and injure my knee, making the walk unattainable. Thoughts echo of the initial abandonment of the Victorian walk, but this time when I cancel there's a new looming shadow over the world. COVID makes its presence felt in Australia and by the time I would have flown, closed state borders render it impossible.

The initial season of COVID is like nothing my generation has experienced. Shocking newsreels of rapidly escalating deaths all over the world lead to community feelings of anxiety and despair for the future. Everyone is told to stay home. Everything is cancelled.

Yet this enforced confinement has its positive aspects. Life slows down, becomes simple. While my current nanny job finishes during COVID, another one started in February with another cute eleven-month-old girl and her five-year-old sister. In August I add a second family, with yet another adorable eleven-month-old girl. Working with young children, while physically demanding, continues to bring joy and laughter to my days. I work long nine-hour days with one family and twelve-hour days with the other. By the end of those days, I really feel my age, but I need the spontaneous fun and innocent entertainment that the girls bring me.

Working in the vegetable garden, cleaning out cupboards, cooking healthy meals, scrapbooking photos of Kari, talking on the phone with friends, spending time with Peter and Maloo fills my days at home during COVID lockdowns. We take the opportunity to give our kitchen a much-needed renovation. While it's wonderful to have a clean, modern space, it's hard to say goodbye to the stove that Kari cooked on, the benches where Kari prepared her school lunches and the cupboards where she reached for her cereal. So many memories tied up in those material structures, memories that will live on long after the cupboards are gone. It's another unexpected aspect of grief.

In amongst the sad, I'm grateful to have a bubbly girl in our granny flat, which we started renting out soon after Tiana moved back to Brisbane. The previous tenant was an older woman who kept to herself, but this girl is a breath of fresh air, so much like Kari-Lee. We have lots of chats, cups of tea and laughter. She brings light and life to our home.

I manage to deliver my letter to Nic's office, asking for forgiveness.

I'm thankful for the activities that continue online. KYB (Know Your Bible) has been an important part of my life for many years. Since Kari died, I've been privileged to take Mum with me to our group. While the group continues to operate through FaceTime, sadly, Mum's unable to leave the nursing home due to COVID restrictions. Even more difficult are the restrictions on visiting her. For several months, there's no visiting at all. Finally, restrictions relax enough to allow us to enter a special room, which is disinfected between visits, restricted to two people for one hour only.

We're seated across from Mum with a huge perspex screen between us. Face masks make conversation difficult, but we're glad to be able to see Mum. In her usual cheerful manner, she's not too bothered by all the restrictions and enjoys looking out her window or reading her books.

As COVID ebbs and flows throughout the year, Peter and I take opportunities for short trips away. They refresh and revive us. When that's not possible due to lockdowns and travel restrictions, we take advantage of the stunning beaches at our doorstep. A regular routine several times a week involves a trip to the dog beach. I take a long solitary walk while Peter throws sticks in the surf for Maloo, followed by coffee together in the park.

These walks on the beach are vital for my mental health. It's where I do my best processing and grief work, as well as often writing chunks of my proposed book in my head. Occasionally we're joined by John and Leanne. They're still in deep grief, missing Mike and working through what it all means. Although I wish neither of us had experienced this, it's interesting for each of us to now be "on the other side". We're now the ones offering comfort and a listening ear while they wrestle with the deep questions and intense longing for their son.

COVID restrictions continue in 2021, but Peter and I manage to get away for several short breaks to beautiful seaside areas or mountains. In May, we spend a week in a cosy B&B with Maloo, then another week hiking through the natural beauty of Carnarvon Gorge, in western Queensland.

June brings Kari's birthday and this year I decide to start a new tradition. Kari may not be here for me to treat on her birthday, but Tiana is. I know she misses Kari-Lee too. I plan a special outing that Kari would have enjoyed. We go to the ballet in Brisbane to see *Sleeping Beauty*. It's a memorable evening, with champagne, fancy clothes and new experiences.

Tiana's made some huge changes in her life recently, starting her own business making healthy, beautifully presented treats for dogs, using her pastry chef skills. She calls her business "Floofy Patisserie". It starts small, but in August she takes her products to several markets in Brisbane and resigns from her chef job to work fulltime in her business. She's an incredibly hard worker, which soon pays off. Her business grows, along with her happiness.

MY CONNECTIONS with the Christian bereaved parents' community in America continue to provide vital support. Throughout the year, I'm involved as a "beta reader", providing feedback for an upcoming devotional book called *Reflections of Hope*, being written by Laura Diehl, who has a ministry called "GPS Hope: Grieving Parents Share Hope". I join in an online study of Nancy Guthrie's book *Holding On to Hope* via Zoom, led by Gary and Laura House who have a ministry called "Our Hearts Are Home". From August to November, I take part in a GriefShare group led by Jennifer Coleman, also on Zoom.

All these interactions with fellow bereaved parents who are believers provide comfort, validation and opportunities to continue processing the many deep questions which arise.

2022 STARTS brightly with a trip to Woodgate Beach. Our faithful Maloo brings us joy frolicking in the ocean, running alongside us on our bikes and accompanying us on all our outings. Such a happy, healthy girl for eight years old.

Soon after our return, she vomits up some blood and what looks like a piece of tooth. We book her in to have her teeth cleaned as we notice her breath starting to smell, a common problem as dogs age.

Without warning, our lives change when the vet rings us with unbelievable news. A stage four oral melanoma is discovered in the roof of her mouth. Her condition is terminal.

It's impossible to comprehend as we look at our boisterous, tail-wagging, lovable companion. This can't be happening. Not Maloo. Our adored fur-baby. Our precious link to Kari-Lee.

Initially, we explore treatment options and special diets to delay the inevitable. Gradually, but persistently, the cancer takes hold, eating away at our once active and thriving puppy. Weight begins to fall off her. Her breathing becomes difficult. She starts to bleed from her mouth.

She still appears to enjoy life, so we fill her days with as much love and happiness as we can. Trips to the beach, walks in the rainforest, hugs on the recliner. She sleeps on our bed, something she's never been allowed to do. Yet even with all our love and determination, with a new diet, drug patches to relieve pain, antibiotics to deter infection, we can't halt the decline.

Eventually, just six weeks after diagnosis, we make the merciful decision that it's time to say goodbye. Surrounded by Peter, Tiana and me, lying on the outdoor couch where she spent time with Kari, we hold our precious girl as the needle in her leg does its work, her eyes close gently amidst our whispers of love, and she leaves us.

The world turns grey and sad again. Tears fall freely. This loss hurts so deeply. Why did we have to say goodbye to Maloo "before her time", just like Kari-Lee? Tiana struggles with deep-seated grief brought to the surface by this fresh loss. She takes a week off work to recover. The pain is intense, not helped by the fact that I'm battling COVID.

As soon as I'm non-infectious, Peter and I get away for a break at the beach. We're haunted by visions of Maloo as we ride our bikes, walk on the beach, or just relax. The hole she's left in our lives is deep and wide. I pray that Randy Alcorn is right in his hope that some pets might go to Heaven. If so, I'm sure Maloo will be included. It comforts my heart to think that perhaps she's been reunited with Kari and they're enjoying all the time together that they missed on earth.

A tiny black fluffball comes scampering into our home in May. Soulful black eyes, a tail with a little kink at the end and teeny floppy ears break through the sadness in our hearts and bring laughter to our lips again. Roma is a thirteen-week-old Seeing Eye Dog puppy and we're going to be her carers for the next year. The paperwork's been in the pipeline for a year with the idea that she'd be a companion for Maloo. Now Maloo is gone, but we're so glad Roma's here, with her playful antics bringing some fun and joy back into our lives. We quickly grow to love her.

Kari's birthday offers another opportunity to bless Tiana. We have a very special high tea at Customs House, overlooking the Brisbane River, with a spectacular view of the Story Bridge. This was Kari's favourite bridge. She and Tiana used to try to hold their breaths for the entire time it took to cross. It's another precious opportunity to reminisce, laugh and cry as we speak her name freely and toast her with bubbly champagne.

A wonderful opportunity to share the story of Kari-Lee with the world presents itself. Gary and Laura House are editing a book, titled *Until Then*, aimed at newly bereaved Christian parents. The thirteen chapters, each written by a bereaved parent, will share their story and how, with God's help, they've survived and hopefully thrived. I'm honoured to be asked to contribute a chapter about Kari-Lee. It seems the time is right.

While I'm not now nor ever will be "over it", I believe I've done the necessary grief work to be able to have something to offer to those coming behind. As 2 Corinthians 1:3-4 (NIV) says: "Praise be to the God … of all comfort, who comforts us in all our troubles, so that we can comfort those in any trouble with the comfort we ourselves have received from God." I've received that comfort, now it's my turn to give back.

I'm working, I'm attending church, I'm helping others where I can, I'm contributing to the world. Yes, the broken pieces of my shattered heart are still clumsily put together, with some pieces permanently missing, but I believe God can use broken vessels like me. Peter and Tiana are building their lives. Nic has a new life with a new wife, new baby, new career. The hole that Kari left will never be erased, we will never stop missing her, but all of us are taking steps forward, carrying her with us as we go.

Father's Day brings unexpected and monumental joy. We've just finished eating dinner with Matt and Tiana when Tiana presents us with a cake box. Not sure what to expect, we open it to find a tiny baby suit covered in corgis and a positive pregnancy test. Whatever we thought might be in that box, we were certainly not expecting that. It's absolutely and utterly the best news.

Their plan had been to spend the next year building up Tiana's business before trying for a baby, but God had other ideas. What an awesome blessing. A baby in May. My heart is full.

∼

22.10.22

Thump-thump. Thump-thump. Thump-thump. Windscreen wipers beating futilely, unable to keep up with the relentless deluge. Torrential rain. I peer through the thick curtain of rain, following the white line illuminated by my headlights, as Kari's little yellow sunshine car bravely pushes forward, carrying me home. It's not the way I wanted to spend the eighth anniversary of her leaving for Heaven, but life has a way of serving up challenges.

After a wonderful weekend in my hometown with my siblings, followed by my nephew's wedding, I'm on my way home. Instead of the usual quiet, reflective day for Kari's Heaven Day, I decided to be brave and accept these invitations.

The weather has been abominable all day. It's been a hard day, a really hard day, but I've learned over the past ten years that I can do hard things. With God, I can do hard things. I may not want to, but I can do hard things.

Today didn't turn out how I'd planned. The last ten years didn't turn out how I'd planned. My life hasn't turned out how I'd planned. As the Steven Curtis Chapman song *Finish What He Started* describes, it sometimes feels like my life is falling apart. As with so many of his songs, the following verses bring hope and comfort, as he reminds me again that God is in control. Somehow, no matter how bad it feels right now, God will redeem this time. Somehow, He will make something beautiful of what seems to be a tangled mess. Somehow, all that has happened will be used and woven into His plan.

I'm choosing to trust that God will use everything in my life for His purpose, even what seems dreadful to me. It's not easy, this trust. Through it all, along with the apostle Paul, I consider that the sufferings of this present life are not worth comparing with the glory that is to be revealed to us and in us and for us, "for I am convinced that neither death nor life, neither angels nor demons, neither the present nor the future, nor any powers, neither height nor depth, nor anything else in all creation, will be able to separate us from the love of God that is in Christ Jesus our Lord." (Romans 8:18, 38–39 NIV)

That's what makes all the difference. That's what's enabled me to survive the indescribably heartbreaking loss of my adored daughter. That's what's enabled me to get up each day, reluctantly at first, day after day, month after month, year after year, until I've reached this day.

I'll continue to rise each morning, seeking to live the life that God has prepared for me, finding joy and meaning where I can, until that glorious day when my work on earth is done and He welcomes me home and I get to experience His promise:

> "God Himself will wipe away every tear from [my] eyes; and death shall be no more, neither shall there be sorrow and mourning nor grief nor pain any more…"
>
> — REVELATION 21:4 (PARAPHRASE)

EPILOGUE

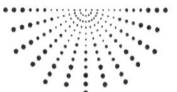

TIMELINE: ONE DAY IN THE FUTURE – ONLY GOD KNOWS WHEN

Out of the fog, two men stride towards me – immensely tall, massively strong and incredibly beautiful. Their radiant faces glow and their hands stretch out in my direction. My mind whirls and spins. Where am I? What just happened? Who are they? I've never seen them before and yet I know them.

Without hesitation I reach forward and place my hands in theirs. I feel myself scooped up in strong, warm arms as the ground falls away beneath us.

The blue of the sky is infused with dazzling light which turns to a kaleidoscope of rainbow colours, permeated with an other-worldly intensity, as we soar through dimensions of time and space. The journey seems to go on and on, yet is over in a moment. Warm breezes embrace me as we approach a scene of indescribable beauty and the air vibrates with a sense of deep peace and belonging.

Massive gates which shine like polished pearls stand before us. A mighty warrior steps forward to block our path. My mouth falls open as I stare in awe and wonder. Nothing is familiar and yet it feels like coming home. My name is asked and given. A giant book with ancient pages is searched before the gates majestically swing open.

Inside, the sound of singing fills the air, like a choir blended from all the choirs that the earth has ever held. Ahead I see a throne. This throne makes all those I've seen before, even the most magnificent thrones built for movie sets, look like children's toys. Around the throne myriad statuesque angels in resplendent apparel soar and bow, raising their hands in praise and adoration to an unseen figure. Lining the way to this throne are thousands upon thousands of people, of every race ever known. They are laughing and singing and clapping and cheering. I crane my head to see who is the focus of their rejoicing, but I see no one except my pitiful figure.

Suddenly, everything goes silent and still. From the throne a man steps forward, a gentle smile on his lips and a glowing crown on his head. The air ripples and crackles and seems to hold its very breath. Pure love radiates from his face, striking me like an atomic explosion. I fall flat on my face, quaking and sobbing, overcome with emotions too jumbled to identify. He reaches out, touching my shoulder. An electric pulse shoots through my body – an encompassing wave of acceptance and, could it be, delight?

"Welcome, child, we have much to talk about, but first…" He pauses.

My heart sinks. Now it's time to face his disappointment. My long list of shortcomings and my failure to live in the way that would please Him brings sadness, even as awareness of forgiveness brings joy and deep gratitude. I start to prepare my thoughts.

But no, I hear a low chuckle.

When I dare to raise my face, he gestures over his shoulder where, in the distance, I see a halo of wild, curly hair flying in the breeze. Beneath it, the face of my beloved Kari-Lee, her smile dazzling, her laughter bubbling in the air, as she bounds towards me, her arms wide, her smile wider. "Mum! You're here! It's so awesome!"

My heart beats so wildly that I feel it will fly out of my chest. My breath leaves me. My knees quiver. My legs lose all feeling. My pulse reaches fever pitch, thumping loudly in my ears. Everything around me fades to dark as I stand to take a shaky step in her direction.

Then, her body slams into mine, my arms crush her to me and I enfold my precious daughter with the ferocity of all those long, long years of missing and yearning, knowing that now we will never be separated again.

This time there is no ending to the story. Instead, it's the beginning of the real beginning…

SELECTED PHOTOGRAPHS

A radiant Kari-Lee on her wedding day. (December 2013) "Her sparkling smile lit up the very air around her."

In hospital as a toddler. This was when I was told Kari-Lee had cepacia bacteria growing in her lungs. (1990)

A bright toddler with a happy heart. (1992)

Our little family. Loving our girl with her "ringlet curls, big eyes and engaging smile". (1994)

Photos of a happy, healthy Kari-Lee were sent to the nursery in Taiwan. (1994)

Kari-Lee and baby Tiana. Kari blossomed as a big sister. (1995)

Kari thrived at school. (1996)

At eight, Kari had the honour of being flower girl. What most wedding guests didn't realise was that underneath her beautiful bouquet of Australian native flowers was a bandage hiding an intravenous cannula. (1997)

During her early school years, dance played a big part in Kari's life, together with Rachel (R). (1998)

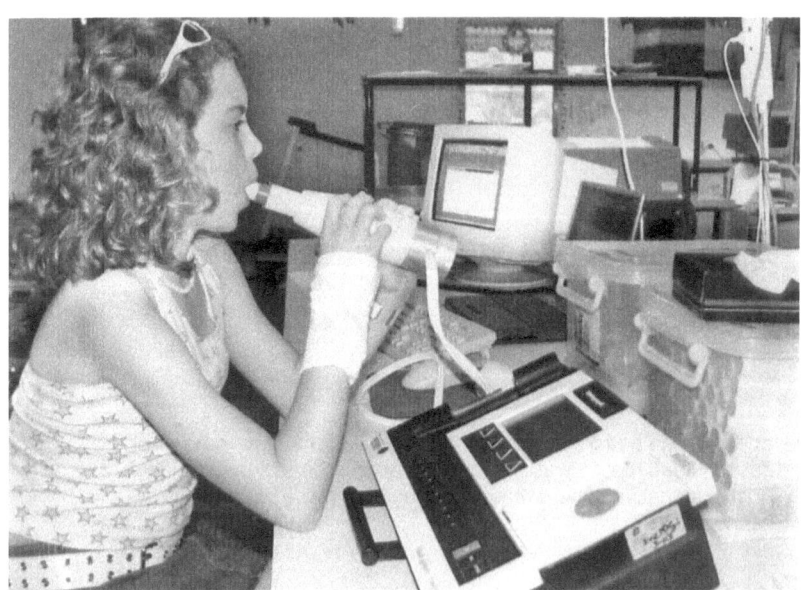

In the respiratory function laboratory at 'breathers', where lung function was measured every six weeks. (2001)

"Soft corkscrew curls tumbled from her loose ponytail ... as Kari-Lee shyly posed for photos prior to her semi-formal dinner." (2003)

Peter (L) supported Kari as he tipped her backwards under the chilly water for her baptism, then raised her up, dripping but triumphant. (2007)

Kari's Make-A-Wish trip to Tahiti was "filled with magical, unforgettable moments". (2007)

At 18, Kari-Lee had her photo taken by the company she would later work for. (2007)

Our family trip to Tiana's birth country of Taiwan was the realisation of years of planning. (2009)

In Rome, Kari stole the show when some "Roman guards" persuaded her to pose with them. (2010)

"HAVING THE BEST TIME!!! I LOOOOOOVE EGYPT!!!!" Kari had hankered to visit ancient Egypt since childhood. (2010)

Kari-Lee glowing with excitement, ready to dance in the Carnival parade in Rio de Janeiro. (2012)

Sisters having fun as they loved to do. (2012)

One of the last photos of we three girls together. On Kari's wedding day. (2013)

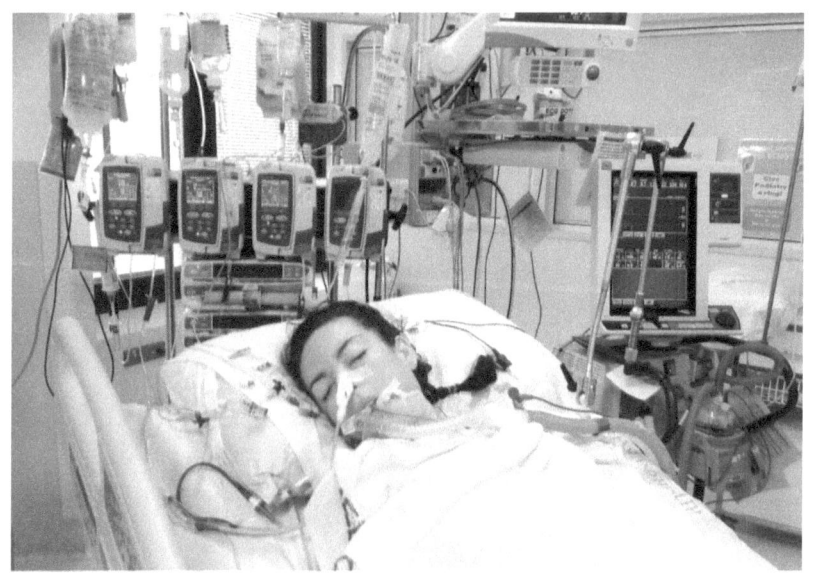

In an open cubicle in ICU, surrounded by countless beeping and flashing machines, lay our precious Kari, eyes closed, looking peaceful following her double-lung transplant. (June 2014)

At Nic's 21st Birthday party. Kari-Lee sparkling and full of life after her transplant. (July 2014)

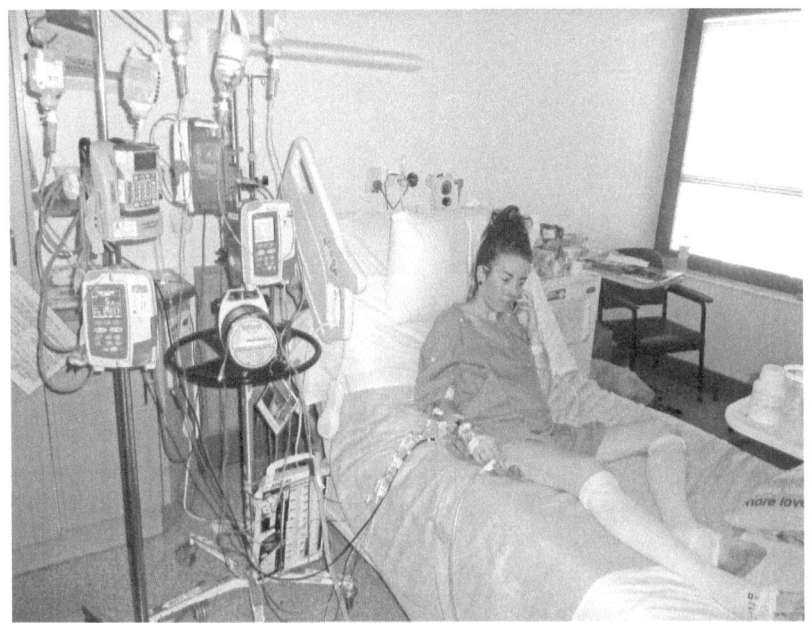

A few days after surgery to remove two lobes of her shiny new lungs. Despite a long row of painful staples marching across her back and the multiple machines pumping copious amounts of strong antibiotics into her veins, Kari happily chats to a friend on her phone. (September 2014)

ABOUT THE AUTHOR

Rhyl Venning lives on the stunning Sunshine Coast in Queensland, Australia. She's been married to Peter for forty years. Their daughter Tiana lives in Brisbane with her husband Matt and baby daughter Kari Florence (known as Florence).

A now-retired Occupational Therapist and nanny, Rhyl loves to make a difference where she can. She volunteers with Ladybird Care Foundation as a peer mentor for bereaved parents; as a Volunteer Care Coordinator with Make-A-Wish; as a support group facilitator for While We're Waiting; as a church representative for Operation

Christmas Child; as a puppy carer for Seeing Eye Dogs Australia and as a blood and plasma donor.

Sunlight on the Ocean is Rhyl's first book, an undertaking she'd never contemplated before Kari-Lee ran ahead to Heaven. Prior to completing this memoir, Rhyl had a chapter published in *Until Then*, a compilation of thirteen life stories shared by bereaved parents and edited by Gary and Laura House. Rhyl has also had poems and prose published in two anthologies called *Courage* and *Change*. These were compiled by Goodlife Writers Group, as fundraisers for local charities.

Rhyl's favourite pastimes include long walks on the beach, KYB Bible study, scrapbooking, swimming, reading and catching up with friends or family for a cuppa and a chat. Her greatest joy is spending time with her precious granddaughter, playing together, laughing and singing lullabies that Rhyl's own grandmother sang to her.

∽

Connect with Rhyl at
sunlightontheocean.com

www.ingramcontent.com/pod-product-compliance
Lightning Source LLC
Chambersburg PA
CBHW020315010526
44107CB00054B/1843